BREAKING WOMEN

Breaking Women

Gender, Race, and the New Politics of Imprisonment

Jill A. McCorkel

NEW YORK UNIVERSITY PRESS

New York and London

NEW YORK UNIVERSITY PRESS
New York and London
www.nyupress.org

References to Internet websites (URLs) were accurate at the time of writing.
Neither the author nor New York University Press is responsible for URLs that
may have expired or changed since the manuscript was prepared.

LIBRARY OF CONGRESS CATALOGING-IN-PUBLICATION DATA
McCorkel, Jill A.
Breaking women : gender, race, and the new politics of imprisonment / Jill A. McCorkel.
pages cm
Includes bibliographical references and index.
ISBN 978-0-8147-6148-9 (cl : alk. paper) — ISBN 978-0-8147-6149-6 (pb : alk. paper)
1. Female offenders—Rehabilitation—United States. 2. Women prisoners—Services for—
United States. 3. Corrections—United States. I. Title.
HV6791.M383   2013
365'.6082—dc23   2012050535

New York University Press books are printed on acid-free paper, and their binding materials
are chosen for strength and durability. We strive to use environmentally responsible suppliers
and materials to the greatest extent possible in publishing our books.

Manufactured in the United States of America
c 10 9 8 7 6 5 4 3 2 1

In loving memory of my grandfathers,

John C. Turnbull and Franklin "Mack" McCorkel

CONTENTS

In January 2009, then governor Arnold Schwarzenegger announced plans to close a $19.9 billion budget gap in California.[1] His proposal to make massive cuts in social services like health care and welfare-to-work programs had all the familiar markings of the Republican Party's brand of fiscal conservatism—with one radical exception. Schwarzenegger took direct aim at prison expansion and overcrowding, promising a constitutional amendment that would prevent the state from spending more than 7% of its annual budget on corrections and plans to reduce the size of the state's prison population by forty thousand persons over a period of two years. Schwarzenegger's proposal was certainly a logical one given that much of California's budget troubles are directly linked to the state's commitment to "getting tough" on crime by incarcerating more people, even those convicted of minor drug offenses, for long periods of time. What made it radical was that in the course of the last three decades few politicians, certainly none of Schwarzenegger's prominence, were willing to risk their political careers by offering anything less than enthusiastic support for the law and order campaign to "lock 'em up and throw away the key." While Democrats and Republicans alike have sought to reduce government spending by gutting social welfare services, they have simultaneously (and unironically) continued to spend staggering amounts of money on prisons. California's budget crisis is the tip of the iceberg. Across the country, states are now scrambling to find solutions to myriad problems associated with costly and overcrowded prisons.

For the first time in nearly thirty years, Americans are rethinking what it means to punish and to incarcerate. Much of the debate has focused on nonviolent drug offenders, since they represent a significant proportion of the increase in the size of the nation's prison population. Proposals include sentence reductions for drug crimes, expanded use of drug treatment programs in prisons and community-based correctional settings, and granting the private prison industry an even greater role in the management and control of prisoners. As a sociologist who studies prisons, I am encouraged by efforts to rethink incarceration, but I am concerned that some of what is being proposed creates a new host of problems and exacerbates existing ones. It is this concern that prompted me to write this book now, a decade after I concluded my research study of an experimental, privately run drug treatment program in a state prison for women located in the Southeast. The program was one of the first of its kind in the country and, with an emphasis on treatment, it appeared to be moving in a decidedly different direction than the usual punitive policies. It was a program I wanted to like and, more important, one I hoped would prove successful in helping women overcome the problems that prompted their involvement in drugs and crime.

Over the course of my research, it became clear to me that the program neither helped the women it claimed to serve, nor did it provide a meaningful alternative to more traditional forms of incarceration. In many respects, its confrontational and coercive tactics effectively collapsed the distinction between treatment and punishment. This was embodied in the program's stated goal of "breaking down" drug offenders whom it claimed suffered from "diseased selves." The program fundamentally destabilized how women understood their experiences with poverty, violence, and social marginalization, and it shattered their sense of themselves as "good" and "respectable" people. In so doing, it left most women worse off than they would have been had they simply done their time in the main prison. They returned to the same streets and neighborhoods without job skills or an education, without the confidence to pursue either of those things, and without a safety net. Not surprisingly, many resumed the same criminal hustles that landed them in prison in the first place.

Although I wrote a few scholarly articles based on this research, I hesitated in writing a book. In the politically charged climate of the nation's War on Drugs, I worried that any critique of a treatment program would be read as a ringing endorsement for mass incarceration. And although I was convinced that this model of drug treatment was a failure, I wondered if what would follow in its wake would be even worse. In the years I had spent in the field, I came to know many of the women very well. I met their friends, families, husbands, boyfriends, girlfriends, baby daddies, and children. I witnessed firsthand their struggles in prison and on the streets. I learned something of what they were up against and how very high the stakes were. I did not want to write anything that would leave them and women like them any worse off. Further, even though the program and the private company that ran it became influential actors within the women's prison, I assumed that officials in the Department of Correction would cut funding if the program proved ineffective in reducing the likelihood that prisoners would resume criminal activity and drug use upon their release. As it turns out, I was wrong. The program survived and prospered even though state-sponsored studies showed that its coercive treatment practices had no effect on prisoner recidivism and relapse rates.

Today the program remains an essential component of correctional programming in the women's prison. Perhaps not coincidentally, the state now has one of the highest incarceration rates of women in the country. This program and others like it continue to gain in popularity in women's prisons and in community-based, alternative-to-incarceration programs across the country. Ultimately, I decided to write the book in order to explore the appeal of a treatment model that aims not to rehabilitate women drug offenders but to "break them down." I argue that coercive therapy is not an alternative to "get tough" policies but a gendered extension of them. It is a failure only if we believe that its purpose is to curb crime and reduce drug use. I aim to show that there are other agendas, beyond crime control, that are at play. This program was born in the same historical moment that poor, African American women were vilified by politicians and media outlets as "crack whores" and "welfare queens." In 1995, for example, former secretary of education William Bennett proclaimed that "if you wanted to reduce crime, you could . . . abort every black baby."[2] Racist stereotypes that took aim at Black women's parenting skills, sexual practices, relationships, and labor market participation obscured how increases in urban poverty, and Black poverty in particular, were a product of shifts in the broader political economy. In essence, such stereotypes turned poverty into a moral problem rather than a political one. This, in turn, undermined whatever sympathy poor families might have garnered from the public and made it possible for politicians to simultaneously dismantle welfare while beefing up the prison system. This paved the way for the prison system to become the primary institutional site for managing and controlling racial minorities and the poor. Treatment programs like the one I studied capitalized on these stereotypes and, by claiming that women offenders were "diseased," added to them. Such claims, in fact, opened up new markets for the private prison industry. I offer this book, then, as a cautionary tale. My intent is not to oppose alternatives to traditional forms of incarceration or to romanticize past systems of control. It is to call for greater interrogation of punishment in all its guises.

ACKNOWLEDGMENTS

This book has been a long time in the making and I am grateful to everyone who has encouraged, inspired, and supported me along the way. My first and largest debt of gratitude belongs to the women incarcerated at East State whose experiences and observations serve as the heart and soul of this book. The questions they asked of the circumstances they found themselves in are what motivated this study. They trusted me with their stories and I took that trust very seriously. One of my greatest regrets is that confidentiality guarantees prevent me from thanking each of you by name. I hope you will recognize yourselves and your contributions in here.

This project has had a number of different institutional homes. I began collecting data when I was a graduate student at the University of Delaware. My mentor, Ruth Horowitz, saw the possibilities in this work long before I did and spent years (*years!*) encouraging me to turn it into a book. I am forever grateful to her. While in graduate school I was influenced and encouraged by a number of wonderful scholars, including Ronnie J. Steinberg, Kathleen Tierney, Sandra Harding, Valerie Hans, Susan Miller, Frank Scarpitti, Heather Smith, Chrissy Saum, and Kristy Miller. Jim Inciardi made this research possible—literally. Although he and I reached different conclusions about the effectiveness of this type of treatment programming, he was steadfast in his support of my work and I am thankful for the many opportunities he afforded me. Rest in peace, Jim, you will always be larger than life to me.

At Northern Illinois University, Jim Thomas took me under his wing and helped me broaden my perspective on U.S. prison policy. Jim and I have logged myriad hours traveling to and touring American prisons together. He continues to be one of my very favorite people to talk shop with. Kristen Myers was a great colleague and friend. She read and commented on early versions of this, well before it blossomed into a book project. At the University of Massachusetts–Amherst, I was fortunate to work in a department where faculty and graduate students enthusiastically engaged with one another's work. I am an infinitely better sociologist because of my time there. Thanks, in particular, to Gianpaolo Baiocchi, Michelle Budig, Eve Darian-Smith, Rob Faulkner, Thomas Hilbink, Joya Misra, Jerry Platt, Randall Stokes, Millie Thayer, Brittnie Aiello, Sarah Becker, Amy Wilkins, Emmanuel Adero, Jason Rodriquez, Shawn McGuffey, Anna Curtis, and Kelan Steel Lowney. Villanova University generously awarded me a yearlong sabbatical to write the manuscript and a summer research grant to complete the follow-up study. Brian Jones is one of my favorite people to talk sociology with and I have benefited from the questions he asks of my work and of ethnography in general. The support I received from Catherine Warrick and Kelly Welch has been unwavering. I could not ask for two better colleagues or friends.

In addition, a number of outstanding scholars have contributed to this work in a multitude of ways. Dana Britton and Lynne Haney have been there virtually every step of the way. They each have read and offered detailed comments on earlier drafts of this manuscript, and we have spent hours debating gendered aspects of the penal-welfare state. I cannot adequately express my gratitude for their input, encouragement, and support. Jeanne Flavin read and commented on several chapters and helped me craft my book proposal. Conversations with Ann Orloff, Kelly Hannah Moffat, and David Garland sharpened my thinking on gender, governance, and the state. Dorothy Burge, Mary Scott-Boria, and Khalil Asad Muhammad (Ervin Davis) pushed me to think more critically about race and provided me with the tools to do it. My editor at New York University Press, Ilene Kalish, was nothing short of magnificent. Her comments were spot-on and her patience was seemingly boundless. Thanks also to the anonymous reviewers. Their suggestions made this a better book.

I benefited from working with a number of fantastic graduate and undergraduate students on this project. Some accompanied me into the field to do interviews, others transcribed those interviews, and many more spent hours slogging through research literature and imprisonment statistics. Thanks especially to Andy Hill, Teena Velez, Julie Yingling, Paige Weller, Erin Kerrison, Cliff Crosley, Tracy Daujotas, and Mitch Bateast. Shericka Ward graciously allowed me to photograph her for the cover of the book. Special thanks must go to Chelsea Moylan. If it weren't for her, this book would be another two years in the making. Her careful editing and methodical approach to referencing were invaluable. So, too, were her YouTube videos. I am also fortunate to have the support of several cohorts of undergraduate and graduate students at three different universities—Northern Illinois University, University of Massachusetts–Amherst, and Villanova University. Thanks so much to all of you. I appreciate your enthusiasm for this project and your willingness to tolerate a seemingly endless number of prison stories. I would particularly like to thank the students and alums at Villanova's "satellite campus"—the Pennsylvania State Correctional Institution at Graterford. Thank you guys for the encouragement and for sharing your own experiences and analyses of incarceration with me. Thanks especially to Charles "Mubdi" Coley for reminding me to always keep punching. I hope this book does all of you guys proud.

Books, of course, are not just born of academic endeavors. They are also the products of personal lives. My friends helped me overcome various obstacles along the way and gave me the confidence to sit down in front of a blank screen and write. I am grateful to be surrounded by such an inspiring, talented, and dedicated group of people. My partners in crime, Kevin Brown and Albert Yee, were always willing to indulge my desire for new adventures and were vigilant about reminding me when it was time to settle down and work. Shawn "Shizz" Charles gave me good advice when I needed it and managed to return me to calm when panic set in. The "entourage" crew (Jamie Blau, Jenny "Hollywood" Perkins, Dawn Eichen, and Anna Smith) kept me sane, kept me laughing, and kept me dancing throughout the last grueling months of writing. Khalil Asad Muhammad (Ervin Davis) was my sounding board throughout much of the writing process—he offered advice, encouragement, and reminded me regularly that he is "always on [my] side." Brittnie Aiello, Kara Baker, Sarah Becker, and Jamie Blau are the living, breathing embodiment of the aphorism "sisterhood is powerful." Whenever I needed them, they were there. I am forever in their debt.

My husband, Brad Mellinger, has been a crucial part of this project from the moment I first walked through those prison doors right up through the evening I wrote the very last lines of the manuscript's conclusion. Words are not enough to express my gratitude for his loyalty, generosity, love, and support. I love you, Mels. Thank you for everything, but most especially, thank you for always believing.

Searching for Red's Self

I'm lost. I've had to surrender my self.
—Red, on the eve of her release from prison

What must one know about oneself in order to be willing to
renounce anything?
—Michel Foucault, "Technologies of the Self"

"I'm lost, I've had to surrender my self." As Red says this, she curls her fingers
into a loose fist and raps her chest as if to indicate the part of her that has
gone missing.[1] We are sitting in a shaded corner of the prison's recreation
yard awaiting word on whether her release paperwork will be processed in
time for her to return home to celebrate her son's fourth birthday. She learned
the day before that she had successfully completed all five of the "transformation phases" of an experimental, intensive drug treatment program that was
housed in a separate wing of East State Women's Correctional Institution.[2]
The program, known as Project Habilitate Women or PHW for short, was
the latest in the prison's arsenal of measures designed to curb chronic prison
overcrowding, high rates of inmate recidivism, prison disciplinary problems,
and spiraling economic costs associated with the state's War on Drugs. PHW
was the creation of Prison Services Company (hereafter the Company),[3] one
of the largest for-profit providers of prison health care services in the country.
Beginning in the early 1990s, the Company began an aggressive campaign to
corner what continues to be a booming market—drug treatment services for
correctional populations. PHW was one of the first in what would become a
growing chain of such programs in prisons, jails, work-release facilities, and
halfway houses across the United States.

Red was one of PHW's most celebrated participants. In the twelve years leading up to her present incarceration, she made a decent living by selling drugs and engaging in small-time hustles like prostitution and petty theft. When her appetite for using drugs exceeded her income from selling them, her criminal activity took a dramatic and some would say "masculine" turn. She developed a penchant for carjacking and armed robbery—crimes that remain almost exclusively a man's game.[4] It was her second armed robbery, the stickup of a convenience store, that landed her in prison. Like previous stints, this one initially seemed to only deepen her involvement with drugs and crime. She began her prison term surreptitiously smoking the crack cocaine she had smuggled into the facility. Her decision to enter the drug treatment program was purely strategic. She was facing a sentence of eight to twenty-seven years on two counts of robbery in the first degree and a prior drug conviction. Successful completion of PHW held out the possibility of a significant sentence reduction.[5]

After nearly four years in prison (two of which were spent in PHW), she seemed well on the way to turning her life around. She had racked up an impressive array of accomplishments, including getting clean, earning certification as a nursing assistant, gaining weekly, supervised visits with her son, getting approval to work outside the prison at a local sanitation facility, and earning credit toward an early release from prison. During PHW's graduation ceremony, she described herself as a changed woman—one with goals, "positive" relationships, and a new outlook on life. She spoke of these changes optimistically and emphasized that she did not regret abandoning the person she once was—a person she described as little more than a "liar, thief, and manipulator." Red's characterization of her "old self" corresponded to the description that company executives and state officials used, although they often punctuated their account with a host of clinical sounding terms like "addictive personality," "codependent," and "criminal thinker." Red's story—particularly her lengthy criminal history and bumpy road to redemption—was one that state actors, from prison administrators to correctional officers, liked to tell. The fact that Red had not yet stepped foot outside the prison as a free woman was beside the point. In these retellings, she was more political allegory than data point. Specifically, they used her story to make two points. The first was that women offenders had changed. They claimed that the incoming tide of prisoners were more aggressive, drug-involved, manipulative, and prone to commit crime than were previous ones. The second point was that the ideology and structure of control in the prison also had to change in order to manage this new population effectively. State officials, in particular, argued that Red's history of recidivism and drug relapse was facilitated, in part, by the limitations of a gendered system of control that had its origins in the 19th-century women's reformatory movement. To overcome this, the Department of Correction closed the old women's prison, a reformatory-era building that dated back to 1929, and replaced it with a new, state-of-the-art facility that resembled, in both appearance and effect, prisons for men. Barbed wire crowned perimeter fences, metal detectors and various surveillance devices were installed in housing blocks and main thoroughfares, and a control unit was built to deal with inmates deemed dangerous and unruly.

This did not mean that gender disappeared as an organizing strategy of control in the prison. It persisted in different forms. Administrators and line staff held fast to the belief that while incoming women prisoners were different from previous cohorts, they were not men. Thus administrators resisted the idea that the women's prison should entirely morph into its male counterpart—an austere, isolating environment designed to warehouse prisoners for the duration of their sentences. They remained committed to the principle that prisons for women should prioritize treatment over punishment. To respond to the challenges presented by inmates who were thought to be more dangerous, drug addicted, and crime prone, administrators worked with executives from Prison Services Company to launch Project Habilitate Women, an intensive, confrontational form of drug treatment that was based on the therapeutic community model.[6] Sociologists have characterized this model as "strong-arm rehab" because it is considerably more coercive than popular self-help programs like Alcoholics and Narcotics Anonymous.[7] PHW made a similar distinction, referring to their system of control as "habilitation" in order to contrast it from "softer" and "more lenient" rehabilitative models. Habilitation is a set of social technologies that mobilize surveillance, confrontation, humiliation, and discipline for the purposes of "breaking down" a self that is thought to be diseased. It is guided by a philosophy of addiction which holds that the self is the ultimate source of social disorder (in the form of crime and poverty), institutional disorder (in the form of prison overcrowding and inmate recidivism), and personal disorder (in the form of drug addiction). According to this framework, women like Red get addicted to drugs and become dependent on criminal lifestyles because they are believed to possess diseased and incomplete selves—selves that are further eroded under the weight of addictions, poverty, and "bad choices." The appeal of this program to prison administrators was that it embodied the spirit of the state's efforts to make prisons tougher and more secure, while simultaneously preserving the logic of gender difference in the application of carceral control. Ultimately, administrators and state officials hoped to alleviate the problem of drugs, crime, recidivism, and overcrowding by engineering nothing short of an institutional takeover of unruly selves.

At the time of our interview, Red had done two major stints in prison, the first beginning in 1989 and the second (and current one) beginning in 1995. Her experiences in prison straddle the divide between the classic rehabilitative system of control and the more coercive system of habilitation. Her first term was spent in the old, reformatory-era facility. She told me that she "slid" through her time there and attributed this primarily to the fact that prison staff were relatively lenient and functioned like quasi-parental figures: "They told us to be good and to read our Bibles." Her current term took place in the new prison. In contrast to her description of her first term as "easy," she characterized her experiences in the new prison, particularly her time spent in PHW, as "intense" and "hard":

> RED: [The old prison] never got in-depth. Inmates will say, "Prison is prison is prison." Well, it's not. I've been around. Prison is one thing—this is another, you know? In here [PHW] they get in real deep. They're in your head and so it's hard time—it's a real tough adjustment. They break you down.
>
> JILL MCCORKEL (HEREAFTER JM): Why do they do that?
>
> RED: Because addicts—addiction fucks with your head. You don't think right, you don't act right, you know? Addiction is my life, it affects my life and so, to get a new life, I've got to surrender my self to their process.

As we talk, I watch one of the PHW counselors moving across the yard to meet us. She's got release paperwork in her hand. The counselor informs Red that she will be transferred to a community-based, work-release program within the month. She won't make it out of prison in time for her son's fourth birthday, but provided things go well in work release, she'll be back home after having served just over half her minimum sentence.[8] As the counselor disappears back into the prison, I remark to Red that she must be happy to have earned an early release from prison. She looks at me blankly and shrugs. "Most people say that prison robs you of time, but this—," she gestures to the green building where PHW is housed, "this is a new kind of punishment. This robs you of something else. When they take away a person's dignity, a person's self-respect, what is left?"

* * *

At the time of my conversation with Red, I had been an ethnographer in this women's prison for nearly four years. It was not the first time that I heard a prisoner pose the question of what this "new kind of punishment" meant for their sense of self. From the start, prisoners had been asking whether habilitation was a form of "brainwashing," designed to make them into something they were not sure they wanted to be. State officials, company executives, prison administrators, and line staff were similarly consumed with the subject of prisoners' selves, though they did not frame this in quite the same terms. For them, the diseased self was a social problem that required immediate intervention. Their questions frequently centered on how best to identify and diagnose the "real" selves of prisoners for the purposes of institutional management and social control.

It is important to emphasize that everyone from prison staff to state officials to prisoners themselves approached the self as if it were a real, empirical thing. That is, they believed in the existence of a "real self," a coherent entity within a person that serves as a sort of inner core from which everything else (e.g., emotion, cognition, behavior, beliefs, attitudes, morality) flows.[9] Where they differed was in their representations of what this self "really" was. Prisoners struggled to be seen as more than drug addicts and criminals. Staff struggled to determine whether the things prisoners did and said were authentic representations of who they "really" were. For the purpose of this analysis, my aim is not to discover whether the staff were right when they diagnosed prisoners as diseased, nor is it to determine whether prisoners were being truthful in the narratives they told about themselves. Such an approach would be a dubious undertaking, particularly since the question of whether a core self lurks under the surface of public identities and managed impressions is a point of theoretical controversy within the social sciences. What is important for my purposes is the fact that individuals interact with one another, and institutions like the prison act on individuals, *as if* a core self exists. The self, in other words, is a socially constructed object.

The institutional preoccupation with the self took me by surprise. I began my fieldwork in this women's prison in 1994. It was at a moment when the "get tough on crime" movement and the mass incarceration it produced appeared to signal the demise of what sociologist David Garland calls the modernist project of penal welfarism.[10] The penal welfare system comprises an interlocking grid of institutions, agencies, and policies that make up the criminal justice system. These include indeterminate sentencing laws, presentence investigation reports that allow courts to individually tailor sentences, specialty courts for juveniles, social work programs for offenders and their families, early release programs from prison, educational and rehabilitative programming in prison, halfway houses, parole, and community-based programs that aim to reintegrate offenders in the social mainstream. The origins of the system can be traced to 18th-century Enlightenment philosophy and the expansion, particularly during the post–World War II era, of social engineering programs. It is organized around two ideas. The first is the reha- bilitative ideal, a core principle that holds that penal measures should aim, whenever possible, to assist offenders in leading law-abiding, productive lives.[11] The second is that the state is responsible for not only the punishment and control of offenders, but also their care and reform. The goal of penal welfarism is an optimistic one—it is to reform and normalize unruly selves rather than to permanently stigmatize and marginalize them.[12] It rests on the belief that offenders are more unfortunate than they are bad or evil.

Although the decline of penal welfarism, and concomitantly the reha- bilitative ideal, was evident as early as the mid-1970s, it was the maturation of the "get tough on crime movement" during the mid-1990s that heralded the collapse of this system. "Get tough" turned penal welfarism on its head at virtually every conceivable level within the criminal justice system. It rejected the rehabilitative ideal in favor of greater punitiveness, infamously symbolized in "three strikes" legislation, mandatory minimum sentences for drug crimes, and expanded use of the death penalty. It bears emphasis that these policies not only sharply upped the ante for those charged with crimes, they did away with judicial discretion and individually tailored sen- tences. For example, California was one of the first states to pass three strikes legislation in 1994 and over the decade, twenty-three other states and the federal government followed suit. Three strikes laws vary by state but typi- cally impose mandatory life sentences on persons convicted of three or more felony offenses.[13] Even more widespread than three strikes legislation was the statewide adoption of mandatory minimum sentences for drug crimes. The War on Drugs was part and parcel of the "get tough" movement. States modeled their drug laws after federal drug schedules created in the Anti– Drug Abuse Acts of 1986 and 1988. This legislation dramatically increased the penalties for drug crimes, particularly for crack cocaine. Indeed, crack cocaine was the only drug that carried a mandatory minimum penalty for a first offense of simple possession. Offenders convicted of possessing five or more grams of crack cocaine were sentenced to a mandatory five-year term in prison.[14] Further, this legislation stipulated that criminal penalties in drug cases were not to be based on an individual's role in the offense, but rather on the volume of the drug in question. Thus an individual who played a more minor role in a drug transaction such as a lookout or delivery person was sentenced as if he or she were one of the main parties to the crime. These laws, combined with aggressive policing tactics associated with the War on Drugs, gave rise to the contemporary phenomenon of mass incarceration. Mass incarceration refers to the fact that more Americans are incarcerated for increasingly longer periods of time—more so than at any other point in this nation's history and defying global comparison. Currently, more than 2.2 million adults are incarcerated in federal and state prisons and county jails in the United States. With an incarceration rate of 743 adults per 100,000, the United States is the world leader in locking up its own citizens.[15]

In many respects, sentencing policies that sent more offenders away for ever-longer periods of time marked the declining significance of the self within the broader terrain of the criminal justice system. The popular crime-control adage "lock 'em up and throw away the key" suggests that within the rubric of the "get tough" movement, unruly selves are considered beyond redemption and repair. The trend toward greater punitiveness was amplified within the prison system, as carceral priorities shifted away from rehabilitation in favor of the "humane incapacitation" of the millions of men and women who were serving time. Indeed, it was not just that more Americans were being sent to prison than ever before, it was that prisons themselves were changing. As prisons became preoccupied with deploying new technologies of surveillance and restraint to control inmates, educational, vocational, and rehabilitative programming all but disappeared. The 1990s and beyond were witness to the widespread use of control units within medium- and maximum-security institutions and the birth of "super max" prisons designed to house a new criminal class of "super predators."[16] These units and facilities typically house prisoners in isolation cells, for up to twenty-three hours a day, with little to no human contact.[17] Research documenting these trends suggests, in men's prisons at least, that what was emerging in the wake of penal welfarism was the antithesis of the rehabilitative ideal.[18]

In their influential 1992 article "The New Penology," sociologists Malcolm Feeley and Jonathan Simon endeavored to map the contours of what they argued was emerging as the system of punishment that would replace penal welfarism.[19] Among their key claims were that the fundamental objectives of the criminal justice system were changing, as were the techniques of control. The goal of rehabilitation was being replaced by the desire to identify and manage risk. The objective of risk management is premised on a much more pessimistic set of beliefs about crime and criminals—specifically, that crime is never going to go away and that serious offenders are incapable of reform. Thus the central task of the criminal justice system must be to manage crime by identifying those groups who are thought to be the most crime prone and subjecting them to high levels of surveillance and control. Feeley and Simon observe, "The new penology is neither about punishing or rehabilitating individuals. It is about identifying and managing unruly groups."[20] With this comes a renewed emphasis on incarceration as the primary technique for neutralizing the threat presented by dangerous groups. In this model, prisons become little more than human warehouses, designed to hold offenders until the risk they pose diminishes or disappears altogether. The internal work of the prison system subsequently redirects itself away from tailoring treatment to improve the individual offender's chances for success upon release and toward finding more cost-effective, efficient means for managing large groups of prisoners for longer periods of time.[21] Feeley and Simon's theory of the new penology has been critiqued for, among other things, its failure to adequately theorize race and gender and its treatment of prisons as homogenous and static institutions.[22] Nonetheless, the term "new penology" remains in use today by prison scholars like Loïc Wacquant to refer to the general and systemic shift away from rehabilitation and toward the management of dangerous groups.[23] I am using the term in a similar way here, to refer to profound shifts in punishment ideologies and techniques of control within prisons.

I began this study with the intention of documenting the impact of the "get tough" movement in the women's prison. As a sociologist who studies gender, I was particularly interested in understanding how such a pronounced shift away from rehabilitation would affect the gender regime of the prison. Research by feminist sociologists and historians makes clear that prisons are gendered organizations in which assumptions about masculinity, femininity, and gender difference are encoded into the practices, ideologies, and distributions of power.[24] For the better part of the nineteenth and twentieth centuries, prisons have operated according to the logic of separate spheres, in which the techniques of surveillance and control and the ends to which both were put were guided by beliefs about men's and women's essential natures, the source of their criminality, and socially constructed assumptions about their needs, capabilities, and their locations vis-à-vis family, market, and state.[25] In many respects, the ideology of rehabilitation has occupied a more central and stable place within the feminine side of the penal system. Criminologists Candace Kruttschnitt and Rosemary Gartner argue that this is because broader cultural assumptions about women criminals and normative expectations of femininity have persisted through time.[26] Crime is not considered an extension of women's essential nature but rather a perversion of it. Thus there has been a tendency to portray women offenders as more mad than bad and, concomitantly, an institutional mandate to prioritize treatment over punishment.

By the mid-1990s, however, the "get tough" movement seemed poised to upend this gendered logic. Restrictions on judicial discretion, primarily in the form of mandatory minimum sentences, meant that tens of thousands of women were being sentenced to lengthy prison terms. From the start of the War on Drugs in the mid-1980s through century's end, the number of women in state and federal prisons increased by over 400%. Much of this increase is attributable to mandatory sentences for drug crimes.[27] Today the number of incarcerated women in the United States stands just under 115,000. More than three-quarters of women prisoners are African American or Latina and the majority are mothers to children under the age of eighteen.[28] Increases like these are historically unprecedented and demonstrate a shifting set of priorities within the criminal justice system.[29] Indeed, the very categories of persons for whom mercy was once reserved—first-time and nonviolent offenders, juveniles, and women—became the fastest growing segment of the prison population. Feminist criminologists were quick to christen the gendered effects of the new penology as "equality with a vengeance."[30]

My primary aim in undertaking an ethnographic study of a women's prison during this period is to understand how punishment, in terms of its constitutive logic and practices, changed, and to document the implications of these changes for prisoners, line staff, and administrators. Most of the scholarship on mass incarceration and the new penology has been produced from afar. Social scientists have analyzed survey data, descriptive statistics, judicial decisions, legislative mandates, administrative decrees, media coverage of crime, and political rhetoric to piece together what is happening. As valuable as these analyses are, none are able to offer an interior account of the punishment process. How did state actors interpret, implement, and legitimate "get tough" policies? How did they reconcile them with the prison's tradition of reform? How, in turn, did prisoners experience, resist, and make sense of what was happening? As the handful of ethnographic studies of men's prisons made clear, the "get tough" movement not only changed *who* is sent to prison, but also *how* punishment is enacted therein.[31] How these changes affected the institution of the women's prison and prisoners like Red is the subject of this book.

Like state officials and executives from Prison Services Company, I am also using Red's story and the stories of women incarcerated alongside her. My purpose in doing so is not, as they did, to legitimate new forms of control; rather, it is to interrogate these forms of control. As the interview excerpt from Red's account of her time in prison suggests, the implications of this "new kind of punishment" within women's prisons are profound. It shapes not only how women prisoners experience the pains of incarceration, but also how they come to experience the self, often with devastating consequences. Beyond this, it suggests that despite the implementation of various "get tough" measures, women's prisons are moving in a distinctly different direction than men's. At the moment when men's prisons became preoccupied with containing the body, the prison I studied became even more deeply invested in the self as the primary object of institutional control. This does not mean, however, that the rehabilitative ideal persisted in women's prisons as it withered in men's. As my analysis will show, rehabilitation quickly lost legitimacy in the wake of various sets of institutional crises reverberating throughout the prison system. Further, habilitation as a technique of control cannot be understood as rehabilitation by another name. I argue that it does indeed signal the arrival of a new system of punishment—one that is deeply gendered and racialized and reflects the growing influence of privatization and market-based sensibilities in the governing logic of punishment.

Gender and Women's Prisons

Even during the height of the "get tough" movement, women's prisons were not moving in lockstep with men's. In their book *Marking Time in the Golden State*, Candace Kruttschnitt and Rosemary Gartner present a comparative historical study of two different women's prisons in California at two different points in time, the 1960s and the 1990s.[32] They report that during the 1990s, vestiges of a rehabilitative framework remained, even as the prisons themselves adapted to the more punitive institutional context in which they found themselves.[33] Prison staff continued to theorize women's criminality in terms of their vulnerability to risky men and their "bad" relationship choices. This is a key distinction from men's prisons, where the logic of "get tough" framed male offenders as rational actors who committed crimes intentionally. Gendered assumptions about subjectivity shape how "get tough" measures are translated into practice within the prisons they studied. What changed then from the 1960s to the 1990s is not so much the belief that women offenders needed to be punished more than rehabilitated, but that offenders themselves, rather than the state, must take up the torch of their own rehabilitation.[34] Scholars call this process "responsibilization." The term refers to a general strategy of governance that shifts responsibility for social problems from the state to the individual and, then in turn, encourages the individual to become self-regulating.[35] In recent years, responsibilization has emerged as a major theme in scholarship on women's prisons.

In her extensive research on women's prisons in Canada, sociologist Kelly Hannah-Moffat examines the implementation of "woman-centered" and "gender responsive" policies aimed at empowering women prisoners.[36]

Although these policies aim to counter some of the harm associated with "equality with a vengeance," they do not, in actual practice, offer women prisoners much in the way of empowerment. Arguably, they do more to disempower women by masking the coercive effects of incarceration. Their failure to improve conditions for women prisoners is linked both to their psychologizing of the inequalities that women confront (e.g., domestic violence is attributed to poor self-esteem rather than structural vulnerabilities) and their tendency to position women as victims.[37] Women are expected to take ownership of their problems and resolve them by learning how to make the "right" choices even when, in many instances, the situations they find themselves in are not an outcome of choice.

Sociologist Lynne Haney explores gender, punishment, and responsibilization in her comparative ethnography of two California-based residential facilities for women offenders.[38] The programs are community-based alternatives to prison for women and their children. Her study spans a ten-year period from the early 1990s through 2005. In both cases, programming was cast as a gender-specific and "empowering" corrective to "get tough" measures. In the program she studied during the 1990s, the focus is on breaking women from their dependency on welfare, crime, and unreliable men by encouraging self-reliance through wage labor and education. Ten years later, the second program she studied promoted a much more restrictive model of citizenship. In the latter case, women were told that their problems are a function of "dangerous desires" (e.g., physical, sexual, and emotional drives) and that in order to improve their circumstances, they must learn to regulate the self. The program operationalized self-regulation solely in terms of managing thoughts and emotions, so much so that therapeutic counseling was prioritized over job training and education.[39] Both of the programs are responsibilization schemes, but the latter, with its efforts to tame women's "dangerous desires," offers a particularly bleak portrait of gendered governance on the feminine side of the penal system.

My study builds on this scholarship but offers two important modifications to the way that responsibilization, as a gendered outcome of the new penology, has been theorized. The key difference between the "new punishment" as it evolved in East State Women's Correctional Institution, and the "empowerment" strategies detailed in these other studies turns on the distinction between rehabilitation and habilitation as techniques of penal control. Executives from Prison Services Company were fond of saying, "Rehabilitation implies a fully formed self." In other words, rehabilitation presumes an otherwise complete self in need of a fix, whether this involves job training, anger management, or improved parenting skills. This can be fitted in with responsibilization schemes like those studied in California and Canada, in the sense that a complete self is regarded by state actors as theoretically capable of taking up the mantle of self-regulation and rehabilitation.[40] As one of the counselors in Haney's study observed of the young women in her care, "They're gonna make it 'cause they're doing things for themselves."[41] This stands in sharp contrast to habilitation, which begins with the premise that the self is incomplete, flawed, and disordered. As my analysis will demonstrate, this is not a self that is regarded as capable of self-regulation. Nor is it a self that the state hopes to normalize. Rather, it is a self that must be "surrendered" to a lifelong process of external management and control.

What does this mean for how social scientists have come to understand responsibilization and the new penology in women's prisons? I argue that framing the self as incapable of self-regulation is an outcome of prison privatization and the racial politics of mass incarceration. Privatization is one of the key elements of the new penology, but it remains under-theorized in feminist analyses of the carceral state. Although we tend to think of prison privatization in terms of facilities that are wholly owned and operated by for-profit companies, privatization is actually a much broader phenomenon. It includes the provision of thousands of goods and services to prisoners as well as to their friends and families. The expanding role of for-profit companies within the prison system, particularly at a moment when incarceration rates are exploding, prompted activists and scholars to declare this new leviathan the "prison–industrial complex." The result is that over the last thirty years, public prisons have evolved into "hybrid institutions," in the sense that they play host to a range of private and nonprofit partnerships.[42] This raises important questions about how market sensibilities and the profit motive influence the ideology and practice of punishment. In the present study, it is hardly coincidence that Prison Services Company is promoting an ideology of addiction which holds that drug-involved offenders can never be "cured." The disordered self is a profitable self in the sense that it requires various forms of external management throughout the lifecourse. As I will show, this ideology and the Company's influence within the prison system were consequential not only for the prison's administrative apparatus but also for how control was enacted and legitimated on a day-to-day basis.

The second way my study modifies previous discussions of responsibilization and the new penology is to center the issue of race. Scholarship on women's prisons has tended to collapse the distinction between race and poverty so that the drug war is analyzed as a method of governing poor women.[43] While it is certainly the case that poor women, compared to working- or middle-class women, are the most likely to be harmed by drug war polices and the "get tough" movement, it is crucial to acknowledge that the most coercive measures and punitive outcomes have been directed at poor, African American women, and that it is African American women who bear the greatest weight of "equality with a vengeance." For example, between the mid-1980s and early 1990s, the demographic group experiencing the greatest increase in its incarceration rate was African American women. The number of Black women in prison increased by a staggering 828%, compared to a 241% increase among white women.[44] By 1995, 31,000 African American women were serving a term of a year or more in state and federal prisons.[45] In the state I studied, one out of every 284 African American women was incarcerated, compared to one out of every 1,448 white women. Further, white women were disproportionately likely to be sentenced to community-based alternative-to-prison programs, while African American women were much more likely to be sentenced to prison. This has implications for how punishment and control are enacted. Scholars like Michelle Alexander and Loïc Wacquant offer sophisticated theorizations of race as it effects African American men and the organization of control within the men's prison system.[46] Wacquant, for example, argues that it is no coincidence that the rehabilitative ideal died at the very same moment when the number of African Americans behind bars surpassed the number of incarcerated whites. He argues that this is linked, in part, to broader economic shifts that serve to remove entire socio-demographic groups from the labor market permanently.[47] Further, as Alexander argues, the mass incarceration of African Americans does more than manage economic inequality—it creates and sustains a social order that systematically privileges whites over Blacks and Latino/as.[48] What remains underdeveloped is how race affects punishment within women's prisons. What are the consequences of racial marginalization and changes in the political economy for ideologies and techniques of control in women's prisons?

In the prison I studied, a shift in the racial demographic of the prison population was as consequential to the emergence of habilation and the "new punishment" as privatization was. As African American women eclipsed white women to become the prison's majority, prison staff began distinguishing inmates who were "good girls" from those who were "real criminals." Race was central to this categorization. In fact, racial stereotypes of Black women, particularly as welfare dependent, crime prone, and drug addicted, became galvanizing symbols for abandoning the rehabilitative ideal and replacing it with control strategies that were both more coercive and more intrusive than earlier practices.

Ethnography on the Inside

This ethnography of East State Women's Correctional Institution is premised on a set of theoretical questions I had about gender, race, and the new penology, as well as a set of questions raised by prisoners regarding the consequences of this new kind of punishment for the self.[49] Data are drawn from three sources: participant observation, semi-structured interviews with a variety of state actors including administrators, line staff, and prisoners, and archival documents kept by the prison. Data collection occurred in two phases. During the primary phase of this research project, I averaged between fifteen and twenty hours per week in the facility, and balanced my time between hanging out in housing units and recreation areas with prisoners and attending administrative events, conferences, and meetings with prison staff and state officials. During the first two years in the field, I had an official role in the setting in that I was brought in as an ethnographer on the university research team charged with evaluating the PHW program. I was granted a high-level security clearance, which meant that I was able to enter the prison at any time, and was given relatively unimpeded access to housing units, recreation areas, the visitation room, and PHW. Beyond the setting of the prison itself, I was also able to attend high-level meetings of state criminal justice officials that brought together wardens, administrators, judges, politicians, decision makers from the Department of Correction, and executives from Prison Services Company. When the evaluation was completed, I received permission from the warden and the director of PHW to remain in the prison to continue collecting data for my own purposes.

In addition to participant observation data, I conducted formal interviews with seventy-four prisoners and twenty-nine administrators and staff members, including correctional officers, counselors, and a number of state officials (e.g., politicians, judges, officials from the Department of Correction, and executives from Prison Services Company). Interviews with state officials, administrators, and line staff explored the evolution of criminal justice policies in the state, the nature of their work, the problems they encountered within the prison system and beyond, their assessment of prison policies, and their observations regarding crime, addiction, gender, race, and poverty. Interviews with prisoners, the overwhelming majority of whom were in PHW at one point or another, typically focused on their experiences in the criminal justice system, particularly their prison experiences, as well as broader discussions of their life histories. Nearly half of all respondents were interviewed more than once over the four-year period. In addition to formal interviews, I had hundreds of informal conversations with prisoners, former prisoners, correctional officers, social workers, administrators, prison activists, family members, and counselors.

I supplemented interview and participant-observation data with archival documents collected by the prison, including population and summary statistics, inmate surveys, case files, disciplinary reports, memoranda, meeting minutes, monthly state of the prison reports, institutional manuals, press releases, and other documents relating to PHW and the contractual relationship between the prison and Prison Services Company.

During the primary phase of this project, PHW admitted 264 prisoners: 77% were African American, 17% percent were white, and 6% were Latina. The median age of women in the program was thirty years, with 50% of participants in this study ranging between the ages of nineteen and thirty. Prior to their incarceration, the vast majority of women in PHW lived in poverty or near-poverty conditions. According to case records compiled by the program, 91% were the survivors of sexual or physical abuse.

The second phase of data collection took place during 2000. Throughout my first four years in the field, the prison was in a period of tremendous upheaval. Prison officials faced increasing pressure to abandon reform efforts in favor of "getting tough." This pressure, combined with overcrowding and budgetary crises, gave rise to a persistent sense among prisoners and staff that the institution's future was up for grabs. By the time I left the field in 1998, it was clear that the rehabilitative ideal had faded in significance and was regarded as little more than an artifact from a distant and moribund past. What was not clear was whether habilitation, as a replacement control strategy, would harden into the foundation of a new penology. I returned two years later to see what had become of the prison and of PHW, and to ascertain the consequences for current and former inmates, staff, and administrators. I did participant observation for six weeks in the prison and conducted interviews with twenty-six current and former prisoners (many of whom were part of the original study) and twelve administrators and staff members, including the former warden, his replacement, counselors, and correctional officers from the original study.

Overview

The ethnographic analysis that follows comprises three parts, each of which considers the emergence of a new penology in the women's prison from different vantage points. In the first part, I take a broad view of the prison and the wider criminal justice system of which it is a part, in order to analyze how and why, over the course of a decade, the structure and ideology of punishment underwent a radical revision. In chapter 1, I trace the rising influence of "get tough" policies and the concomitant decline of the reha- bilitative ideal within the local context of the women's prison. The focus in this chapter is on prison administrators and line staff, most of who were trained according to a rehabilitative paradigm and who were vested, both organizationally and ideologically, in the reform of women offenders. In the early years of the drug war, these state actors refused to implement "get tough" measures, on the grounds that such policies were gender inappropri- ate and undermined the institution's tradition of reform. In the wake of a severe and persistent overcrowding problem, however, they began to doubt the effectiveness and viability of the institution's reformist mission. What ini- tially emerged as a resource crisis broadened into a crisis of meaning as staff and administrators struggled to understand the obstacles that confronted them, the responses available to them, and their own stake in various out- comes. It is within the crucible of institutional crisis that reformist ideolo- gies and practices were abandoned, a process the warden characterized as the "unfounding" of rehabilitation.

Chapters 2 and 3 examine the strategies state actors pursued in response to the resource and ideological crises that plagued the prison. I demonstrate that while their responses were constrained by larger institutional forces, those forces did not determine their responses. The choices they made in light of the constraints they faced reconfigured the prison's structural arrangements and discursive forms and set the stage for the emergence of a new penology. Chapter 2 attends to the prison's resource crisis, with par- ticular emphasis on how a private company offered a resource bailout to the prison. Prison Services Company received federal grant monies to develop an experimental drug treatment program targeting incarcerated, "drug addicted" women. Although the proposed treatment program was contro- versial on a variety of fronts, the deal was too good for prison administrators to pass up. The chapter details the deal that was brokered and considers the organizational implications of privatization. Chapter 3 attends to the prison's ideological crisis and the racial politics that fueled it. In the early years of the drug war, staff were unable to reconcile political pressures to "get tough" with their own beliefs about the nature of women's criminality. All this changed, however, when a shift in the racial demographic of the prisoner population coincided with a rise in institutional disorder and overcrowding. Staff began to distinguish between prisoners of old ("good girls") and an incoming tide of "real criminals." Race was central to this distinction and, ultimately, to legitimating a change in the prison's control apparatus. I argue that Prison Services Company capitalized on this crisis by providing staff with a clinical discourse that offered quasi-scientific validation for racist constructions of "real criminals" and their needs. In short order, the disease concept became the central ideological register for justifying changes to the practice and objective of control within the prison.

In part 2 I examine the social technologies that constitute habilitation. Habilitation relies on a distinct power/knowledge apparatus. In contrast to rehabilitation, the object of habilitative control strategies is not to repair or restore a self that has been damaged; rather, it is to "break down" a self that is incomplete and disordered. In this sense, the endgame of habilitation is not to normalize the deviant self, but to manage the unruly one. Chapter 4 brings readers inside Project Habilitate Women and examines the mechanisms of power that program staff use to control prisoners' bodies and minds. These mechanisms include surveillance, confrontation, discipline, and humiliation. I demonstrate that power strategies serve both repressive and probative functions. They ensure behavioral conformity by detecting and sanctioning prohibited acts. They simultaneously generate knowledge of prisoners' habits and customs that serve as one basis for the program's efforts to diagnose and manage the self. Chapter 5 scrutinizes the kinds of knowledge about the self that the habilitative control apparatus yields. While the previous chapter analyzes how program staff know what they know about prisoners' selves, this chapter inventories the contents of that knowledge. The images of internal disorder that counselors "mirror" back to prisoners draw on racially controlling images of African American women across three domains: motherhood, sexuality, and labor market.

In the final section of the book, I consider the consequences of this new system of punishment from the perspective of those who are its targets—predominantly poor, African American women with some connection to the illicit drug economy. Most women resisted the program's efforts to change their identities, others surrendered, but all struggled to navigate the new penology in ways that minimized their exposure to routine humiliations and maximized their efforts to achieve respectability. In chapter 6 I examine how prisoners experienced and made sense of habilitation. They likened the experience to "renting out one's head" and revealed that they pursued one of three strategies in response to it. These included "surrendering to the process," "faking it to make it," and open defiance. The remainder of the chapter considers the first of these paths, surrender, and identifies the various factors that pushed some women into accepting the program's addiction ideology and abandoning their claims to an autonomous self. Chapter 7 documents the struggles of women who rejected the PHW's addiction philosophy in whole or in part. These women pursued one of two strategies. Either they engaged in open defiance or they "faked it." Women who engaged in open defiance did so to simultaneously (1) achieve an autonomous self and (2) provoke program staff into releasing them back into the prison's general population. For women who were sentenced directly into the program or those who faced additional years in prison should they fail to successfully complete it, open defiance was not an option. Instead, they engaged in a strategy of "faking it to make it," which involved a complex set of distinctions between public conformity and private unruliness, the "rented head" and the "real" self.

The conclusion reports on what happened to Red and other women in the years following their release from prison and traces the expanding influence of habilation and disease rhetoric throughout the prison. Since I left the field, PHW's treatment modality has been replicated in women's prisons and in community correctional settings across the country.[50] Yet the habilitative model could hardly be considered a success. Most of the women I studied resisted the program's efforts to change their identities, and they did so in ways that were often dramatic and consequential. Substantively, their acts of resistance were not so much organized in defense of either their drug use or criminal careers, but in defense of the integrity and essential goodness of their "real" selves. While their struggle presents a compelling portrait of the resilience of the self, it invites sustained reflection and debate on the punitive character of the new penology.

PART I

The End of Rehabilitation

1

Getting Tough on Women

How Punishment Changed

Everything's changing. We're not supposed to call the warden "Daddy" anymore.
—Prisoner, on the transition to the new prison

Unfounding is like rewriting history.
—Warden Richardson

Warden Richardson looked uncomfortable during the press conference. He was a large man with a commanding presence, but today, as he waited to be introduced, he was decidedly unsettled. He alternately shifted his weight forward onto the balls of his feet and then backward onto his heels until he lost his balance and had to be steadied by a correctional officer. He fumbled with his watchband, wiped his eyeglasses, and elaborately folded and refolded his handkerchief before returning it to his pocket. When it was finally his turn to speak, he appeared startled and asked a well-dressed man to his left if he would prefer to introduce himself. The man smiled faintly and nodded for the warden to begin. The warden cleared his throat, welcomed everyone to East State Women's Correctional Institution, and declared, "Today is the sixty-fifth anniversary of our founding as the first and only women's prison in the state. I am also pleased to announce that we are here to celebrate not one but two anniversaries, for today is the first anniversary of our future." He spoke briefly of the prison's origins in the 19th-century reformatory movement and its long-standing commitment to rehabilitating women prisoners. He then motioned the well-dressed man to come forward and introduced him as a "partner and pioneer in correctional innovation" and a "strategic resource for winning the War on Drugs."

The press conference took place in January 1994, a year considered by many state officials to be a turning point in the War on Drugs. Arrests and convictions of drug offenders had reached unprecedented highs. The punishments associated with drug crimes, particularly cocaine-related incidents, had become demonstrably harsher, and most carried mandatory multiyear prison sentences. Men and women convicted of drug offenses were now more likely to be sentenced to prison and, while there, serve considerably longer terms. Prisons across the state had also changed. Funding for rehabilitation, vocational, and education programs was sharply reduced and in many of the men's prisons dropped altogether. Surplus funding went to new prison construction and the acquisition of surveillance and restraint technologies like ceiling-mounted cameras and fortified cell doors. In annual criminal justice reports and political stump speeches, politicians and bureaucrats presented increases in arrest and incarceration rates and the "hardening" of prisons as good things, signs that local agencies and the state government were winning the War on Drugs.

The flaw in this formulation—one that had recently come to dominant political discourse behind the doors of the state capitol—was a sizeable and politically unwieldy overcrowding problem in the state's only prison for women. Poor conditions in the prison had attracted national attention, prompting investigations by human rights groups and a series of class action lawsuits charging the state with violating the 8th Amendment's ban on cruel and unusual punishment. State officials responded by building a new, larger facility for women in 1992. When, just eighteen months later, it too became overcrowded, both prison administrators and state officials faced a formidable problem—how to reduce the size of the prison population without appearing soft on crime? Mandatory sentencing policies meant that early release and community-based rehabilitation programs were out of the question. The political climate in the state, particularly widespread support for a punitive response to drug offenders, positioned reform as not only the antithesis of punishment, but as a failed and pointless endeavor. What was needed was a response to the overcrowding problem that would embody the ideals of the "tough on crime" movement while serving to shrink the size of the prisoner population.

The strategy prison administrators would come to pursue was embodied in the form of the well-dressed man whom Warden Richardson was in the process of introducing to guests at the press conference. His name was Dr. Michael Nesbitt, and he was vice president in charge of the clinical division of Prison Services Company. His company was the lone supplier of health care services to inmates throughout the state and one of the largest providers of correctional medical care in the country.[1] The Company was a joint sponsor of the press conference and, it would seem, of the future of punishment more generally. Invitations to the event billed it as a coming-out party in honor of the "promising future of women's corrections," and a celebration of the "strategic" partnering of government and private industry to resolve the interrelated problems of drug addiction, crime, and prison overcrowding.

The press conference was staged inside one of the prison's largest housing units and attended by a mix of criminal justice insiders and professional outsiders, among them journalists, politicians, judges, prosecutors, administrators of social service agencies, university researchers, and community organizers. The focus of the day's festivities was not on either of the most visible and costly developments that had recently taken root at East State Women's Correctional Institution. The press release made no mention of the fact that the facility where we all assembled was barely two years old and was the architectural antithesis of its reformatory-era predecessor. Nor did any of the day's speakers address the installation of new surveillance equipment, even though this had been the subject of an intense and ultimately successful campaign by officials from the state Department of Correction to convince prison administrators of its utility. As the day's proceedings wore on, it became clear that the key harbinger of the penological future was not to be found in electronics or architecture. Rather, the future was in social technologies that advanced the possibility of both organizational and individual transformation. Speaker after speaker revealed that these technologies held the promise of remaking women drug offenders into law-abiding citizens, and antiquated, seemingly ineffectual total institutions like the prison into "bottom line" organizations. Both sets of transformations would be realized in and through Project Habilitate Women, an experimental drug treatment program that was designed and managed by the Company and housed and operated within the institutional environs of the prison. When asked by a reporter how the program would bring about such sweeping changes, Dr. Nesbitt leaned forward to reply but was interrupted by the warden, who said with a wink, "We're unfounding rehabilitation."

It was an intriguing turn of phrase. "Unfounding" is part of the lexicon of the criminal justice system, although the warden's use of the term was a creative appropriation from its customary usage. The term traditionally refers to a formal statement issued by police departments declaring that a crime previously thought to have occurred never actually took place. As a record-keeping practice, unfounding is intended to correct for crime reports that turn out to be false or erroneous (e.g., "police unfounded the crime after learning the report was false"). But it is a political practice as well. Unfounding offers police a strategic means of manipulating the official crime rate in order to accomplish any number of political objectives.[2] When I spoke with the warden after the press conference, I asked why he used this term to characterize the transition from older, rehabilitative styles of control to a new penology. He explained that he meant the phrase as an "inside joke" about the zero-sum politics of the drug war. He elaborated:

> WARDEN: It's wrecking havoc on how we run things in here. Look, there isn't any room anymore for civil debate. You're either tough on crime or you're not. If you say rehabilitation, you're soft. And if you're soft, you're out. They don't give a damn about what actually goes on in prison or what works in terms of managing inmates. . . . That's why this new program is called [Project] *Habilitate* [his emphasis]. The executives at [the Company] are not stupid, they're not going to try to sell something that nobody wants.
>
> JM: So "unfounding rehabilitation" means renaming it? Repackaging it for political purposes?
>
> WARDEN: No, it's more than that. What I meant is that there's tremendous pressure to rethink everything—who we are, what we do. It's like the past is not a part of us—of this the current enterprise. . . . Unfounding is like rewriting history.

The warden's comments on the politics of institutional change in the prison system offer a unique vantage from which to consider current debates over the evolving character of punishment in the United States. The War on Drugs and the emergence of the "get tough" movement mark a stunning reversal of the dominant ideology of punishment. That ideology, referred to as "correctionalism" or "penal welfarism," is characterized by a modernist commitment to reforming and normalizing criminal offenders.[3] As a philosophy, correctionalism survived, prospered, and ascended to penal orthodoxy over the better part of a century.[4] Although it is certainly the case that practical concerns with order and control have often outstripped the central tenets of correctionalism in shaping the ways that prisons are actually run, reform and rehabilitation have endured as legitimating ideals, serving to guide and justify the larger project of confinement.[5]

At the center of current debates is the question of whether the punitive policies of the drug war signal the end of the rehabilitative ideal and the correctionalist regime of which it is a part. Those who argue that we are in the midst of a "new" or "postmodern" penology point out that prisons no longer pursue the "technical transformation" of individual offenders.[6] Instead, the phenomenon of mass incarceration and the rise of supermax facilities suggest that today's prisons operate as little more than human warehouses, committed to risk management and institutional security.[7] In her book *Total Confinement*, anthropologist Lorna Rhodes reports that maximum security prisons for men offer little in the way of rehabilitative programming or possibilities for self-improvement. Indeed, the very logic of control in these prisons would appear to undermine a philosophy of correctionalism, since rehabilitation is here posited as the very antithesis of security and order.

Other scholars caution against such a reading. Treating current punitive policies as if they represent a definitive break with the past or the coalescence of a new, postmodern penology obscures the extent to which various features of correctionalism endure.[8] This is particularly salient for considering the apparatus of control on the feminine side of the penal system. Women's prisons have proven historically resistant to political and intellectual fads. As criminologists Kruttschnitt and Gartner argue in *Marking Time in the Golden State*, these institutions are remarkable in terms of their continuities and, in particular, their long-standing prioritization of gendered logics of reform.

Nonetheless, continuity in women's prisons is at least partly attributable to stability in the size of the inmate population. For much of the 20th century, the number of women sentenced to state prisons grew very little. The drug war, of course, changed all this—increasing the overall incarceration rate to five times its average from the early 1970s.[9] Among women, the rate of increase has been roughly double that of men from the 1980s through the turn of the century.[10] It seems likely that explosive population growth over a very short period would destabilize even long-standing patterns of control. This, combined with the zero-sum politics of the drug war, suggest that at the end of the century women's prisons faced, if not a period of profound transformation, then at least an institutional rupture with the continuities of the past. This is in fact precisely what the warden meant when he remarked that current policies were "unfounding" the rehabilitative ideal in the prison. Indeed, the challenge that the "get tough" movement poses for correctionalism lies not only in its demand that prisons adopt punitive technologies of control, but also in its insistence that they dispense with past logics of reform.

I am interested in what happened to the rehabilitative ideal within the local context of the women's prison. Most scholarly accounts locate the source of rehabilitation's collapse within larger structural arrangements, most notably welfare state restructuring and the cultural anxieties of late modernism.[11] This chapter offers an alternative account, one that emphasizes the crucial role played by state actors on the ground. Shifts in the political economy and broader cultural sensibilities debut as crises within institutions, and it is precisely in these moments of crisis that routine practices and working ideologies are disrupted, and subject to challenge and debate. In these moments, local actors endeavor to identify and define the kind of problems they face, develop strategic and meaningful responses to those problems, and construct new vocabularies of motive to legitimate changes in organizational practice. Although their responses are constrained by larger structural forces, those forces do not determine these responses.[12] In this sense, state policy is given its form in and through the struggles of its agents to overcome creatively and strategically the crises that confront them. To gauge whether the drug war has indeed ushered in a new penology, it is necessary to first examine how these local agents interpreted and reconciled the "get tough" mandate in light of institutional traditions and ongoing organizational concerns.

My focus in this chapter is on prison administrators and line staff, most of whom were trained within a correctionalist paradigm and who were vested, both organizationally and ideologically, in the reform of the women prisoners.[13] What challenges did the overcrowding problem pose for their sense of the prison's mission? How did they reconcile the punitive demands of "get tough" with the prison's reformist traditions? The future with the past? The sections that follow demonstrate that although prison staff were early critics of "get tough" policies, the politics and circumstances of the drug war sparked a series of resource and ideological crises that undermined their support for correctionalism and weakened their commitment to preserving the prison's reformist legacy. I argue that it is within this crucible of crisis and rupture that the staff abandoned long-standing ideologies and practices, and "unfounded" rehabilitation.

The New Prison

Prior to the construction of the new prison, incarcerated women were held in an unwalled, 19th-century facility that had originally been designed to accommodate forty-five prisoners. Over the years, the facility had been expanded to hold almost double this number, but staggering increases in the women's incarceration rate meant that by the late 1980s the inmate population well exceeded the facility's expanded capacity.[14] In lawsuits filed against the warden and the Department of Correction, prisoners complained of being "packed like cattle" in the old facility and of having to sleep on the floor of a converted activity room. Attorneys representing the inmates contended that these conditions amounted to cruel and unusual punishment and were therefore unconstitutional. In the interest of settling the lawsuits and avoiding future overcrowding problems, state legislators quickly approved the Department of Correction's request to build a larger, "state of the art" prison for women. Although the warden requested that the original facility be retained to serve as a secondary space to deal with "population overflow," state officials denied the request. In his memorandum to the warden, the commissioner of correction explained that the old facility was "insufficiently secure."[15]

From the beginning, the new prison was a catalyst for an increasingly antagonistic relationship between East State's senior administrative staff and officials from the Department of Correction. Senior staff complained that they were left out of design decisions and that state officials ignored their suggestions for the new facility. Prison staff were particularly aggrieved by what they regarded as the security-conscious and "masculine" design of the new prison. Staff Lieutenant Miriam Johnson recounted some of these concerns in an interview:

> It was just too much, too much on the security end of things. It looks like a concrete bunker, like a place you'd put the worst of the worst in. You don't need all that for women. The old prison didn't even have a fence until a few years ago. Even back then, it was rarely a problem. . . . Women just don't present the same kind of problems that men do.

Echoing these sentiments, Deputy Warden Harriet Pearson recalled that she filed a report with the Department of Correction to complain that the new design was "masculine" and "inappropriate for women." Despite these and other complaints, construction on the facility went forward as planned.

Upon completion, the new prison bore little resemblance to its predecessor. There were no curtains on the windows, outdoor picnic tables, or flowerbeds. Instead, featureless, low-rise, green and gray buildings rose up from a grassy clearing and were set apart from the landscape by perimeter fencing and razor wire. The only notable aspect of the new facility was that it was so *prison-like*, a newcomer might mistakenly assume that the inmates held there were men. That was, of course, precisely the point. Among other things, the overcrowding lawsuits urged the state to adopt an "equal treatment" framework for making resources and opportunities available to women prisoners. The Department of Correction endeavored to do so, although it expanded the definition of "equal treatment" to include not only access to resources and opportunities, but also parity in the conditions of confinement. In a memo to Warden Richardson, a high-ranking state official described the "equal treatment" policy this way: "Prisons for either men or women are not

vacations from life. They should exhibit toughness, consistency, and consequences." Women prisoners received a much-needed law library as a result
of this policy, but subsequent years brought what many prisoners and staff
regarded as far less desirable "equivalencies," including boot camps, razor
wire fences, and body cavity searches.

In fact, the Department of Correction's version of "equal treatment"
did not produce gender neutrality in the prison system so much as it universally masculinized the physical structure of incarceration.[16] In designing the new prison the way that they had, the Department of Correction
made men's prisons the model for *all* prisons. This represented a significant
departure from past policy. Since the 19th century, the prison system in East
State and throughout much of the country was patterned on a "separate
spheres" model in which presumed differences between men and women
necessitated the use of separate prison facilities and gender-specific forms
of control.[17] While "heavy walls and strong locks" were regarded as necessary to counter hypothetical dangers posed by male prisoners, women
occasioned few of the same concerns. Indeed, separate spheres meant that
women's prisons were less immediately bound to prevailing trends in penology since these trends were premised on theories about men's criminality,
and were therefore considered inapplicable or inappropriate for women.
Gender distinctions were symbolized in the architectures of 19th- and early
20th-century men's and women's facilities, particularly the designation of
foreboding, fortresslike penitentiaries for men and unwalled, cottage-style
reformatories for women.[18]

The iconography of the new women's prison challenged the logic of separate spheres by adopting many of the features in use in the state's prisons
for men. This is evident in the glittering razor wire and heavy steel doors
that greet visitors as they enter the new prison and in isolation cells, control booths, and mechanized gates that regulate the movement of prisoners
and staff within the interior of the facility. Although senior prison staff complained that women did not warrant the same kinds of security precautions
as men, the state's equal treatment framework disallows formal recognition
of gender difference. Instead, the Department of Correction endeavored
to make all prisons within a given security classification (e.g., maximum,
medium, minimum) the same. The new women's prison is designated
"medium plus," meaning that the facility has a special "max" unit to house
prisoners who are considered security risks. As a medium security facility,
the new women's prison is, as the commissioner of the Department of Correction told a group of foreign dignitaries during a tour, "indistinguishable
from the medium-rated facilities for men." He continued proudly, "We could

easily house high risk men in the max unit here without having to make additional fortifications."

One of the state officials I interviewed acknowledged that the design of the new prison was "probably overkill." Nonetheless, she and other decision makers made a point to emphasize in interviews with me, as well as in meetings with prison administrators, that they had good reasons for designing the facility in the way that they had. First, they hoped that by making the facility the structural equivalent of medium-rated facilities for men, they could avoid lawsuits over sex discrimination. During one meeting with prison administrators, this official reported:

> Sex discrimination is a two-way street. Look, men could file suit, claiming the women have it easier, have more freedoms, that they [women] aren't subject to same degree of regulation. . . . So either way you look at it, it's important that a medium facility is the same, whichever group you're dealing with.

Second, the state intended the design of the facility to both symbolize and facilitate the transition from correctionalism to "get tough." The commissioner of correction explained in an interview:

> The state decided to go forward with this ["get tough"] as early as 1986. And since 1986 we've been working with our facilities to increase security, enhance public safety, emphasize accountability and discipline for our prisoners, and make prison an unpleasant—humane but unpleasant place. They [those at the women's prison] have not done that. They have continued to do the same thing they've always done—which I'm becoming convinced doesn't accomplish what it needs to. They're the last of our facilities to have not taken steps toward this. . . . The [new] facility is helping them implement changes by prioritizing security and order.

What the women's prison had "always done," according to the commissioner, was emphasize rehabilitation and reform over punishment and security. Rehabilitation came under fire both in the state and across the nation as early as the mid-1970s with the publication of Robert Martinson's "What Works?" report.[19] The Martinson report surveyed 231 social science studies examining the impact of a variety of prison-based treatment programs on the likelihood that prisoners would commit new crimes following their release from prison. Based on negative correlations in those studies, Martinson and his colleagues argued that prison rehabilitation programs had no salutary effect on recidivism rates. The report concluded with the infamous declaration that when it comes to prison rehabilitation programs, "nothing works."[20] Several state officials invoked both the Martinson report and rising crime rates to account for the emergence and popularity of "get tough" policies in the state. A Department of Correction official noted in an interview:

> "Nothing works" made intuitive sense, I think. Crime rates were going up, the incarceration rate was going up and you didn't have to commission a study to come to the conclusion that what we were doing, and I mean "we" in terms of prisons in general, was not working.

In the wake of "nothing works," the Department of Correction endorsed a report released by a state sentencing commission that concluded that the goals of punishment should be (in order of priority): incapacitation of offenders, restoration of victims' rights, and rehabilitation. Rehabilitation was, in fact, a very distant third. A projected expenditure report released by the Department for the ten-year period 1987–1996 revealed that over 90% of the expanded budget was earmarked for new prison construction, facility improvement, and personnel, with less than 7% designated for rehabilitative programs including education, vocational training, counseling services, and drug treatment.[21] Rehabilitation was ideologically overspent as well. Administrators from the state's men's prisons claimed that it contributed to violence and disorder, while at least two high-ranking state officials publicly characterized it as a "proven failure" and "soft."

Department of Correction officials hoped the design of the new facility would encourage East State's administrators to prioritize "security and order" over "reform and rehabilitation." Architecture, however, is not always a reliable guide to penal regimes. New systems evolve in advance of replacement buildings, and antiquated structures endure well beyond the era for which they were designed. In East State's case, the rehabilitative ethos did not end with the closing of the original, reformatory-era facility in 1992. East State's administrators and correctional officers were largely unpersuaded by rehabilitation's critics and tough-talking state officials. Supervisory personnel like Jim, a staff lieutenant whose entire career was spent in the women's prison, criticized "get tough" measures in terms of gender distinctions and organizational integrity:

> I'm not gonna dis the commissioner. He's a smart man and what he's done in [men's prison] has been effective in cutting down on assaults on officers and inmate on inmate violence. But his telling us that we're not doing right

is . . . it hurts, it's a smack in the face. It's kinda like if somebody said everything you've been doing with your life is wrong. How can he say that? He
doesn't know these women or what they need. He doesn't know the best
way to handle them and, yeah, I'll say it right now—this is my training, my
experience. It's what *I do best*. [his emphasis]

In their recollections of this period, senior staff echoed Jim's observation
that the new prison and the "get tough" movement of which it was a part were
problematic, in terms of both their failure to honor gender differences among
prisoners as well as their failure to honor the prison's organizational culture
and history. When I asked one correctional officer if he thought the new
prison ensured equal treatment for women, he shook his head negatively and
said, "No, it just treats women as if they're men. That's not progress at all, it
ignores our history." Indeed, their reluctance to embrace "get tough" was not
born of a general criticism of security enhancements or even efforts to make
prisons "unpleasant." Like Jim, many officers and administrators felt that
such measures improved conditions in men's prisons. Instead, their criticism
of "get tough" and of the design of the new prison was anchored in their belief
that the prison's history was also its destiny. When I asked them to elaborate,
one staff member after another would tell me the story of East State's origins,
which they referred to as the "founder's tale."

The Founder's Tale

Throughout the first several months of my fieldwork, almost every senior-
level staff member I came into regular contact with made a point to ask me
if I was familiar with the "founder's tale" and whether I had seen the deputy
warden's collection of early, black-and-white photographs of the original
facility. Even when, some months later, I began to answer these questions in
the affirmative, many staff members proceeded to tell me the story of East
State's origins anyway. Their narratives differed very little from one another,
and virtually all began with the observation that prison scandals are "nothing new." Harriet Pearson, the deputy warden whose career spanned nearly
forty years in the women's prison, elaborated in an early interview:

All prisons have scandals, there's nothing new in that. This overcrowding
thing has people talking . . . but it's not a scandal. I'll bet you didn't know
this prison began with a scandal. It did . . . there was no such things as
women's prisons back then, back in the 1800s. They kept the women with
the men, in the same prison, that's exactly what they did. There weren't the

numbers we have today but there was still a good lot of women, living up in a section of [men's prison]. Well, I can't even begin to tell you what went on up in there, Lord! There was supposedly prostitution rings, the warden running a prostitution ring with some of them girls, I don't know who for, but I think it was his good old boys, you know? But the scandal really hit when some of those girls got pregnant, you know, 'cause the men and women prisoners weren't supposed to have no kind of contact. And, you know, those girls didn't come in pregnant so it was a big scandal.

Staff members identified the period when the scandals took place in vague terms—usually as the "1800s" or "late 1800s." Records from the 1890 convention of the Women's Christian Temperance Union show that members of that group proposed that the state erect a separate reformatory for women in order to improve the conditions of women's confinement.[22] The state initially agreed to provide a separate work-farm facility for women, but later rescinded this offer due to budgetary constraints. It was not until 1929 that prison reform groups were able to secure the financial resources and political support necessary to open the first and only correctional facility for women in the state. According to Harriet Pearson, this only happened because of pressure exerted by "society ladies":

> Back then you had a situation where women offenders were truly considered the worst of the worst. They were worse than men in terms of how the public thought of them. They were really despised and, really, people thought of them as evil, as not worth the effort to improve. But a group of society ladies here in [the state] took up their cause, because they believed these women were reformable and because conditions were just so bad, someone had to reach out to them. . . . They believed that if you treated women like women, you know, created a homelike environment, they could be reformed. So that's what they did. They set out to create a place specifically for troubled women to provide what they needed and to be run by woman. They [society ladies] fought for those girls. They had resources. They had money and family influence and they were some of the key players in the [prison] reform movement at the time. . . . So this prison is truly what they created, a reformatory, a women's reformatory. Those reformers made us what we are, made this prison into a place where troubled women can get healed. That's our history . . . this isn't just any old prison.

The central claim in the founder's tale is that East State was one of the progenitors of the 19th-century women's reformatory movement. That movement had two goals—institutional improvement and individual redemption.[23] Reformers believed that both could be achieved by cleaving the penal system into masculine and feminine spheres. Abuse and neglect at the hands of male prison guards was to be eliminated by relocating women prisoners into separate, "feminine" facilities that were to be administered and run by women. The creation of separate institutions enabled the second goal, individual redemption, by providing a "homelike" institutional space and a set of familial relationships that encouraged the emergence of prisoner's "true," feminine nature. In contrast to the penitentiary with its large, congregate buildings encircled by an imposing perimeter wall, reformatories consisted of several small cottages, each boasting domestic amenities like flowers, music, and children's nurseries. The cottages were situated amid gardens and groves on multi-acre, unwalled campuses, most located outside rural farming communities. Within the cottages, small groups of inmates lived and interacted as "families" with matrons and their assistants performing the role of maternal custodians. Reformatories recruited a specific category of offender, young women charged with petty misdemeanors, whom they claimed were the best candidates for change.[24]

While it was surely the case that the prison's origins are linked in fundamental ways to Progressive-era activism, East State Women's Correctional Institution was never a reformatory in the archetypal sense, and this was reflected in its name. In fact, the facility opened in 1929, a period when historians suggest that the reformatory model was collapsing under the weight of resource limitations and contradictory institutional imperatives.[25] By the late 1930s, most reformatories had morphed into quasi-custodial institutions. In many ways, East State's earliest guise embraced these contradictions. Living space was not distributed among various cottages but was located within a congregate facility that, for the most part, resembled facilities for men, except that it had curtains on the windows and lacked perimeter fencing and gun towers. Although women were the primary caretakers of the facility, they did not enjoy autonomy within the wider prison system. Prior to the 1950s, the wife of the warden from a nearby men's workhouse was designated as head matron of the women's facility, but her husband supervised her work. East State's inmate population represented yet another crucial modification on the reformatory ideal. Shortly after the facility was built, judges not only sentenced young, female misdemeanants to prison terms but also immediately began transferring the entire population of adult women from jails and prisons to the new facility. In the years that followed, all women sentenced to prison terms were sent there, not just those convicted of misdemeanor crimes.

Staff members downplayed these differences in the founder's narrative through symbolic displays of institutional lineage. In 1994, the year of the press conference, a purple banner hung from the ceiling of the prison cafeteria that read, "Celebrating 65 Years of Reform." Grainy, black-and-white photographs of the original facility and of matrons with young, predominantly white inmates were featured in reception areas and the corridor leading to administrators' offices. What senior staff members made a point to emphasize when they claimed a reformatory pedigree was not building architecture or inmate characteristics, but a doctrine of separate spheres that marked a division between "masculine" and "feminine" sides of the penal system and of the objective and practice of control therein. What made East State a reformatory, according to senior staff, was that its founders established "healing" and treatment as control mechanisms suited to women. As Ms. Barker, the senior prison counselor, explained in an interview, this emphasis on healing and "change" stands in sharp contrast to the security concerns that continue to animate punishment practices in men's facilities:

A women's prison is different from most men's facilities because most females aren't dangerous and they know they've done something wrong— you don't have to punish them to get them to see that. Here, we try to correct behavior by creating a space for change and they can only change with support from us, their kids, and their families.

This distinction between men's and women's prisons is, of course, as much rhetorical as it is reflective of actual differences in practice. As historians have noted of even model reformatories, mundane custodial concerns with security, order, and discipline rivaled "sisterly" reform efforts in the day-to-day interactions between the matrons and their "wayward" charges.[26] East State's original facility, a congregate building rather than cottages, suggests that the reformist goal of providing prisoners with "homelike" living arrangements was outweighed by a custodial interest in maximizing surveillance.[27] In a parallel sense, administrators of men's prisons have, since the 19th century, relied on the language of reform and rehabilitation to shore up the legitimacy of punishment practices, even when such practices appear as counter to these goals.[28] My point here is that the founder's tale and East State's symbolic representations of the reformatory movement should not be regarded as a reliable guide to how control was actually deployed in the institution's past, but should be seen instead as constitutive features of the institution's vocabulary of motive in the present.[29] This vocabulary has implications for the gendered organization of penal practice—particularly in terms of the arrangements and mechanisms through which control is and can be accomplished. The reformist goals of "change" and "support" were realized through discipline and surveillance—the same mechanisms used to accomplish security and punishment in men's prisons—but the apparatus through which these operate is different. As staff members explained, the goal of rehabilitation was not to contain dangerous offenders or to deter unwitting ones but to "support" and restore women to their "true," "feminine" nature, and this was accomplished through a control apparatus that mimicked familial arrangements.

Good Girls and Their Warden Daddy: Rehabilitative Paternalism and the Idiom of Need

During one of my earliest visits to East State, I spent the better part of an afternoon hanging out with two prisoners who were considered "old-timers" among their peers. Both women were in their early forties and each had served the first several years of her current sentence in the "old" prison. The warden and the deputy warden, along with a number of other administrators and correctional officers, were transplanted from the old facility into the new one and a good bit of our conversation that day involved the perks both women felt they enjoyed from knowing high-ranking staff members for the better part of a decade. I asked for an example and Terasia offered the following:

> You're supposed to go through . . . [the] classification [committee] to get work assignments, even housing. . . . Now everyone who's been around knows that yeah, ya gotta put in a request through classification, but you really go straight to Daddy or Mom if you can. If you got good relations with them, you go to them and tell them what you need.

I asked her to clarify and Terasia chuckled: "Mom is Deputy Warden [Pearson] . . . she still likes to be called that, 'Mom,' and the warden—some girls still call him 'Daddy' but since moving [to the new prison] we're not supposed to anymore."

Inmates like Terasia and other old-timers were unable to tell me the origin of the nicknames, only that the names had been in use for as long as they could remember.[30] Most of the women I spoke with had no objection to the nicknames because the warden treated them as if they were "his own." Senior staff, including the warden, routinely echoed this sentiment, referring to inmates in the possessive, as "our girls" or "my girls." More than once I heard the deputy warden characterize her job as "taking care of my girls." When I asked Frank, a correctional officer with seven years on the job, to describe his work he said, "They [inmates] are scared . . . of men because they've been abused. So I work to gain their trust, the good ones, and let them know that I'm here to help them whatever they need—take care of them and look after them while they're here."

Familial imagery—particularly of parents and their children—remained a prominent feature of prison vernacular throughout the first couple of years of my fieldwork. Studies of women's prisons undertaken as early as the 1960s and through the turn of the century report on the pervasiveness and persistence of familial references among inmates and between inmates and staff.[31] Although it has long been the case that women's prisons are institutions that rarely seem to outrun their own pasts, there is something more than linguistic inertia at work here. Family talk reveals a particular set of control practices and arrangements that are premised on a logic of gender difference, feminine subjectivity, and moral accountability. Staff members characterized this power/knowledge apparatus in ideological terms as "rehabilitative" or "reform oriented," while prisoners identified it in terms of the structure of their relations with staff (e.g., "a family system" or "when the warden was Daddy"). Both characterizations are narrow in scope, and therefore I have chosen to refer to this particular constellation of control practices, discourses, and relations as "rehabilitative paternalism."

Rehabilitative paternalism is the system of control that was in place in the period prior to the drug war. Its logic and arrangements were what staff endeavored to preserve in the wake of the Department of Correction's demands that they "get tough" and to encode in the design of the new prison. Rehabilitative paternalism is the gendered counterpart of correctionalism. Like correctionalism, it is guided by the rehabilitative ideal—the belief that the central task of the prison is the normalization of criminal offenders. What distinguishes rehabilitative paternalism from the correctionalist forms encountered in men's prisons is that it operates through quasi-familial arrangements that reflect both the institutional conditions of East State's founding and a logic of gender difference and feminine subjectivity. Further, it is legitimated according to the staff's construction of the needs of women prisoners.

Difference, Subjectivity, and the Structure of Control

In situating themselves as parental figures and caretakers, staff members downplayed the custodial aspects of their work. Several went so far as to argue that prison—as an institutional environment and a disciplinary arrangement—was inappropriate for the "girls." One correctional officer who had recently been transferred from the men's prison said:

CO: Most of these girls don't need to be in prison. In the short time I'm here, I know we can't treat them like regular inmates, like men. Their issues are different and that makes our job different. . . . Here the goal is and has been about rehabilitation rather than just security alone.

JM: But isn't rehabilitation a goal in men's facilities as well?

CO: Yeah, in a way, but rehab is not the main thing—it's a side dish. Security is the priority over there. Men and women are different. In some ways, it's like these girls are more fucked up than men and less fucked up than men, you know? They've got a whole lot going on—a lot of abuse and bad stuff—but they can't really be thought of as dangerous because they're not about proving, you know, toughness and manliness. Here it's not a contest of wills.

This officer's distinction between willful (male) inmates and "fucked up" girls is quite useful for understanding why quasi-familial arrangements carried over from the reformatory era remained a useful apparatus for deploying discipline and surveillance in the name of rehabilitation rather than punishment. In contrasting male and female prisoners, he suggests women are not "regular" inmates because they have been on the receiving end of abuse and "bad stuff." Administrators often made a point to note in press conferences and statewide warden's meetings that what primarily distinguished women offenders from their male counterparts was women's extensive histories of physical and sexual abuse.[32] Deputy Warden Pearson took this a step further, suggesting that women inmates could not "really" be considered criminals because they were "scared and confused." Other staff members characterized "the girls" along similar lines—for example, as "emotionally out of control," "vulnerable," "weak," or "psychiatrically unstable." In contrast, male inmates were regarded as the stuff of badness—staff described them as "dangerous," "tough," and "willful" even in the face of the totalizing power of the prison. In distinguishing men and women in terms of their capacity to act willfully and, concomitantly, their relation to crime (as criminals or victims), the comments offered by the correctional officer and other staff members reaffirm the logic behind splintering the penal system into divided and gendered halves.

But the distinction moves beyond merely reflecting the structural divisions of the penal system, it encodes gender into the ongoing meanings and practices associated with punishment and rehabilitation. In this sense, rehabilitation can only be a "side dish" in men's prisons because it is regarded as form of caretaking suited for those who do not choose their behavior.[33] To the extent that staff in men's prisons conflate masculinity with willfulness, this limits the possibilities for care and support since both generate a relational and emotional proximity that could be exploited by "dangerous" inmates.[34] Conversely, security measures in the form of perimeter gun towers and custodial conventions like lockdown and cell extractions were not present at East State during the early months of my fieldwork. Their absence was not so much a function of women's actual rule-breaking behavior (or lack thereof), but of the staff's abiding sense that such gestures were deeply inappropriate when directed at women.[35] In interviews, staff members offered two reasons for this. First, they indicated that security measures directed punitiveness toward offenders whose moral blameworthiness for their crimes was diminished by real or hypothetical victimization and hardships. A prison counselor explained her reluctance to lockdown the prison following one prisoner's successful escape attempt this way:

> We're talking about women who've suffered years of abuse, from the time they were little girls. Most of them are in trouble because of abusive men, you think they just went out and pulled off some carjacking on their own? We have that kind in here, but most of them aren't really criminals and it's hard to justify treating them as if they are.

Second, staff contended that security measures "revictimized" women by subjecting them to "masculine" punishments and, therefore, treated them as if they were men. At one meeting with Department of Correction officials, the deputy warden observed, "Punishment has got to fit the crime. If we adopt your policies, the punishment doesn't fit because we'll be treating them as if they are the same as the men . . . that's double jeopardy, it revictimizes these girls, and I object to it." Another officer with four years of experience at East State observed in an interview:

> Women are different, pure and simple. We all know that, you know that. They respond differently, they're here for different reasons. You can't "get tough" with them. I mean, you can, but that's not going to fix anything in terms of whether they reoffend when they get out of here. In fact, if you do . . . more of them is gonna end up back in here. Why? Cause they were abused before they got in here and they committed crimes. Now, we're gonna take them in and get tough, treat them like men? Forget it, you can't do that to these girls. It's not gonna work.

Of course, this is not to suggest that security measures and custodial practices were nonexistent in the institution. Staff routinely used standard disciplinary and surveillance measures like unannounced searches and solitary
confinement. More often than not, however, staff framed these measures as
rehabilitative in function though perhaps not in form. As the staff lieutenant said of sending an inmate to solitary confinement, "It's not being used
as punishment for punishment's sake but to get her to calm down so we can
figure out together what is the best course of action."[36]

Needs Talk

Staff legitimated differences in institutional priority between punishment
and rehabilitation through the idiom of need. In *Discipline and Punish*,
Foucault observed that the 19th-century penitentiary system relied on need
as a political instrument, one that was "meticulously prepared, calculated
and used."[37] In the contemporary prison system, the language of needs has
become the primary vehicle through which control policies and practices
are legitimated as socially desirable, institutionally necessary, and politically
neutral.[38] Although needs talk serves the same ends in men's and women's
prisons, its configuration varies between the two. In men's prisons, it is the
presumptive needs of the general public or the prison staff that are used to
legitimate control policy. In Rhodes' study of one such prison, she reports
that the decision to acquire stun belts was based on correctional officers'
need of "clean" forms of coercion.[39] In this instance, staff's needs were not
only prioritized relative to inmates but were regarded as antithetical to the
needs of inmates: "They [inmates] know in the long run they are gonna lose
. . . It is that basic dog psychology right there."

Needs talk was and is ubiquitous in East State, but it was not the needs
of staff or the general public that were used to legitimate control practices.
Rather, the system of rehabilitative paternalism was legitimated in terms of
the needs of inmates themselves. This was the case even when an inmate's
behavior ran counter to the image of the scared and powerless "good girl."
Consider the following exchange between the senior counselor and a staff
lieutenant following a fistfight between two inmates in the prison cafeteria:

COUNSELOR: I don't think disciplining her by relocating her to [a security
    housing unit] is appropriate. It's not what she needs at this point.
LIEUTENANT: I understand that. I only suggested it because I'm foggy on
    what caused her to act out with violence. She could be feeling insecure
    over there . . .

COUNSELOR: I'll have a talk with her. I do think this is about her insecurity, I know her well, but I want to be certain that whatever we do is in
response to that. Discipline is pointless if it doesn't take into account
where she's at.

In this example, staff recast violent behavior in terms of the dominant images
of the good girl—her insecurity and vulnerability. It is notable that both parties to this exchange immediately rejected an overt disciplinary response,
and that neither raised concerns about what the incident meant for staff
safety or institutional order. Instead, they endeavored to address the inmate's
needs arising from her insecurity. Note, too, that the counselor's diagnosis of
the problem and identification of need is not clinically rendered in terms of
psychiatric/medical expertise, but according to her personal knowledge of
the inmate garnered through the strength of a personal relationship.

The framing of needs talk based on personal, rather than clinical or custodial, relations was linked, in very immediate ways, to the paternalistic structure of staff–inmate relations. These relationships were facilitated through
the reform-oriented programs in the prison, particularly religious programming that regularly brought staff members, including administrators, into
informal contact with prisoners. Senior administrative staff, counselors,
and correctional officers participated alongside inmates in weekly Bible
study groups, Sunday church services, and prayer sessions.[40] The prevalence
of religious programming reflected senior staff's religiosity, but it also created opportunities for staff to learn more about prisoners' personal histories,
experiences, relationships, beliefs, and aspirations. In addition to generat-
ing knowledge, familial relations created the possibility for more immediate
and intimate forms of observation and discipline. Doris, a correctional officer with twelve years of experience at East State, explained that the warden
expected her and other officers to be "role models,"

I'm also seen as a role model by the warden and his staff and the inmates.
I'm encouraged to be a support person and a guide for them [prisoners], to
help them with anything they need to talk about.

The deputy warden echoed this by explaining to me the prison's reformist
mission:

To correct behavior that is deviant and to create a level of responsibility in
their minds. But also to teach the girls right from wrong by serving as role
models. Our [staff] behavior demonstrates how upstanding citizens are to

act, how men and women are to relate to one another. They [prisoners] learned how to act like bright, respectable young ladies and they learned to respect society and respect God.

Teaching "responsibility" and "respectability" meant that staff could and did admonish inmates for a variety of petty transgressions that ranged from dress code violations to disrespect.[41] Further, it involved them in the broader terrains of their charges' lives beyond the prison. In several instances, the deputy warden, senior counselor, and several correctional officers arranged transportation so that relatives and other caregivers could bring children to visit their mothers in prison. The deputy warden visited one inmate's ailing mother in the hospital and returned with pictures and "motherly advice" for the inmate.

Although staff members were quite sincere when they characterized these practices as "rehabilitative," "supportive," and "in the best interest of inmates," inmates were a bit more circumspect. One prisoner character-ized the familial arrangements and associated control practices as "vanilla" power. Indeed, while familial relations opened up lines of communication between staff and prisoners, the medium of their relationship—needs talk—masked the exercise of power.[42] As Terasia pointed out at the start of this section, informal relations with staff did offer inmates access to high-level administrators without having to steer through the prison bureaucracy. But that same informality meant they had to frame their requests in terms of needs rather than rights. One inmate, for example, told me that she had declined to meet with the attorneys involved in filing a class action over-crowding lawsuit against the prison because she didn't want to "hurt Mom's feelings." Many more, particularly those who did not enjoy close relations with the warden or deputy warden, complained that staff's widespread use of discretion amounted to favoritism and inconsistency. In the end, of course, it was staff who decided what inmates needed, and often there was a discon-nect between what inmates said they needed and how staff interpreted these needs. This was the case with inmate demands for a law library—something staff refused to take seriously despite the fact that access to legal materials is constitutionally mandated.

In those instances where staff and prisoners agreed on prisoners' needs, the outcomes were somewhat dubious. This was particularly the case with pharmacological drugs. Prisoners regularly requested these drugs for every-thing ranging from menstrual cramps, depression, and anxiety to "vio-lent thoughts." Although many women were diagnosed with depression or anxiety, many more were not. They frequently told me that they requested tranquilizers and other psychotropics to make life in the institution more bearable. One local newspaper reported that 70–80% of inmates in East State had been prescribed psychotropic medication since their arrival.[43] The doctor who supervised all medical treatment in the facility explained to me that the high prescription rate was linked to individual and institutional needs:

> [Medications are] an acceptable method of treating unacceptable behavior. . . . I don't prescribe it in every case, of course, but many refuse to begin working on their behavior until it's provided. . . . They come over here screaming and will not leave. They are emotionally unstable. . . . They are like bad little children screaming for candy.

Although staff characterized this system as "rehabilitative," it bore little resemblance to what prison scholars might recognize as the standard fare of rehabilitation. There were more religious programs than educational, vocational, and counseling services combined. Vocational training was often in name only, existing primarily to serve the needs of the institution rather than to provide real training for decent jobs.[44] Inmates rarely received counseling services. This was attributable, in part, to a lack of resources (each prison counselor had a caseload of one hundred inmates and numerous other duties, including administering and processing classification surveys). Arguably, it was also due to a lack of therapeutic vision. Staff regarded inmates as "girls" whose moral accountability for their crimes was diminished by their feminine subjectivity and past victimization. Staff positioned themselves as the guardians of inmates' needs, and it was through the idiom of need and the relations and mechanisms that supported it that the regime of rehabilitative paternalism flourished. This power/knowledge regime drew its legitimacy from the "separate sphere" arrangements of the reformatory era and an ongoing, gendered logic of practice in which "rehabilitation" was regarded as central to the project of confining women.

Institutional Crises and the Decline of the Rehabilitative Ideal

Twelve months after the press conference described at the opening of this chapter, administrators amended prison policy to make the use of "informal and/or familiar" forms of address a rule violation. Although the rule was only spottily enforced, prisoners who used terms like "Mom" or "Daddy" as a direct reference to the deputy warden and the warden were cited for "disrespect," a Category II offense that carried disciplinary penalties like the loss of recreation or phone time. When the rule change was announced, I asked

Terasia, an "old-timer," what impact she thought the rule change would have for staff–inmate relations. She answered me with uncharacteristic brevity: "Everything's changing. We're not supposed to call the warden 'Daddy' anymore. That says it all."

What was changing was rehabilitative paternalism, a system of control that had been in place prior to the drug war and one that administrators traced back to the prison's reformatory origins. It had been under attack for some time in the state, and signs of its deterioration were evident at the press conference. Indeed, the warden, his staff, and the business executives who cosponsored the event made a point to emphasize that the future of "women's corrections" was premised on a clear and distinct break from the past, and in particular, the rehabilitative ideal. At the same time, as this chapter has shown, prison staff and administrators were critical of "get tough" mandates and endeavored to find ways to preserve old arrangements. They were not successful.

It is important to emphasize that rehabilitative paternalism was not a passing fad; rather, it was literally built into the structural arrangements of the prison. To understand its end, we must attend to the institutional structure and the resources, meanings, and relations that sustained it. Political currents and larger policy mandates were not enough, in and of themselves, to wreck these arrangements. Instead, a series of resource and ideological crises destabilized these relations and subsequently undermined the structural and motivational supports necessary to maintain rehabilitative paternalism as a penal regime.

A Crisis of Resources

A resource crisis brewing in the state prison system became apparent in East State by the end of the 1980s and grew steadily worse throughout the 1990s and beyond. Drug war policies made themselves evident in the prison in the form of persistent and severe overcrowding—a condition with implications for every conceivable aspect of the prison budget, ranging from building maintenance to overtime allowances for line staff. It was overcrowding, of course, that ultimately forced the closure of the reformatory-era facility. The new facility, boasting four times the bed space of its predecessor, was overcrowded within a year and half of its opening.

Prison administrators petitioned the state for funds to construct an "overflow" wing. Their request was denied on the grounds that women constituted less than 10% of the total inmate population and, according to an internal Department of Correction memo, presented a "less urgent" set of needs and priorities than did male prisoners.[45] Compounding matters, a Department spokesperson noted that funds for the new, $25 million facility had been "borrowed against future appropriations," meaning that East State's slice of the corrections budget would grow proportionally smaller in coming years. Even more troubling for administrators and staff was the fact that the drug war showed no signs of slowing down. State politicians, liberal and conservative alike, continued to stump on a platform of law and order, and newspaper opinion polls reported that the vast majority of citizens in the state favored mandatory sentences for drug offenders and curtailment of early release programs. Projections from an independent research group predicted that within five years, the population of incarcerated women in the state would more than double.

In addition to a lack of material support and funding, the prison's resource crisis included dwindling administrative and political capital. Within total institutions like the prison, order is a valuable administrative resource. Wardens who are able to maintain order in their facilities use it as political leverage to secure various resources from the state and various forms of compliance from prisoners.[46] Overcrowding in the new prison gave rise to several forms of internal disorder. For example, a group of fourteen inmates with the assistance of a local inmate advocacy group and the American Civil Liberties Union threatened to file an additional round of lawsuits charging that overcrowding in the new facility had reached unconstitutional levels. Other prisoners loudly complained to correctional officers and administrators that overcrowding reduced privacy, limited opportunities for recreation, contributed to "petty" fights, and disrupted their strategies for "doing time." Several "old-timers" made a point to problematize the consequences of overcrowding for the "warden's system" (i.e., rehabilitative paternalism). Sofie explained:

> Overcrowding means little or no access, and the warden's system ran on access. So with more girls, what you think is gonna happen? Fewer of us got access to "Daddy" [she grimaces and gestures for quotation marks as she speaks], even girls with legit needs, and everyone starts complaining about favoritism. . . . And the pettiness, oh, it was a real trip. People start beefing with each other, lots of disrespect.

Indeed, inmate "beefs" (i.e., verbal threats that periodically led to physical confrontations) contributed to a surge in disciplinary problems that prompted some correctional officers, particularly newer ones, to voice doubts about the effectiveness of rehabilitative paternalism. Jon, a shift supervisor who had recently been promoted from the men's prison, complained to me about East State's gender differentiated system of control, "Look, I've been telling them we need to get real. It's not the 1950s anymore and we can't keep treating inmates like they're these innocent, little girls. They're not girls, they're criminals."

Incidents of disorder exacerbated the growing divide between East State's administrators and Department of Correction officials, and eroded whatever political capital prison administrators were once able to muster. Indeed, the Department had historically granted administrators at East State a fair degree of autonomy, but the overcrowding crisis and associated lawsuits ended that practice.[47] Following the construction of the new facility, Department of Correction officials commissioned an internal study to identify the causes of overcrowding in the women's prison. That report concluded that the majority of incoming inmates were sentenced to prison as a result of the state's mandatory sentencing laws. Nonetheless, state officials used the *fact* of overcrowding to speculate loudly and publicly on the effectiveness of the prison's paternalistic relations and reformist ideologies. At a statewide meeting of wardens and Department of Correction officials, the chief of the prison bureau diagnosed East State's overcrowding woes as the product of "too many softies on a mission."

The Department's solution to East State's problems with overcrowding and disorder was, of course, to do away with a gendered system of rehabilitation in favor of a "get tough," "equal treatment" approach to punishment. To overcome administrators' reluctance, officials approached East State administrators with both carrots and sticks. For example, the Department refused to approve emergency funds to build an addition to the facility, and they cut funding to rehabilitative programs that could not provide convincing proof that they were a cost-effective way to reduce inmate recidivism. Most programs that did not or could not provide this evidence were subsequently abandoned.[48] However, the Department did grant funds to support the acquisition of new surveillance technologies and security devices—items they regarded as instrumental for "emphasizing sanctions" and improving institutional order. The warden recounted the theme of his conversations with state officials during this period:

> Their message was consistent. It was, "Try our way or you won't get the funds. We'll release funds to support 'get tough' even if that does nothing to stop overcrowding." But they let it be known that overcrowding was our problem, not the state's, and that they weren't going to bail us out by building another wing even if it meant another lawsuit for all of us.

Beyond the Department of Correction, prison administrators lacked broader political support for rehabilitative models. As I noted earlier, political rhetoric in the state was organized with few exceptions around tough talk and tough images. Campaigning politicians and their brethren in the statehouse cloaked speeches, party platforms, and legislative proposals in the language of combat, mortal and otherwise: "eye for an eye," "three strikes and you're out," "zero tolerance," "get tough," and "lock 'em up." While the state did have a few high-ranking public officials who supported rehabilitative measures, particularly for first-time drug offenders, most of the state's legislators, judges, and other policy-making officials found themselves responding to the public's outcry for harsher prisons and longer sentences. A state senator who was a long-standing proponent of rehabilitative strategies told me, "The terms of this debate have been set. Forget anything approaching rehabilitation, it's get tough versus get tougher."

A Crisis of Meaning

Overcrowding and resource limitations were fomenting another sort of crisis—specifically, a crisis over the meaning of punishment. Although staff members were critical of "get tough" policies and the Department of Correction's encroachment on what they regarded as their professional terrain, many began to express frustration and anger at what they perceived as persistent lapses in institutional control. During a meeting of supervisory staff, a staff lieutenant commented, "I'm being called upon to defend a system that I'm losing confidence in. How can I legitimate something that doesn't appear to be working?"

In an effort to improve staff morale and to assuage concerns regarding the effectiveness of the rehabilitative system, Warden Richardson contacted researchers from a nearby state university to conduct an independent study of the overcrowding problem. The results from this study proved more embarrassing than the Department's earlier study. Although the university report identified mandatory sentencing as a significant factor contributing to overcrowding, it revealed a second reason for the dramatic population growth—inmate recidivism. Over 40% of incoming inmates had previously served time in the prison, with a mean of 3.5 prior incarcerations. Staff and administrators were certainly aware that recidivism was an issue before the release of the university report. Indeed, the "revolving door" frequently crept into their discussions of inmate disciplinary problems. In one classification meeting, for example, the senior counselor gestured to a pile of disciplinary reports and said, "It just seems that we're getting more girls who are making a career outta this. It's the revolving door problem." As her remark indicates, staff did not initially regard recidivism as a problem whose source was lodged in the prison. Rather, the source of recidivism was attributable to the influx of certain type of offender—career criminals.

In the politically charged context of the drug war, however, recidivism began to look more and more like an indicator of organizational failure. If rehabilitation was working, inmates would lead productive lives upon their release and would not return to prison on new charges. If rehabilitation was failing, it would be reflected in the recidivism rate. This was certainly the conclusion that Department of Correction officials were drawing in state-wide policy meetings when they characterized rehabilitation and treatment efforts as "soft," "ineffective," and "costly." The university report did little to counter this interpretation of recidivism data. In fact, it bolstered the conclusion that what staff did or failed to do had a direct bearing on inmate behavior. In one particularly damning section, researchers reported that 20% of the inmates at East State acknowledged using drugs or alcohol *during* their period of incarceration. It was hard to avoid the conclusion that prison staff were implicated in the criminality of their charges

In many ways, the university report served as the final nail in rehabilitation's coffin. It did so by calling into question the very thing that staff and administrators had struggled so hard to assert—the legitimacy of rehabilitation as a penal strategy. Administrators expressed surprise and dismay about the report's findings. Although several senior staff members remained stalwart defenders of rehabilitation, the release of the report encouraged other staff members to voice their concerns about the limitations of the institution's control structure. At one meeting following the release of the university report, the warden reiterated to senior staff the comments he had made earlier to me during an interview:

> Recidivism, in particular, is *our* problem [his emphasis]. Whether it is in reality our fault or not doesn't matter. That's how it looks to the public and to the DOC. High recidivism rates make us look like we could be doing more with them in here, though nobody wants to give us the funds to get something off the ground.

Despite their misgivings about "treating women like men," administrative staff acknowledged that overcrowding, limited resources, declining morale, and pressure from prisoners, state criminal justice officials, politicians, and the public were collectively bringing East State's tradition of reform to an unceremonious end. The senior counselor commented to me, "The writing is on the wall [laughing]. Literally! Look, we can't pretend that things can just go on the way they've been. The center ain't holding, you know?"

Unfounding Rehabilitation

The sheer magnitude of resource and legitimation crises did not mean that administrators were poised to accept the implementation of "get tough" penal strategies, but it did mean that they were prepared for the first time in their professional careers to break with the institution's past. This was by all accounts an unprecedented and heretofore inconceivable event. They inherited from the reformatory era a structural set of arrangements in the form of gender-segregated institutions and a two-tiered punishment system in which gender served as a proxy to organize and justify various disciplinary and surveillance practices. Their inheritance was also discursive, in that reform became the central rhetorical mechanism to legitimate practices on the feminine side of the penal system. Although a number of measures were reformist in name only, the concept was essential to the institution's vocabulary of motive. Both elements—the gendered arrangements and rhetorics of legitimation—were at the heart of what it meant to punish and confine women. The press conference that I described earlier in the chapter made it clear that each of these elements was abandoned to a distant and moribund past. The future, it seemed, was up for grabs, while the past was "unfounded."

Unfounding is an apt metaphor to characterize a process that is neither entirely deliberative nor accidental. In the same way that the unfounding of crime is simultaneously driven by practical and political ends, so too is the unfounding of a penal regime a multifaceted enterprise. On one level, pressure to abandon rehabilitation, to declare its logic and practices erroneous, reflects practical concerns with overcoming resource crises through reducing crime and prison overcrowding. On another level, the assault on rehabilitation serves a variety of political interests, ranging from those of prisoners anxious to frame their issues around rights rather than needs, to state officials and politicians who aim to restore integrity and public confidence to the penal system. But the warden's use of the term unfounding refers not only to the dualistic nature of the effort to dismantle rehabilitation, it also indicates the consequences of doing so. Specifically, it signals a rupture in the prison's relationship with its own past. Indeed, to the extent that the founder's tale and other symbolic artifacts of the reformatory era were used to inform and legitimate the apparatus of control in the present, unfounding complicates this relationship, and it does so by eroding the motivational and structural supports necessary to maintain it.

It is within this crucible of crisis that both the logic and practice of punishment were remade. The rupture with the past and the pervasive sense that the future could no longer be charted along the beaten path of the rehabilitative ideal had structural consequences, reconfiguring the prison's administrative apparatus and cultural logic. Both sets of changes were linked to state actors' efforts to overcome resource and ideological crises. Together these reconfigured sets of relations altered, in significant ways, the scaffolding and arrangements on which the prison hung and made the emergence of a new penology possible.

2

Taking Over

The Private Company in the Public Prison

There are in our prisons many things for which a very high price is
paid to the contractor.
—Gustave de Beaumont and Alexis de Tocqueville,
On the Penitentiary System in the United States
and Its Application in France

I want to know who the hell they answer to.
—Staff lieutenant, on the status of Company employees in the prison

Accountability committee meetings are held once a month in the conference
room adjacent to the warden's office. Attendance is by invitation only and
limited to supervisory staff from various units and departments within the
prison. All told, there are eleven regular attendees who are "accountable" to
the warden, including the deputy warden, the heads of the education and
medical departments, the prison chaplain, the senior prison counselor, the
records clerk, the head of the classification committee, and the lieutenants
and staff lieutenants who oversee the small army of correctional officers and
support personnel throughout the prison. The meetings follow the same format—the warden or his deputy make announcements, the department heads
offer clipped reports, and, in whatever time remains, the floor is open for
"problems." Problems run the gamut from trivial and mundane (the cold
water faucet in the kitchen has sprung a slow leak) to grim and substantial
(a portion of illicit drugs confiscated from prisoners has gone missing). Discussions of problems are rarely philosophical—they keenly hew to the whats
and hows of prison policy, rarely the whys and wherefores.

For this reason it was a noteworthy event when, at one such accountability
meeting, a lieutenant indicated that he had a problem that was both proce-
dural and philosophical. The problem stemmed from a series of complaints

filed by prisoners assigned to Project Habilitate Women, the new drug treatment program that the Company was running in the prison. Specifically, prisoners contended that they had been forced to watch "pro-Nazi propaganda" by a counselor in the treatment program. After receiving the complaints, the lieutenant contacted Joanne Torrence, the director of the program and a Company employee. She did not respond to any of his initial inquiries. When the prisoners did not receive a timely response from the lieutenant, they had concerned family members notify the American Civil Liberties Union. A lawyer from the organization contacted the warden about the incident. It was only then that an investigation was conducted into the event, one that was run by staff from the Company, not state prison employees.

As reported to the warden, the Company's investigation revealed that one of its counselors had required prisoners in the program to watch *Schindler's List*, a movie about the Holocaust.[1] She told them the film was about "cultural diversity" before popping the tape into the VCR and returning to her office. When the movie was over, she sent the prisoners to the cafeteria for dinner with no discussion of the movie, the historical context of Nazi Germany, or invitations for the women to talk with her if they had questions, concerns, or reactions to the film. Following the investigation, the counselor was disciplined by the Company for failure to do "direct therapeutic work" following the screening of the film.

The incident proved embarrassing for prison administrators because it suggested they were ultimately not in control of what was happening in PHW, a program that housed nearly one quarter of the prison's inmate population. As the lieutenant commented in his remarks at the accountability meeting, "Look, I want to know who the hell they answer to. The complaint comes to me, I try to investigate and get nowhere because the program director supposedly doesn't work for us. However, it's my ass on the line with the DOC [Department of Correction] when the ACLU gets involved." A chorus of voices rose up in agreement as the lieutenant looked at the warden and asked, "Do they answer to us or are they truly independent contractors?"

Before the lieutenant could finish his thought, Warden Richardson was shaking his head saying, "No, no, no. We're responsible. It doesn't matter who signs her check, we have the final word. *We* contracted *them*" (his emphasis). His response provoked a second, then a third round of questions from the other administrators in attendance, many of whom noted that Ms. Torrence, the director of PHW, did not attend accountability meetings even though she held a supervisory position that was roughly analogous to the supervisory positions held by state employees in charge of educational and vocational programs in the prison.[2] As the meeting wore on, the administrators' questions about the presence of a private company in a state prison grew increasingly reflective and philosophical. Among them: Why are they here? What is their official status? How much autonomy do they have? Who controls what they do?

There were more questions than answers at that meeting and in the accountability meetings that followed. The only thing that was clear to everyone was that the prison's newly hatched partnership with the Company had significant implications not only for prisoners, but also for staff. What was at stake was not just the overcrowding problem, but the very way that the prison and punishment were governed.

In this chapter, I argue that the Company's presence and growing influence in East State Women's Correctional Institution was chiefly in response to the prison's resource crisis. Specifically, the Company offered prison administrators a resource bailout in one of two ways. First, it provided a service, in the form of PHW, that targeted the rising tide of drug-involved prisoners, many of whom had come to symbolize the prison's "revolving door" problem. Second, it assumed responsibility for a quarter of the prisoner population, offering some relief to the problem of institutional overcrowding. In the sections that follow, I discuss these arrangements in more detail and focus specifically on how a private company came to act as a bailout to the resource crisis, as well as the implications of a private contractor's presence on the governance structure of the prison.

Privatizing Punishment

The presence of private interests in the state and federal prison system is often treated as if it is a new phenomenon, but it is not. Public–private partnerships have been present in some form or other throughout this country's nearly 240-year prison odyssey and in some European societies since the 1600s. Perhaps the most notorious example of this partnership is the convict lease system that emerged in the South in the aftermath of the Civil War. Bankrupted from the war, southern states could not afford to build and operate the large, penitentiary-style facilities that were emerging in the North. Northern penitentiaries were built, at least initially, on the premise that prisoners could be reformed through a combination of hard work, discipline, religiosity, and surveillance. Southern states, whose prisoner population was composed primarily of former slaves, had little interest in reforming prisoners. Prevailing racial ideologies held that people of African descent were intellectually, physically, and morally inferior to whites. This ideology, long used by Europeans to justify colonialism and slavery, was further bolstered by the popularity of criminal anthropology—a set of theories premised on the belief that criminals were "throwbacks" to a biologically inferior and more primitive race of people.[3] In this framework, reform made little sense since "primitives" were incapable of controlling their "savage" impulses.[4] Beyond this, the broader southern economy was on the brink of collapse in the absence of slave labor. The solution that emerged was convict leasing. It existed in various guises but at its core, convict leasing involved private businesses (typically plantation owners) paying the state for the use of prisoners' labor.[5] Prisoners were not compensated for their work. In organizing the penal system in this way, southern states were able to balance their crime-control budgets (and in some cases turn a profit) while simultaneously shoring up plantation economies by providing a ready supply of cheap labor.

Thus it is not the *presence* of private interests that distinguishes the current moment from other eras in American prison history. Rather, it is their growing influence and the multifarious extent of their reach. By the end of the 1990s, the spread of private interests in the prison system became so pronounced that scholars and activists observed that the drug war, coupled with the mass incarceration it produced, fueled a historically unprecedented influx of corporate vendors and private interests.[6] Scholars like Angela Davis characterize these labyrinthine public–private relationships as a "prison-industrial complex" and suggest that it has rapidly eclipsed the "military-industrial complex" of the Cold War era.[7]

Today, the concept of privatization refers to at least three distinct strands of activity: private prison facilities, private financing of public facilities, and the selling of goods and services to prisoners, their families, and the state. In each case, the exchange of money is reversed relative to the convict lease system. For example, in the post–Civil War period, private companies paid states a fee for the use of inmate labor. Today, state and federal governments pay private companies in exchange for housing inmates or providing goods and services.

The most well-known variant of privatization involves entire correctional facilities that are owned and operated on a for-profit basis by companies like Corrections Corporation of America and GEO Group (formerly Wackenhut). There are currently 415 private facilities in use in the federal and state prison systems, holding approximately 7% of the nation's adult prisoners.[8] The growth and development of private prisons began during the War on Drugs in the mid-1980s and boomed throughout the decade that followed. In 1985, private prison facilities held a total of 1,345 prisoners, but over the course of a decade that number jumped to 49,154 prisoners.[9] During this period, the majority of states had inmate populations that were at or above their prisons' rated capacity, and some were under court supervision because overcrowding had reached unconstitutional limits. Compounding matters, many of these same states faced budget shortfalls from, among other things, corrections spending. Private prisons offered a politically expedient solution to the overcrowding problem. By turning over a percentage of state prisoners to a private facility in exchange for a fee, state politicians avoided the use of public bonds to finance new prison construction. Instead, the fees paid to private prisons came from operating budgets rather than capital budgets.[10] Privatizing whole prison facilities allowed politicians to appear tough on crime without confronting either pressing economic concerns about financing or decarceration initiatives. Further, private prisons appealed to market sensibilities—private companies argued that they could run a prison as well as the state, and at less expense.[11] Since the mid-1980s, GEO Group and Corrections Corporation of America have enjoyed two decades of growing profits. In 2010, their combined revenue for the year was over $2.9 billion.[12]

Although much of the scholarly and political debate about privatization focuses on privately run facilities, privatization refers also to the use of independent contractors inside prisons, particularly in the provision of goods and services to prisoners and in the utilization of prisoners as laborers. In this variant, private companies hold contracts with the state and sell their product within the walls of a public prison. It is this latter variant of privatization—the private provision of services—that is the focus of the present chapter. Although it was not the case at the beginning of this study, this form of privatization has since become one of the fastest growing and most stable sources of profit for private vendors.[13] The story of the Company's entrée into the world of independent prison contractors offers insight as to why this is the case.

From Riot to Rehabilitation: The Company's Founder's Tale

In the early years of the nation's drug war, the Company was a relative unknown among a handful of much larger companies involved in prison privatization. In fact, it was pioneering a quite distinct course compared to industry giants like Corrections Corporation of America and Wackenhut. Instead of running an entire prison on its own, the Company aimed to provide health care and related services to already existing, publicly run correctional facilities. This ultimately proved a prescient and lucrative course of action. While companies running private facilities have foundered in the wake of high-profile escapes and costly lawsuits arising from unconstitutional conditions, the Company and service providers like it have witnessed steady growth and stable profits.[14] Today the Company is considered a leader among prison health care providers, an industry worth over a billion dollars per year.[15]

Like prison administrators at East State, Company executives have a "founder's tale." It is one they enjoy telling, particularly at the conferences they host for state-level Department of Correction decision makers and at the "cross-training" sessions they run for prison employees. In the tale, executives link the Company's founding to the bloody aftermath of the 1971 Attica Prison riot. PowerPoint presentations feature several gruesome photos taken during the riot, and Company speakers are quick to emphasize that the chaos and disorder the riot unleashed extended well beyond the walls of the prison.

Attica is the most infamous prison riot in American history. This is primarily due to the number of fatalities the riot generated, as well as the fact that most of the bloodshed was caused by police and National Guard troops, not inmates.[16] Attica's notoriety is also linked to the high levels of solidarity exhibited among the prisoners. The riot began on the morning of September 9, when 1,300 male prisoners at a maximum security prison in upstate New York took over a section of the facility and held forty correctional officers hostage for several days. It was sparked by a scuffle between prisoners and officers, but tension had been brewing for some time over Attica's extreme levels of overcrowding, unsanitary conditions, racism, inadequate health care, and lack of education, rehabilitation, and vocational programs. Among their demands, rioting prisoners requested better rehabilitation programs, education for correctional officers to facilitate better relations, a "modernized" education system, and improved health care services.[17] Unfortunately, Governor Nelson Rockefeller refused all efforts at negotiation. The riot ended following orders from his office to state police and National Guard troops to take the prison by force. In the course of doing so, officers shot and killed thirty-nine of the hostages, bringing the total death toll from the riot to forty-three men.

Attica was, in many ways, the ultimate criminal justice nightmare. The prison system—a symbol of order and control, an impenetrable gulag designed to discipline and contain the dangerous classes—turned on itself. In the ensuing chaos, the keepers and the kept traded places and, in the riot's denouement, those charged with upholding the law at Attica lost sight of it. In their presentations, Company employees emphasized these contradictions. One photograph displayed repeatedly throughout the presentation depicts a densely packed crowd of predominantly African American prisoners, extending as far back into the prison yard as the eye can see. Their fists are raised in solidarity and many cover their faces with towels and blankets. On a few occasions, I have heard members of the audience gasp when this photo was introduced. More frequently, the audience reacted to the photo and the discussion of Attica as if it were counterintuitive to wrap a sales pitch for prison health care services into a graphic summary of a prison riot. At one such presentation for DOC officials, a woman who worked as a statistician for the state furrowed her brow and whispered to me, "What an odd historical event to link one's company to?" It was more of a question than a statement.

Company executives were accustomed to this kind of reaction. At one such presentation, Dr. Nesbitt paused and grinned at a person who asked, "What does Attica have to do with drug treatment?" His response began, "In chaos, we saw possibility." He went on to emphasize that precipitating conditions for the riot included a lack of adequate medical care, as well as the nonexistence of "therapeutic" and clinical services. He continued, "The chaos and contradictions of Attica are only secondarily about the riot. What the riot is a by-product of is the beginning of what we now know is the phenomenon of trans-institutionalization." Here, Dr. Nesbitt reviewed a series of statistics about the number of beds in state psychiatric hospitals, compared to the number of beds in prisons and jails over a given time period.[18] The implication was that as states shuttered facilities serving persons with mental health problems, the prison system had to pick up much of the slack. Of course, doing so has not been easy for the prison system, as any number of research studies and public scandals involving the egregious treatment of mentally ill inmates demonstrate.[19] Beyond this, Dr. Nesbitt asserted that prison facilities and staff are simply ill equipped to deal with a sizeable population of prisoners suffering from what he referred to as "dual diagnosis disorder" (i.e., a history of mental health problems and criminal offending).[20] It is in this niche within the penal system that the clinical and therapeutic services of the Company are, according to company executives, perfectly fitted.

In linking their founding to one of the most violent uprisings in American prison history, company executives are asserting a new vision of social order that has two interrelated components. The first is that order cannot simply be achieved through brute repression of unruly prisoners, but rather through medical and, more specifically, therapeutic intervention into all varieties of prisoner deviance. It is a vision that echoes the design logic of philosopher Jeremy Bentham's 18th-century Panopticon, in which control of a prisoner's mind is at least as important as control of her body.[21] The Panopticon was a congregate facility that was designed so that a single guard could, at any given time, observe numerous prisoners while remaining unseen. Since prisoners never knew if or when they were being watched, they were forced to take up the mantle of their own surveillance. In so doing, they viewed themselves from the normative perspective of the guards and thus began to regulate and police their own behavior. For Bentham, law and order could be better achieved through this kind of intervention into prisoners' minds rather than through the torture and execution of their bodies.[22]

In the late 1970s, when the Company got its start, selling therapeutic programming was certainly a bold position to stake. States were divesting in rehabilitation programs in favor of hardened security measures, increasingly sophisticated surveillance devices, and supermax prisons. For most correctional services companies, the clearest path to profitability was away from rehabilitation and toward new security and restraint technologies. Most contemporary prison scholars hold that the steady creep of prison privatization is itself partly to blame for the decline of the rehabilitative ideal in the criminal justice system. Their argument is that privatization, because it commodifies prisoners and depends on the expansion of the prison system, is antithetical to rehabilitation, given that rehabilitation ultimately aims to reduce the number of prisoners by restoring them to productive citizenship.[23] The argument is analytically correct—on the surface, privatization and rehabilitation are antithetical. But what if rehabilitation could be repackaged? What if rather than signaling the return of the deviant to a "normal" state, rehabilitation or some version thereof meant that deviance and disorder were permanent conditions—conditions that could be treated but never cured? What if criminality and drug abuse were diseases that required a lifetime of external management and control? If this were the case, profitability need not stop at the door of rehabilitation.

This brings us to the second component of the Company's vision of social order, one organized along the lines of race and class. The Company's extensive reliance on the imagery of Attica—angry, organized groups of African American prisoners prepared for violence—was hardly accidental. At the same time, the content of these photographs did not, as audience members noted, offer a clear, logical link to the sale of therapeutic services. In using this racial imagery, the Company was selling more than therapeutic services—it was selling a vision of a particular social and racial order. As Michelle Alexander argues, contemporary stereotypes of young Black men as aggressive, unruly, and predatory can be traced to the post–Civil War South, in which a collapsing economy and the presence of four million newly freed slaves threatened whites' privileged position. Unfounded fears of Black violence among whites contributed to the rise of a criminal justice apparatus, notably in the form of convict leasing, that aimed to restore key elements of slavery's economic and racial order.[24] Criminologists like Dimitri Bogazianos argue the passage of contemporary "get tough" laws would have been inconceivable without extensive use of similar racial stereotypes,[25] particularly those that linked African Americans and Latinos with drugs, street crime, and violence. In their presentations, the Company used the racial imagery of Attica to similar effect. Executives argued that the source of the crime, poverty, and violence that plagued poor, urban neighborhoods was not deindustrialization and broader shifts in the political economy, but rather was located within racially marginalized communities themselves. I explore these racial claims in detail in the chapter that follows. My point here is that the Company used race, particularly long-standing racial fears, as a way to reimagine the source of and solution to social disorder.

At its heart, the Attica Prison riot was about politics—it was a challenge from those at the bottom of the social order to race and class domination as well as to state brutality. Yet, in Company presentations of Attica, politics drop out almost entirely. Instead, they frame the riot as a by-product of mental illness that went untreated. Attica simply represented another kind of disorder, one that American prisons, with their lopsided emphasis on security and "getting tough," were ill equipped to handle. Ultimately, the "possibility" that Dr. Nesbitt saw in Attica was symbolic. That is, the Company aimed to reframe discussions about criminality and offer an expanded vision of social control, one that stoked racial fears and shifted the responsibility for managing disorder out of the hands of the individual and the state and into the realm of the market.

Getting In

In many respects, East State was ground zero for the realization of the Company's unique vision of disorder and control. During the 1980s, the Company found success primarily by providing prison health care and clinical services (in the form of diagnostic evaluations and pharmacological treatment regimes) to state prisons. In the course of ten years, however, other, bigger firms began to enter the game of prison health care services. To survive, the Company needed to expand into new territories, and none seemed more lucrative than the possibilities offered by the War on Drugs. Indeed, the number of annual drug arrests tripled between 1980 and 2005, while the number of drug arrests resulting in prison sentences quadrupled. Today, approximately a half a million prisoners are currently serving a prison or jail sentence for a drug offense.[26]

Nonetheless, as lucrative as the drug war appeared to be for a burgeoning prison–industrial complex, it remained unclear how a company promoting therapeutic services over security measures would fare. After all, this same period ushered in the "get tough/three strikes" movement; the rise of rational choice criminology, which framed criminals as utilitarian, deliberative actors; and the near-universal critique of rehabilitation from both the political left and right.[27] Public opinion in East State mirrored the nation in that few citizens favored prisons modeled on rehabilitative ideals, preferring instead punitive punishments and military-style boot camps.[28] While the state did have a handful of high-ranking public officials who supported treatment programs, most of the state's legislators, judges, and other policy makers affirmed the public's outcry for harsher prisons and longer sentences, particularly for drug offenders. The only "rehabilitative" services to survive in the state's prison system were those that fulfilled basic educational requirements such as literacy courses, high school diploma and General Education Development (GED) classes, vocational training programs, and programs like Alcoholics and Narcotics Anonymous (and these were typically staffed by volunteers). How then, in this pro-punishment environment, did the Company manage to convince prison administrators at East State that their "treatment services and therapeutic interventions" were a wise and sound investment?

The answer comes in two parts. First, the drug treatment program they were promoting was based on a therapeutic community model that effectively collapsed the distinction between "treatment" and "punishment."[29] PHW was a good bit closer to a military-style boot camp than it was to earlier rehabilitation programs that had been derided by some politicians and state officials as "soft" and "touchy feely." As already noted, the Company did not refer to their program as "rehabilitative." Project *Habilitate* Women (my emphasis) distinguished "habilitation" as something fundamentally distinct from "soft" and "ineffective" rehabilitative programs. As we will see in the chapters that follow, their "habilitative" treatment model was tough, confrontational, and punitive.

The second part of the answer regarding how the Company got into the prison had to do with the resource crisis. The grim reality of the resource crisis was that it left prison administrators with very few options. They needed a solution to the overcrowding problem and they needed it fast. As a result, executives did not have to work all that hard to sell their therapeutic vision. More important than their product was the fact that they, in conjunction with a state agency and a federal grant, were offering what amounted to a resource bailout, one that would indirectly shift responsibility for up to a quarter of the prison's ever-expanding population of prisoners from the state to the Company.

The Art of the Deal

By the mid-1990s as the drug war kicked into high gear, the Company had developed a profitable and friendly relationship with the Department of Correction. The Company held an exclusive contract to provide health care for the state's entire inmate population. In addition, it ran an experimental, prison-based drug treatment program for nonviolent, male offenders. Similar to the popularity of prison boot camps, the men's program enjoyed a significant amount of public support in the state because it did not "coddle" inmates. Instead, the program combated addiction through a therapeutic community model that prioritized surveillance, discipline, and personal responsibility.[30] Even in a "get tough" political climate, the program appealed to state officials because it was cost-effective and boasted better-than-average results with respect to recidivism, reoffending, and drug relapse.

During this same period, administrators at the women's prison found themselves in a difficult situation. As the previous chapter demonstrated, the number of women sentenced to prison continued to increase exponentially, which in turn nudged overcrowding past constitutional limits and unleashed a host of disciplinary problems. Despite this, state officials made it clear that they would not finance additional construction to expand the facility, nor would they support control measures that were not directly tied to a "get tough" platform. While prison administrators ultimately accepted funds that supported "hardened" security measures like razor wire fencing and metal detectors, many staff members critiqued the gender appropriateness of "get tough" efforts. Staff acknowledged that they had a real problem on their hands with the escalation of inmate beefs and the "revolving door problem," but virtually no one believed that these problems were going to be solved by treating women as if they were men.

It was in this context that Warden Richardson participated in a series of meetings with Company executives.[31] By his own admission, he was, like many other wardens around the country, "desperate" to find a solution to the twin problems of recidivism and overcrowding.[32] Beyond this, he was looking for a solution that resonated with the institution's reformist legacy and the gendered assumptions on which it was based. As he recalled in an interview with me, "I accept that we have to run things differently, that rehabilitation in a traditional sense is not viable. However, I wasn't trying to throw the baby out with the bathwater."

Given these concerns, his decision to negotiate with the Company for a drug treatment program, rather than with other firms for other services, was logical. First, the Company's therapeutic community model had the potential of appealing to both "get tough" advocates at the Department of Correction and to reform-oriented staffers at the women's prison. As one prison staffer described it, PHW's emphasis on transforming the "addict self" through confrontation, discipline, therapy, and surveillance represented the "perfect blend" of "treatment and punishment." Second, the Company promised a "gender specific" approach, meaning that it would not simply replicate the program from the men's facility, but would target women's "unique" needs. This perfectly corresponded to the prison's "separate spheres" legacy and to a punishment ideology organized principally in terms of gender. Third, the Company had not only established a successful track record within the Department of Correction, it had also made significant inroads with state legislators, policy makers, and the state sentencing commission. Given these considerations, the warden was reasonably optimistic he could overcome state officials' restrictions on funding treatment programs.

For their part, Company executives were eager to design and implement drug treatment programming in the women's prison. Not only would PHW serve as an additional contract with the state, it would be the prototype for gender-specific drug treatment programming.[33] Indeed, the development of a treatment program specifically tailored to women's "gender specific needs" would allow the Company to expand the scope of its drug treatment services across all twenty-two states with which it had pre-existing contracts, and potentially to even more states. To help persuade prison administrators and reluctant state officials of the need for treatment programming, the Company teamed up with a state sentencing commission to survey currently incarcerated women on their drug use, criminal histories, and prior treatment experience. Among the findings highlighted in the commission's report were that 75% of women prisoners in the state were regular users of crack and cocaine, 70% of women prisoners required treatment for their drug use,[34] and nearly 80% of women prisoners had never received substance abuse treatment of any kind.

Despite the commission's report and pressure from the warden and Company executives, the Department of Correction remained unwilling to set aside the funds necessary to bring a residential treatment facility into the women's prison. Its relationship with the Company notwithstanding, state officials had broadly assumed an anti-treatment stance when it came to corrections in general and the women's prison in particular. As I noted in chapter 1, several state officials had publicly characterized rehabilitation programs and treatment efforts as "soft," "ineffective," "costly," and "touchy-feely." Indeed, the Department of Correction took the position that overcrowding problems in the women's prison were a product of a failed treatment regime.

Their message to Warden Richardson was consistent and firm: the only way to overcome overcrowding was to jettison the old system of reformist-era paternalism with a "hardened" system of "get tough" punishment.

Ultimately what persuaded the Department of Correction to shift its position was money—more specifically, the promise of federal grant monies that would absorb 100% of the program's costs during its first three years of operation. The brokered deal involved a web of overlapping relationships across state and federal agencies, the women's prison, and the Company. A state agency called Social Service Access Committee (hereafter the Committee) played the pivotal role in securing the funds necessary to make PHW a reality in the prison. Created by legislative mandate in 1992, the Committee was a "bridge" agency housed within a division of the Department of Health and Social Services.[35]

Bridge agencies began popping up within state governments in the early 1990s in response to the byzantine bureaucratic structures of criminal justice and welfare systems. They emerged from the recognition that although there is considerable overlap between the population of adults under correctional supervision and the population of adults receiving some form of social service assistance, there is little coordination across agencies. The Committee's job was to identify suitable services for offenders and their families and to coordinate case processing and surveillance across the criminal justice and social welfare systems.[36] Members of its board included the commissioner of corrections, the secretary of health and social services, and the secretary of services to children and their families.

Following a series of planning meetings with Warden Richardson and Company executives, Betty Thompson, director of the Committee, agreed that the agency would apply for a federal demonstration grant that would in turn fund an "experimental," "gender specific," and "culturally sensitive" drug treatment program that was expected to house up to a quarter of the prison's inmates. Upon receipt of grant monies, the Committee planned to contract the Company to develop, staff, and run the program. The Committee was to be responsible for project supervision, staff training, and coordination with prison officials. Despite their anti-treatment stance, state officials were not hostile to this plan. They agreed to make the prison's newest, largest, and as-yet unused housing unit available for the sole use of the program. In addition, they agreed to staff the program with four correctional officers who would provide an around-the-clock security detail. By the time the final round of negotiations concluded, state officials had also agreed to consider funding the program following the end of the three-year demonstration grant. One official explained to me, "We agreed to pick up the tab if they [the

Company] could demonstrate some successes, particularly in terms of our recidivism rate. That's not politics, it's smart business."

With federal grant money in tow, the Committee promptly contracted the Company to bring its experimental drug treatment program into the facility. The program was staffed by a director, five counselors, and a secretary, all of whom were Company employees. The only state employees present in the program were correctional officers, and their influence on the day-to-day operations of the program was minimal.[37] PHW opened its doors on January 31, 1994, and accepted a "trial group" of sixteen women from the prison's general population. Within eighteen months, the program was running at double that capacity, with thirty to thirty-five prisoners enrolled at any given time.

The new program and the grant that supported it eased the resource crisis considerably, though not by reducing the actual size of the prison's total population, at least not in the short term. Rather, PHW served as a resource bailout in three ways. First and most important, the program initially relocated just over 15% of the inmate population and later, over the course of three years, more than a quarter. While the number of incarcerated women in the state did not change during this time, responsibility for them did. Costs associated with their care and supervision were paid out of grant monies, not the state's operating budget. In addition, the significance of their relocation was more than fiscal. As one correctional officer explained:

> The number of prisoners in this prison did not change. What changed is how we count them and the consequences of this. . . . In a way, they're hiding in plain sight because they're no longer in the mix we supervise. For us, they disappeared. They're not our direct responsibility anymore, that honor belongs to [PHW].

Because these prisoners were removed to a separate unit that was itself physically isolated from the rest of the facility, they were no longer present in the main hallway, central cell blocks, cafeteria, gym, or recreation yard. There were, from the perspective of the officers, fewer inmates to guard throughout the prison. Further, since responsibility for the daily supervision and care of up to a quarter of the inmate population shifted to PHW, the overall ratio of officers to general population inmates improved, allowing for greater supervision and control.

The second way the program presented a resource bailout was in the provision of additional staff. PHW employed seven staff members (a program director, five counselors, and a secretary). Their salaries and benefits were paid out of the grant. In addition, the program employed four "therapeutic" officers to provide security on the unit. These officers were state employees but the Company provided their "therapeutic" training, with the expenses associated with that training coming out of the grant.

The Company offered a third set of resources to the prison in the form of provision of services. For example, the federal grant stipulated that PHW would provide HIV testing and counseling to all prisoners, regardless of their drug use histories or eligibility for the drug treatment program. Beyond this, PHW counselors screened all incoming prisoners regarding their history of substance use and abuse. They then assisted the prison's classification committee in determining housing arrangements and programming for all newly sentenced prisoners. This reduced the workload for the prison's counseling staff considerably. As the senior counselor explained to me, "There's only two of us [counselors] for this entire prison. We have to screen everyone. . . . Having them [PHW counselors] do intake assessments doubled our staff size. My inbox is still overflowing, but their taking this on definitely helps on that front."

In the resource-starved environment of an overcrowded prison, these contributions were significant. Of course, Company executives were promising much bigger returns in the future. In the short term, they planned to work with local judges to reduce the size of the prison population by expediting early release for women who successfully completed the treatment program. Beyond this, they anticipated a significant, long-term reduction in the recidivism rate of program graduates. Since nearly two-thirds of the prison's new commits were former inmates, any reduction in recidivism would have a noticeable impact on the size of the prison population.

While the warden and his top-level administrators were pleased with the additional resources the Company's drug treatment program brought to the prison, most staff members remained deeply ambivalent about their presence. Chief among their earliest concerns was the role Company employees would assume in the prison's hierarchy of organizational power. As the lieutenant demanded in the accountability meeting described at the opening of this chapter, "I want to know who the hell they answer to."

The Private Contractor in the Public Prison

One of the defining characteristics of mass incarceration is the growing influence of commercial companies in the criminal justice system, particularly prisons. The story of exploding incarceration rates in the 1990s and beyond cannot be told without pointed reference to these business interests. Indeed, the term "prison–industrial complex" refers to the structural linkages and mutually reinforcing interests among penal institutions, politicians, the media, and private companies.[38] Within this framework, the bodies of prisoners become a source of profit for politicians, the media, and, of course, the companies that provide goods and services to the penal system.

There is, however, more to privatization than the passage of punitive legislation that sends more Americans to prison for longer periods of time. Scholars like David Garland, Jonathon Simon, and Malcolm Feeley argue that privatization alters decision-making structures within criminal justice agencies by replacing a modernist ethos of rehabilitation with one that prioritizes managerialism, fiscal conservatism, and organizational efficiency.[39] This shift in focus has implications for how prison administrators respond not only to prisoners but also to their own staff. Garland observes, "What were once state-monopolized powers have increasingly been devolved to private, 'for-profit' contractors, who are allowed to pursue their commercial interests so long as they remain within the constraints established by their contract with the government authorities."[40]

In the case of East State, it was entirely unclear to staff, even administrators, what these constraints would be. Indeed, confusion about organizational boundaries and fear of the loss of autonomy were the primary sources of the anxiety among administrators in attendance at the warden's accountability meeting discussed at the opening of this chapter. Their concerns were exacerbated by the fact that the contract between the Company and the Committee did not specify the terms of the Company's day-to-day role in the prison, beyond noting that the ultimate responsibility for prisoners enrolled in PHW remained with the state. There were no explicit instructions requiring Company employees to share information about prisoners with prison staff, nor were there any guidelines with respect to the Company's participation in broader administrative functions like the warden's accountability meetings. This proved a serious oversight given that in institutions like prisons, organizational power frequently derives from the number of prisoners under a given staff person's command. With the Company poised to take command over a quarter of East State's prisoners, administrators and staff had good reason to question what role they would play in the prison and where Company employees stood in the prison's chain of command.

Over the course of this study, the Company's actual role shifted considerably within the institution, often in tandem with the number of prisoners under its control. In the wake of what prison staffers referred to as the "Nazi incident," described at the top of this chapter, Warden Richardson sought more explicit control and access to the director of PHW and the program's

Table 2.1. Privatization and shifts in the prison's governance structure

	1994	1997	2000
Prison administrative structure	"Accountability meetings" run by warden with attendance limited to key members of his administrative staff.	PHW director and Company executive are nonvoting "consultants" at accountability meetings	PHW Director and Company executive are regular, voting members at accountability meetings
Supervision of PHW	PHW director reports to warden and Company executive. Orders from correctional officers supersede directives from PHW staff.	PHW director reports to Company executive, who reports to Committee director. Committee director issues report to granting agency and warden. "Therapeutic training" mandatory for correctional officers assigned to PHW. Orders from officers supersede directives from PHW staff.	PHW director reports to Company executive, who in turn reports to warden. "Therapeutic officers" take orders from clinical staff. Supervision of these officers is shared between PHW director and warden.
PHW's funding source	Federal demonstration grant	Federal demonstration grant	State contract
% prisoner population in PHW	15	20	25
% prisoner population eligible for PHW*	80	85	90

* According to Company estimates.

drug treatment counselors. This meant, for example, that Joanne Torrence, PHW's director, was required to provide monthly progress reports on the program and the prisoners in it to Dr. Nesbitt, Betty Thompson, and Warden Richardson. In addition, administrators at that early accountability meeting agreed that orders from correctional officers in the prison would always supersede program directives. Although PHW staff protested this latter rule on the premise it was "not conducive to treatment," it remained in play throughout most of the duration of the research study.

By 1997, the configuration of the accountability meetings changed, as did PHW's reporting practices. Just three years earlier, the accountability meetings comprised the warden and key members of his administrative staff. The attendance of others, including the director of PHW, was by invitation only. This was true even after administrators at the meeting described above agreed that the director should be present at the meetings. Although she was more regularly present after the "Nazi incident," she was not always invited, nor did she have a vote when she was. When I asked the warden about why she was not given a permanent seat at the meetings, he replied simply, "She's a contractor, she doesn't work for the state. She doesn't have a right to participate in matters outside of the [drug treatment] program."

Three years later, however, both Joanne Torrence and Dr. Nesbitt were regular attendees at the meetings. In the meeting minutes, they were listed as "consultants." This change in status did not give them a vote, but it did grant them monthly representation and they were allowed to share their perspective on matters pertaining to broader prison policies that were related to their role in the institution. For example, Torrence often weighed in on matters pertaining to the medical department's practice of prescribing psychotropic medications to inmates with drug abuse histories.

Ironically, the Company's greater access to prison administrators brought about a fairly significant shift in reporting practices. Instead of submitting progress reports directly to the warden, the PHW director submitted a report to her supervisor at the Company, who in turn submitted it to the director of the Committee. The Committee director then submitted the report to both the granting agency and the warden. This change in reporting was initiated by the Company over and against the wishes of the warden. Company employees complained that the warden and his staff were trying to interfere with the treatment program but that they did not have sufficient experience and knowledge in the field of addiction counseling to legitimately do so. As Dr. Nesbitt explained to me in an interview, "We've got the contract to provide the service. They obviously don't get how to fix the [drug] problem or they would have. They needed to step aside and let us do our thing."

The change in the reporting practice would have been inconceivable three years earlier, when PHW was a newcomer in the prison. In the intervening years, however, the Company had gained some institutional traction. By 1995, Company representatives supervised 20% of the prison population and had persuaded both Committee and state officials that they had to be granted sufficient autonomy from the warden to "do their thing." This primarily meant that prisoners in PHW did not follow the same schedule as general population inmates. Instead, they spent much of their day in various therapeutic groups in lieu of working or going to educational and vocational training programs. As Dr. Nesbitt reminded prison administrators at an accountability meeting, "If we're wrong, if we fail to provide effective drug treatment, we're out and your bosses at the DOC will see to it that we're out."

Reporting to the warden through the Committee effectively ended the warden's supervision of the program. If the warden or his staff had concerns about the program, they were forced to communicate it through

Betty Thompson, the Committee's director, who very often served as a buffer, deciding which remarks to pass on and which to challenge or ignore. She explained to me, "They [prison staff] simply don't have the kind of background in drug treatment needed to make the call. Until they are more familiar with addiction, they're not in a position to call shots in a treatment program."

The power of prison administrators was further eroded by the Company's demand that all correctional officers in the institution receive "cross-training" to improve their knowledge of drug addiction and treatment. The Company vigorously pursued this policy initiative after several unsuccessful attempts to overturn the prison's rule that orders from correctional officers superseded those of treatment staff. If Company officials could not upend officers' power, they would endeavor to increase the likelihood that officer's orders would be more consistent with their own treatment ideology. The primary focus of the sessions was to convince officers that prisoners suffered from "damaged selves" and that past "rehabilitative" practices like Bible study and paternalism were ineffective responses to the problem. Instead, trainers instructed officers to consistently enforce both the prison's and the program's rules and to sanction and report all rule violations. Although they were unable to mandate that all officers participate in training, they did convince the warden to make "therapeutic training" mandatory for all officers assigned to the PHW unit. Nearly two-thirds of all officers attended at least one training session, often at the insistence of the warden or his deputy.[41]

By the time this study concluded six years later, the Company's institutional power had expanded considerably. By that time, the Company was directly under contract with the state Department of Correction and had increased its share of the prisoner population to 25%. There was a new warden in place and two Company employees (the vice president of clinical services and the director of PHW) had a regular seat at the accountability meetings. The program's reporting practices had once again shifted. The director of the program issued monthly reports to the Company's vice president of clinical services, who in turn submitted them to the warden. Any issues were discussed at the accountability meeting, where the two representatives from the Company had voting rights.

Perhaps the most significant change was in the supervision of correctional officers assigned to the program unit. The Company had earlier negotiated that only "therapeutic officers" could work in PHW. These officers were state employees but graduates of the Company's officer training program. Notably, they were now specifically required to take orders from clinical staff in the program. Further, supervision of these officers was shared between the Company and prison administrators. In just six years, the Company's role vis-à-vis prison staff had changed from being under the warden's direct (if attenuated) supervision to gaining some autonomy and influence over prison policy and select performance appraisals of state personnel.

Conclusion

Research on the boom in prison privatization suggests that much of it was fueled by overcrowding problems that were themselves generated by drug war policies. This was certainly the case in East State Women's Correctional Institution. But the story of the Company's emergence as a major player in the prison is a good bit more nuanced than theoretical constructs of the prison–industrial complex allow for. In this case, privatization was not imposed from above. While the larger forces that gave rise to the resource crisis constrained the actions of administrators and staff in the women's prison, they did not determine them. Staff and administrators in the women's prison strenuously and creatively resisted the demands of state officials to "get tough." It was their resistance in combination with the resource crisis that paved the way for privatization.

While the warden's motivation in utilizing the Company's drug treatment program was to overcome overcrowding and recidivism in a way that resonated with the institution's reformist traditions and gendered ideologies, it was clear to virtually everyone that the presence of private contractors was the beginning of the end of rehabilitative paternalism and the informal governance structure that supported it. Indeed, the Company's presence altered the structure of governance in the prison in a way that made the old system of control impossible to sustain. Specifically, PHW laid claim to a quarter of the prison's inmates and, with it, institutional policies and ideologies of control. This changed the practice of punishment in the prison, but it also changed the way staff saw women prisoners and the communities from which they came. This had important implications for not only how the institution responded to the resource crisis but also to another, larger crisis that was brewing—a crisis of meaning.

3

From Good Girls to Real Criminals

Race Made Visible

In the drug war, the enemy is racially defined.
—Michelle Alexander, *The New Jim Crow*

They're a different breed and you can see that 'cause jail don't have
no effect on them. They keep coming back.
—Deputy warden, on perceived changes among the population of
women prisoners

The warden's office is nestled in the corner of the prison's administration
wing, which lies to the far right of the prison's main hallway and is comfortably removed from the noise and bustle that characterizes the rest
of the facility. Were it not for the sound of the ponderous metal door that
announces the arrival and departure of staff and visitors alike with a thun-
derous clang and the buzz of a passing correctional officer's walkie-talkie, a
person standing in the administration wing could readily forget that he or
she was in a medium security prison. The pale yellow walls of the hallway
are decorated with paintings of nature scenes, the carpeted floors render the
cadence of footsteps notably silent, and everywhere the sound of easy listening music hangs in the air. Other than worn fabric on the arms of the chairs
in the reception area and the layer of dust that has settled on the leaves of a
plastic tree in the corner, the setting is remarkably corporate.

Inside his office, Warden Richardson is comfortably seated in a leather
chair behind a massive wooden desk. It has been nine months since Project Habilitate Women opened in the prison and I am there to interview
the warden about mounting tensions between prison staff and PHW counselors. Initially these disputes were about organizational power and ter-
ritory, and frequently involved correctional officers asserting their right

to discipline and communicate with PHW prisoners without the explicit permission of the program's counseling staff. More recently, their hostility toward PHW had broadened to include substantive criticisms of the program itself, particularly that it was more punitive than rehabilitative. At base, their critique reflected a fundamental divide over how best to comprehend the identities and needs of the incoming tide of women prisoners. Were they the good girls that prison staff had long been accustomed to dealing with? Or did they represent a different sort of criminal offender, one whose behavior and subjectivity was more in line with the predatory bugbear of drug war mythology?

The divide over how to view women prisoners, and by extension how to deal with them, is evident in a story the warden told me during our interview about Alicia, a thirty-one-year-old African American prisoner. Alicia had been in and out of prison and community-based correctional facilities throughout her adult life. Most of her convictions were for relatively minor offenses like petty theft, prostitution, and forgery, but over the last few years, she had begun to rack up a series of drug charges beginning with simple possession and extending to drug trafficking. Her most recent conviction, for possession of crack cocaine with intent to sell, resulted in a sentence of three to five years in prison. The sentencing judge left open the possibility of an early release from prison, provided that Alicia complete the PHW program.

Alicia was among the first cohort of prisoners admitted into PHW, and by all accounts she appeared to be doing well there. It was a surprise to everyone when, just a few months shy of her program graduation date, Alicia wrote a letter to administrators requesting to be transferred from the program to the general prison population. Doing so meant that she would be ineligible for an early release from prison and that she ran the risk of having to serve a maximum sentence of five years. While her request was unanticipated, it was not the request itself that brought about the controversy. Rather, it was that she had listed "abuse" as the reason for her request. I was not present as Alicia was escorted out of PHW by two correctional officers, but Alicia, a counselor from PHW, and several general population prisoners claimed that as she was lead to "max,"[1] a crowd of approximately thirty people (including COs, staff members, and inmates) lined either side of the main hallway, clapped, and shouted congratulatory remarks. Joellen, a prisoner who witnessed the event, recounted to me that although inmates were normally prohibited from lining the hallways in a cluster formation, the officers on duty that day relaxed the rules. In our interview, the warden downplayed the number of staff involved in the event, but he did acknowledge that officers on duty were under investigation for violating procedure.[2]

At the urging of PHW's director, Warden Richardson called an accountability meeting so that all the affected parties could air their grievances regarding Alicia's departure from the program. Over the course of the meeting (which I was present for), Director Torrence claimed that both line staff and administrators were attempting to "sabotage" PHW by encouraging prisoners to leave and by spreading false rumors about abuse to dissuade others from entering. While vehemently denying the charge of sabotage, several high-ranking staff members acknowledged that they had questions regarding whether PHW was actually providing "rehabilitation" to the prisoners. Their concerns reflected confusion over PHW's unconventional approach to treatment. As an example, they cited their outtake interview with Alicia, who claimed that PHW counselors called her a "crack ho" and subjected her to what she felt were "abusive" disciplinary measures like having to scrub the floor with a toothbrush. In fact, the program, which was based on the therapeutic community model, did not claim to "rehabilitate" drug users but, rather, to "habilitate" them.[3] From the perspective of many prisoners and staff members, habilitation bore a much closer resemblance to the punitive forms of control associated with "get tough" punishment than to treatment. This, of course, violated long-standing organizational constructions of prisoners as "good girls" who were undeserving of "harsh" and "masculine" control measures like confrontational therapy.

As the meeting wore on, two things became increasingly clear. The first was that PHW counselors had a radically different view of women prisoners when compared against organizational constructions of "the girls." Director Torrence, for example, countered Alicia's claims that she had been a victim of abuse within PHW by saying, "Abuse is what *she* put her children through during her addiction. Abuse is what *she* has done to her own body. Habilitation means holding her accountable for her own actions. That's not abuse, it's treatment" (her emphasis). This stood in stark contrast to those staff members who characterized Alicia as a "good girl" and who argued that her extensive history of physical and sexual abuse rendered her too "fragile" for "confrontational therapy."

Second, prison staff's constructions of Alicia as fragile notwithstanding, it was also evident that the image of the "good girl" and the ideology of gender difference and feminine subjectivity that informed it were in crisis. Virtually everyone at the meeting acknowledged that Alicia's lengthy criminal record and multiple incarcerations meant that past attempts to reform her had failed. A staff lieutenant went so far as to suggest that Alicia was a "poster child" for the prison's revolving door problem. She was, he added, as much "victimizer" as "victim." With these seemingly contradictory constructions of Alicia's identity in play, no one could agree on whether the decision to process her request for a transfer out of PHW had been the most appropriate course of action to take. The only thing they did agree on was that something about the population of women prisoners had changed, and that this change had profound repercussions for the integrity of the prison's control apparatus.

In this chapter, I turn to the second major crisis that confronted the prison—the crisis over the meaning. Overcrowding, recidivism, and an outbreak of disciplinary problems strained not only the prison's material resources but its ideological ones as well. Prison staff began to question, for the first time in their professional careers, who women prisoners were and what was needed to control them. I argue that race is essential to understanding why staff ultimately lost faith in rehabilitative paternalism and became increasingly willing to entertain a new ideology of punishment. In the first half of this chapter, I examine how a shift in the racial demographic of the prison population coincided with the staff's perception that incoming prisoners were "real" criminals rather than good girls. This, in turn, undermined the staff's ideological commitment to rehabilitation. In the second half of the chapter, I explore how Company executives capitalized on racist constructions of "real" criminals to promote a new ideology of control—one that attributed drug addiction and criminal behavior to a diseased self.

Taking Notice: Women's Visibility and the Drug War

In the decades leading up to the War on Drugs, feminist criminologists observed that women offenders were "invisible" across the wider the criminal justice system and, within the prison system specifically, were little more than "afterthoughts."[4] While it is certainly the case that the history of women's prisons is constituted by institutionalized patterns of neglect and indifference, the tide began to turn when extreme levels of overcrowding forced policy makers and academics alike to take notice of trends in women's offending. From 1980 to 1994, for example, the number of women incarcerated in state and federal prisons grew by 386% and continued through 2004 to increase at a rate roughly double to that of men.[5] This increase hit African American women particularly hard. From 1986 through 2003, the incarceration rate among Black women increased by 800% compared to an increase of 400% over the same period for non-Black women.[6] By 2009, the incarceration rate for African American women was 142 per 100,000 compared to a rate of 50 per 100,000 white women.[7]

During the course of the drug war, East State had one of the highest incarceration rates in the country. From the mid-1980s through the mid-1990s, the number of incarcerated women in East State tripled and continued to rise over the next decade, such that by 2000 they constituted about a tenth of the state's prison population.[8] Much of the explosive growth in the overall incarceration in the state, as well as women's rate in particular, was attributable to increases in the number of drug offenders sentenced to prison. In 1980, drug offenders constituted just over 4% of the state's prison population but by 1990, amid the drug war, they represented nearly 20% of the prison population.[9] African Americans bore the brunt of both the state's incarceration boom and, in particular, the "get tough" penalties for drug crime. In 2000, African Americans made up 20% of the state's general population, 64% of its prison population, and 87% of those serving time on a drug offense. Over the twenty-year period from 1980 to 2000, incarceration rates for both whites and Blacks grew, but the number of incarcerated Blacks grew much faster while the overall proportion of whites in the prison population declined. This was true for both male and female prisoners. In terms of gender, African American women in East State were incarcerated at five times the rate of white women.[10] Indeed, by 2000 roughly two-thirds of women prisoners were African American.[11] While African American women have always been overrepresented among the state's prison population, the drug war marked the first time that they became a clear majority of women sentenced to prison. It bears noting that these statistics, particularly trends in race, drug offenses, and incarceration among women, mirror national trends from 1980 through 2000.[12]

Social scientists attribute national increases in the number of women doing time primarily to drug war policies (in particular, aggressive policing in predominantly African American and Latino/a neighborhoods and mandatory sentencing schedules for drug offenses), and secondarily to changes in the structure of crack-cocaine markets that made it easier for women to find work selling and distributing drugs.[13] Early into East State's overcrowding crisis, the state sponsored a series of studies investigating why the number of women in prison was skyrocketing. These studies focused exclusively on women's involvement in the drugs–crime nexus. For example, a 1991 survey of 128 incarcerated women administered by a state sentencing commission reported that 55% had been convicted of at least one drug-related crime and 100% admitted to using heroin, cocaine, or speed in the six months prior to their incarceration. In a follow-up study of 258 incarcerated women done by the DOC four years later, nearly one-third reported either selling or trafficking illicit drugs.

Overcrowding gave incarcerated women newfound visibility among state actors. However, instead of balancing survey data about drug involvement against research examining the impact of mandatory sentencing policies, state policy makers focused exclusively on drug use statistics. This exaggerated the extent to which the increase in the number of incoming prisoners was a function of changes in women's behavior. Staff officials and prison administrators interpreted the data as indicative of a drug epidemic the likes of which had never been seen in East State. According to one state official:

> The surveys are showing that we've got a real crisis on our hands. One that is affecting not just men, but for the first time, women. Among our new commitments [to the women's prison] 90% report using a drug other than alcohol in the last ninety days. That's shocking and what's worse, they're not getting any drug treatment.

The perception of a drug epidemic among women went beyond the statistics the DOC and the sentencing commission had collected. Many staff members in the prison hypothesized that surges in the prison population were an immediate consequence of changes in women's offending. They linked these changes to what they presumed was an expansion of drug use in urban areas, particularly within African American neighborhoods. Kelly, an African American officer with four years of experience in the women's prison, observed:

> Drugs, yes, I'd say that drugs is the major reason for building a new [women's] prison. There's almost no place you can go in [nearby city] without being able to get drugs. And guess what? Nowadays you're as likely to buy it from a woman as a man. A lot of them girls up there are sellers, not just dope freaks. . . . Drugs are the number one reason for all the crime in the city.

Deputy Warden Pearson, an African American woman in her sixties, also attributed the increase in the prison's population to drugs:

> The late 1980s, early 1990s is when the whole thing began. Or at least, among women, the drugs, crack, and crime got started and just took off. It's sweeping across the state, I've been seeing more girls from [rural area] caught up in it, coming in here recently. It's, what do you call it when you've got a disease that nobody can cure? An epidemic? I think what we saw in the 1980s is only the beginning.

Fred, a white correctional officer who lived in East State his entire life and had seventeen years of experience working in corrections (seven years of which were spent in the women's prison), described the situation:

> FRED: In the sixties and seventies, drugs were recreational, the kids were using them in school, people were experimenting. It wasn't serious, people weren't getting killed. Now, it seems like every day I turn on the news and some little Black kid got shot in a drive-by or something.
>
> JM: Did things change in here [prison] because of it?
>
> FRED: Oh, yeah. These girls are crazy, some of them. Yeah, girls, err, women are involved in this stuff like never before and that's making it worse. Nobody's teaching those kids growing up in the city about what's right and what's wrong. Used to be at least their mothers would do that. Now they grow up and kill each other. . . . I don't know what's gonna happen with it all, it just seems to me this thing is out of control.
>
> JM: So the changes involve behavior of inmates?
>
> FRED: Well, there's two major changes that I have seen. First, and most obviously, is the fact we had to build a new prison to house all of 'em. Numbers is the first thing, we started dealing with more and more convicted offenders in here since I'd guess the beginning was, 1985. The second change, yes, is behavioral. Some of them are the same we got before—good girls—but there's a lot of ones who will act crazy, question your authority, we didn't see that so much before.

It bears emphasizing that their perceptions regarding a drug epidemic among African Americans are flawed. Survey data consistently demonstrate that a greater percentage of whites use drugs than do African Americans across virtually every drug category. So, for example, the National Household Survey on Drug Abuse reports that in 1998, there were an estimated 9.9 million whites and 2 million African Americans using illicit drugs. Four times as many whites used cocaine compared to African Americans. Even in the case of crack cocaine, the number of white users exceed African American users by three times. Nonetheless, a comparison of drug users to drug arrests reveals that between 1979 and 1998, a disproportionately higher percentage of African American drug offenders were arrested compared to white drug offenders. This is true for both men and women.[14]

Three themes are evident from these excerpted interviews as well as others that I conducted with the policy makers and those correctional officers who were employed in the prison system during the period 1985–1995. The first is that beginning in the mid-1980s, women offenders acquired sudden visibility in the state. Their drug use, criminal involvement, and prison admissions were the subject of several internal DOC reports and state-sponsored research studies. Although women certainly did not occupy center stage in the theater of policy makers' concerns (young, African American men continued to hold this spot), they were no longer the correctional afterthoughts of a decade before. Second, state actors, particularly prison staff, were quick to point out that incoming prisoners were different, in terms of their offense history and behavior in prison, than were the "girls" of the past. Drug use figured prominently in this distinction. Third, race and the presumed moral decay of Black and Latino/a urban neighborhoods became a central frame of reference as state actors endeavored to make sense of all of it—the rates of women's incarceration, their participation in drug crime, and the perception that they were "acting crazy" in prison. Collectively, they sourced the crises erupting in the prison system to a larger social problem involving morality, drugs, and crime in impoverished urban neighborhoods. Within this framework, they identified young, poor, undereducated African American women as a central set of scapegoats and "folk devils."[15]

Race and the "Real" Criminal

By the mid-1990s, the image of the "good girl" was under siege and with it, the legitimacy of rehabilitative paternalism. Only a small number of prison staff continued to refer to prisoners as "girls" and even then, they were quick to make a distinction between "the girls" and a new type of prisoner: "real criminals." While staff members often described "the girls" as vulnerable, innocent, and suffering from psychological problems attributed to childhood traumas, physical violence, and sexual victimization, they characterized the incoming cohort of prisoners as, in their words, "manipulative," "predatory," "aggressive," "addicted," and "tough." For example, consider the deputy warden's explanation to me of why she endorsed Alicia's transfer request out of PHW and would do so again for any of her "girls":

> Oh, for a long time now the girls we've had in here have basically been good girls. I mean that honestly, I look on some of them as my own. . . . The typical girl had some real bad things happen to her during her life. A lot of them was abused as kids, and got into a lot of bad relationships with men, usually the men was why they were in here. I shouldn't even say "was" 'cause most of them is still in here because of something their man did that they got caught up in. They aren't criminals so much as just confused and scared.

In this excerpt, the deputy warden, like so many other prison staffers, distinguishes the "girls" from the "criminals." In the same interview, the deputy warden goes so far as to refer to incoming prisoners as a "different breed":

> What we noticed was that there's a new type of offender among us, one with a lot more problems and with a lot more anger than what we've seen here before. It requires someone with specialized knowledge about drug addicts. We've had drug problems for as long as I can remember and we've been successful dealing with it, but this is a criminally involved addict, they're a different breed and you can see that 'cause jail don't have no effect on them. They keep comin' back.

The contrast in her description of the "girls" and the "criminals" is striking. Girls are the victims of abuse who get "caught up" in men's criminal activity. Criminals are "angry," and impervious to the effects of incarceration. The senior prison counselor, an African American woman in her mid-fifties, makes a similar distinction between the passivity of "the girls" and the aggressiveness of incoming "antisocial types":

> Before you saw a lot of girls who just wanted to be good, to fit in. They might've ended up in the wrong crowd or with the wrong guy and bam, they find themselves in jail. But they was always basically good. . . . Nowadays, there's a lot of problem cases in here, women that just don't want to fit in with nobody, real antisocial types in my opinion. They will victimize some of the real innocents in here, just like they victimized their mothers, grandmothers, and for some of them, their kids.

An African American correctional officer in her thirties described incoming prisoners in terms of their unruliness within the prison: "Some of them are hard to control, they have no respect, they'll be up in your face when you try to discipline them. It's a contest, it seems like between them and us."

Distinctions between "good girls" and "real criminals" coincided with the emergence of the overcrowding problem and a rise in disciplinary issues in the prison, particularly inmate "beefs."[16] It also coincided with a shift in the racial demographics of the prisoner population. In the decades leading up to the 1980s, the majority of women serving time in prison were white. Ten years later, African American women became the majority in the prison, and in the decade that followed, they increased their proportion to a two-thirds majority. The impact of the racial shift was evident in how staff formulated the distinction between "good girls" and "real criminals."

Indeed, the staff's claims about the "immorality," "badness" and unruliness of the incoming tide of "real criminals" were fueled by racist stereotypes. While most higher-level state actors would not come right out and say this (though some did), the link between immorality, race, and class was made clear by the outright use or strong allusion to racially charged, controlling images of African American women as crack whores and welfare queens.[17] Sociologist Patricia Hill Collins explains that controlling images are part of a "generalized ideology of domination" that function to make racism, sexism, and poverty appear as inevitable and normal outcomes for certain socio-demographic groups.[18] In the prison, these images made the increase in African American women's incarceration rate appear to be an inevitable consequence of their own behavior and choices rather than as a function of poverty or broader changes in criminal justice policy. For example, during my interview with the warden, he explained that the source of the prison's problems with overcrowding, recidivism, and disorder lay in poor, predominantly African American neighborhoods in the city. He said, "Drugs are destroying these inner-city communities and are spilling the predatory types into *our* communities, *our* playgrounds" (my emphasis). When I asked him to clarify his point about "inner-city" communities, the warden took a long pause before speaking:

> What's going on out there is crack cocaine. It's destroying urban communities and morality. You don't have to look very far to see that. The women in here have done some desperate things for their crack. Selling their bodies, the bodies of their children. . . . The problem is not just overcrowding, this thing will take over *our* communities if we don't do something to stop it now. [My emphasis]

The warden's repeated references to "our" communities in contrast to the "inner-city" are intentional. The warden and I are both white. As he talks, he points to three African American women walking by his window, signaling that our conversation has shifted into a thinly veiled form of "race talk" where "us" and "our" refers to middle- and working-class whites and "them" and "their" refers to mostly poor, African American women.[19] In his description, the "real criminals" coming into the prison are simultaneously "desperate" and "predatory." He never mentions changes in sentencing policy.

The director of the Committee, a white woman in her early forties, drew on similar racial stereotypes, though she emphasized the criminality, "dependency," and "failures" of incoming prisoners rather than their immorality per se:

The women that we're talking about, the ones we're really trying to do something for are those ultra poor, ultra down and out group from [nearby city]. They've got the same MO. Repeat offenders, probation failure, parole failure, juvenile rap sheet, on and off welfare, in and out of prison, you know? They're working the system, welfare, criminal justice, they're living their lives going from one institution to the next . . . and they can't get it together because they've become dependent on this system we've set up.

In response to my follow-up question about what she meant by "dependent," her allusions to race became more explicit:

I think PHW is gonna do it, is gonna break the dependency cycle because it requires them to hold themselves accountable for what they've done. They're *not victims*, and they're not powerless, and that's the program's message [her emphasis] . . . unlike other drug treatment programs, cultural programming and increasing sensitivity is very important over there [PHW]. Hiring staff who look like them and can relate to them,[20] that . . . tells them that they can make it.

While the Committee's director never explicitly identifies the "ultra poor," "ultra down and out" group as African American, she makes this link when she mentions staff "who look like them." A high-ranking, white, Department of Correction official was even more direct when I asked him about changes in the inmate population. He responded by summarizing an article he had recently read about the "psychopharmacological" properties of crack cocaine and the high prevalence of crack use among "inner-city Blacks." Based on his recollection of the article, he hypothesized that out-of-wedlock births and incidences of infants born addicted to crack were likely the product of the drug's ability to decrease sexual inhibitions and create a "craving" for sexual activity. The consequence, according to the DOC official, was that urban areas were facing a "morality crisis" that not only exacerbated the drug-crime problem but also threatened the "integrity" of the welfare system and the "stability" of the prison system. A white correctional officer in his late twenties was even more blunt:

Problem is sex, drugs, and rock and roll, or rap [laughs], whatever they're listening to. We see a lot of girls that have done just about anything to get their drug, whatever it is—heroin, cocaine, crack, pot, speed. They leave up outta here and they're right back out on the street again. Lot of crack whores up in [the city] or up and down route [interstate road with several truck stops]. . . . Others will just have babies and cheat the system, you know, the queens of welfare.

It is important to note that most of the above excerpts are taken from interviews I conducted with administrators and state officials, the overwhelming majority of whom are white. Their remarks regarding race and class were more explicit in interviews and conversations with me than what I observed in meetings, press conferences, and other professional settings. In professional settings, particularly those that included correctional officers and support staff (a much more racially diverse group),[21] references to race persisted but were less explicit and were coded using terms like "cultural differences" and "urban." A rare exception to this occurred at a national conference on prison drug treatment, when a Company executive told an audience of legislators, clinicians, academics, wardens, and state officials that PHW was unique because its programming was tailored to meet the "culturally specific" needs of "Negroes." Following his statement, Tynice, an African American counselor from PHW, leaned over to me and noted that white decision makers frequently use the phrase "cultural differences" to mask racist sentiments about poor Blacks. Such statements, she noted, were rife with "recycled stereotypes" about African Americans. Laughing, Tynice suggested that the executive's ideas about race must be more antiquated than most, since "nobody informed him we're not going by the name of 'Negroes' anymore!"

Broad generalizations about "cultural differences" or "culturally specific programming" were almost always made by white policy makers and academics and were frequently met with informal, private criticism by African American staff members at all levels. Indeed, after the incident at the prison drug treatment conference, four African American prison staffers told me that they felt that white executives at the Company "perpetuated racial stereotypes" and "[didn't] quite get it." This did not necessarily empower them to raise such objections publicly, as I was never aware of an incident in which racial attitudes and beliefs among high-ranking decision makers were challenged by anyone at any level. For example, when executives from the Company questioned why an African American counselor was holding seminars in PHW about slavery and the history of race in the United States, the counselor explained that it was "culturally specific programming." Executives rejected this explanation (one of whom complained that the sessions were more "radical politics" than treatment), and in response the counselor voluntarily agreed to terminate the sessions. Among the African American prison employees with whom I discussed this issue, many felt that challenging racial stereotypes and "cultural programming" would cost them their jobs.[22]

Although a number of Black administrators and staff members privately objected to raced-based explanations of the drug-crime problem, they did not necessarily challenge the larger framework within which distinctions between the "good girl" and the "real criminal" were made. Typifications about welfare dependency and sexual promiscuity arising from crack use figured prominently in discussions with Black decision makers and employees, as it did with whites. A much larger portion of Blacks than whites, however, stressed the class-based dimensions to the drug-crime problem. Indeed, while many of the Black employees interviewed for this study used adjectives like "immoral," "dependent," "crazy," and "manipulative" to describe incoming prisoners, most were careful to stress that such behaviors were not the result of cultural/racial differences, but were generated from the strains imposed by enduring poverty. For example, one African American CO who heard about the "Negro" comment through the prison grapevine explained to me why she objected to race-based explanations that did not account for class:

> You hear a lot of them [white employees] use race to explain increases in the general pop statistics.[23] They see a lot of Black women and they think race has got something to do with it. Well, race *has* something to do with it when you talk about poverty [her emphasis]. A lot of these women are wicked bad, I'm certainly not denying that, but they've had to survive on almost nothing but their wits, and maybe their butts, and how well, or if, they can con some john or junkie. Blacks make up a large percentage of the poor in this country, more so than we rightly should, so you should expect to see a lot of Black women in here 'cause they're coming from poor neighborhoods and fucked-up situations. Must be some of the white folks in here are a little color-blind when it comes to their own [laughing] 'cause I'm seeing quite a few white girls in here still! How do they account for them if this is just about race?

In closing this section, one final issue needs to be addressed, and that is the racial status of the "good girl" in comparison with the "real criminal." It is clearly the case that constructions of "real criminals" are racialized. Indeed, interviews and conversations with staff suggest that the "real criminal" is a racially exclusive category. Blackness is the central referent most staff used for describing the incoming cohort of prisoners, as is evident from private interviews in which race was explicitly identified (e.g., "inner-city Blacks") to public discussions in which race was alluded to using coded language (e.g., "them," "rap," "urban," "culturally distinct"). Of course, it was not the case that the incoming tide of prisoners was racially monolithic. Large numbers of white women were also convicted of drug crimes and sentenced to prison.[24] They were implicated in the category of "real criminals," but as a racial exception rather than the rule. For example, when staff members described "real criminals" as drug addicted and welfare dependent, they would occasionally offer statements similar to this one made by a white correctional officer: "Nowadays you even see white women getting heavy into crack." The use of the qualifier "even white women" suggests an implicit link between African Americans and drug abuse, despite a significant volume of research evidence that demonstrates that rates of drug use are remarkably similar across race. Studies that report racial differences in drug use reveal that whites use at greater rates than do African Americans.[25]

This begs the question: if "real criminals" are Black, does this mean that "good girls" are white? The answer is yes but with an important proviso. The social construction of the "good girl" has its origins in the original reformatory movement and is premised on a set of beliefs about gender difference and feminine subjectivity that are themselves informed by cultural expectations regarding white women's place in social life.[26] The category "good girl" was born of a historical moment when white women constituted the majority of prisoners in the state. It was their purported needs around which the institution crafted and legitimated its control policies. Nonetheless, the category "good girls" is not racially exclusive in the sense that it was used by staff to refer to both African American and white prisoners without qualification. This is evident in administrators' descriptions of Alicia, who is African American, as a "good girl." The difference between the racially exclusive category of the "real criminal" versus the racially inflected category "good girl" lies in the prison's historical relationship to the broader political economy. Simply put, prison in the current moment functions as a racial caste system, a holding pen for persons permanently displaced from the labor market and civic participation.[27] This is distinct from previous eras, particularly on the feminine side of the system, where the focus was on restoring women to a productive citizenship vis-à-vis their place in the home and within the "pink collar" of the labor market.[28] The image of the "real (Black) criminal" is an important legitimating symbol for the current racial caste system because it obscures the ways in which welfare state restructuring shapes women's access to and participation within the labor market and the state.

Confrontational Therapy and Gender

The social construction of a problem involving drug crime in poor, predominantly African American neighborhoods and the belief that incoming prisoners were "real criminals" laid the groundwork for a shift in the prison's system of control. The prison, once designed to meet the socially constructed needs of "girls," was now home to both "girls" and a newcomer—the "real criminal." Among the policy makers and line staff I talked with, all agreed that the emergence of a new type of prisoner necessitated changes in the institution. The Department of Correction's solution was to "get tough" by jettisoning treatment programs in favor of greater punitiveness. Although most administrators and line staff objected to these measures on the premise that they were gender inappropriate, they ultimately assented to a number of changes that hardened security. Barbed wire was secured to the tops of both inside and outside fencing, the glass walls of the central control booth were blackened to allow officers to view out into the hall but prevented others from viewing in, and an imposing metal detector was erected just inside the front gate. Isolation cells were created to house women charged with serious disciplinary offenses, and a policy of prison-wide, twenty-four-hour lockdown was implemented to discourage outbreaks of unruly behavior.[29]

Prison officials maintained that these changes were not in themselves sufficient. Since so much of what was problematic about the "real criminal" was her drug use, decision makers argued that a specialized program was necessary to deal exclusively with addiction. Thus PHW's appeal. PHW was initially welcomed into the institution not only because it was "free," but also because of the extensive public relations campaign Company executives waged with administrators that emphasized the success of therapeutic communities in reducing recidivism rates among male prisoners. That PHW emphasized discipline and personal responsibility under the banner of drug treatment was an added bonus as it offered a politically palatable form of treatment in the era of "get tough." Nonetheless, problems quickly emerged within the prison over PHW's "confrontational" techniques, and this was primarily because no one had a clear sense of what addiction was or how to respond to it. Ironically, while there was a great deal of consensus among administrators and line staff about the nature of the social problem (drug crime) and the characteristics of the social villain (real criminals), there were serious disputes over how to best reconfigure control within the institution. All of this contributed to the bad blood that emerged between prison staff and PHW during the first year of the program's operation in the prison.

The earliest disputes between PHW and the prison staff involved terri-
tory and PHW's right to institutional sovereignty. Such was the case when
the deputy warden objected to the program requirement that PHW counselors be notified of all communications taking place between prisoners in the
program and prison staff (including communications initiated by administrators). A similar dispute arose between a lieutenant and the PHW director when the director admonished two correctional officers on duty in the
prison cafeteria for disciplining a PHW prisoner without first notifying and
receiving permission from PHW counselors. Behind prison staff's concern
about who was *actually* in charge of the prisoners housed in PHW, however,
lay more fundamental misgivings about the appropriateness of confrontational treatment for women.

Amid a number of sensational, unfounded rumors about disciplinary
practices in PHW, a few prominent and influential staff members questioned
the legitimacy of the program and charged PHW with engaging in coercive
punishment practices in the name of therapy. The most inflammatory and
widely circulated rumors were that prisoners in PHW were made to get on
their hands and knees and bark like dogs for medication, and that to punish
certain prisoners, counselors shackled them to their beds at night. Neither
rumor was true, and the latter was completely implausible given that PHW
counselors did not have access to shackles, handcuffs, or any other restraint
device. Nonetheless, the persistence of these and similar rumors reflected the
level of anxiety among both staff and inmates in relation to a changing control structure within the prison.

The staff's climactic display of opposition to PHW came with the very
public departure of Alicia from the program, discussed earlier in the chapter.
Following the warden's accountability meeting in which PHW's director dis-
missed charges of abuse as something prisoners like Alicia did to themselves
on the street, these staff members shifted their criticism to emphasize the
inappropriateness of any sort of "confrontational" therapy for women. In a
meeting with PHW staff and Company executives, the senior prison counselor argued that confrontational tactics, combined with yelling, were inappropriate forms of communication with "battered" and "abused" women.
Following her statement, the deputy warden demanded to know why PHW
did not consider women's abuse histories when planning treatment interventions. Shortly following this meeting, two of the prison's counselors took it
on themselves to interview prisoners who had dropped out of PHW, in order
to determine whether they had done so because the yelling reminded them
of previous abuse. Though they would not say how many women they interviewed or discuss the specifics of the interviews with me,[30] they contacted

the warden and called a special session to discuss their findings, claiming that the program was profoundly disturbing to women who had been victims of abuse. Notably, neither PHW's director nor Company executives were invited.

I will explore prisoners' reasons for dropping out of PHW in a later chapter; my point in including this issue here is to highlight the irony of this particular line of criticism. Charging PHW's style of treatment as "inappropriate" for the victims of battering and abuse reinvigorates the imagery of the "good girl" and thereby violates the reasoning that went into bringing PHW into the prison in the first place. The criticism was an interesting one, for it called into question the accuracy of institutional constructions of real criminals as "victimizers" and not "victims," and reasserted the prison's paternalistic commitment to "taking care of the girls." In the wake of this session, line staff and general population prisoners regularly forecast PHW's "decline" and a few administrators took great delight in monitoring the program's dropout rates. The Company's response to this was to relaunch its public relations efforts, this time with an eye toward winning over both line staff and administrators. Their aim was to "educate" prison employees about the unique character of addiction among "crime-involved women." Although they continued to include statistics about the "successes" of the therapeutic community model, the emphasis in these sessions was on why it was necessary to provide addiction treatment that was not only "gender responsive" but also "culturally specific."

The Person Is the Problem

In many respects, the PHW program can be summed up in two statements that executives and PHW counselors repeat with considerable fanfare in all their presentations, training sessions, and written materials. The first statement describes the characteristics of the disease of addiction: "Addiction is a disorder of the whole person. The problem is the person, not the drug." The second concerns addiction treatment: "Rehabilitation implies a fully formed self. Crime-involved addicts suffer from incomplete and underdeveloped selves. Therefore, they cannot be rehabilitated, they must be habilitated." Both statements make the case that something is intrinsically wrong with the self. The Company's cross-training sessions with prison staff build on each of these statements by elaborating on what is wrong with the self and what can be done to manage it. They do so first by creating a composite sketch of the addict—her lifestyle, drug use, and criminal participation—and then cataloging her cognitive, emotional, social, and moral deficits. The remainder of these sessions is spent showcasing how habilitation, as a treatment modality, is the only effective means of simultaneously controlling and intervening in the disordered selves of women who are drug addicts and "criminal thinkers." Woven throughout are a series of ongoing concerns about race, class, and gender, particularly as these interpolate the disordered self and the implications for treatment strategy.

The composite sketch of the "inmate in need" presented by the Company at the cross-training sessions echoed the prison staff's constructions of the "real criminal." The difference was that Company trainers aimed to legitimate these constructions by drawing on statistical data and pseudoscientific claims about addiction.[31] The first part of the training session featured statistical data that detailed women's drug use, criminal activity, and demographic characteristics. Trainers claimed that 80% of women prisoners in the state suffered from a substance abuse problem, and that 70% of women prisoners had a drug problem that was serious enough to warrant residential substance abuse treatment. They attributed these estimates to earlier studies conducted by the DOC and a state sentencing commission. Among the findings highlighted: 90% of women prisoners reported using an illegal drug in the ninety-day period prior to their incarceration (and 100% had used one in the last six months), and among that group, 75% had reported the use of crack cocaine "one or more times." This latter statistic often drew vigorous nods of agreement among the audience of prison staff. Although it was never clear to me how that particular survey item spoke to addiction and the need for treatment, any reported use of crack cocaine was broadly assumed by Company trainers, state officials, and prison employees to be a proxy for addiction.[32] Indeed, crack cocaine was the ultimate boogeyman in these training sessions, in much the same way it was featured as the galvanizing symbol of the drug war.[33] As one CO sitting near me said to a companion, "No one up and *tries* crack. You gotta be an addict already to even touch that stuff" (his emphasis). Although the Company's official line on addiction held that a person could be addicted to any drug (since addiction is "about the person, not the drug"), nothing the trainers did or said in those sessions contradicted the popular myth that crack cocaine was pharmacologically more addictive, and by extension more dangerous, than other substances.

In addition to presenting data on women's drug use, trainers also offered a detailed account of their participation in crime and involvement in the criminal justice system. They claimed that incoming prisoners were "persistent" offenders who possessed "criminogenic" personality traits. As evidence, they again featured Department of Correction survey data. The subset of prisoners who were deemed "in need" of residential drug treatment averaged just over seven adult criminal charges and had been in prison at least three times during their adulthood. Among this same subset, 41% had a violent crime on their record and 55% had been convicted of a drug crime. Finally, to make the link among addiction, criminality, and race explicit, trainers presented demographic data emphasizing that three-quarters of the women prisoners identified as "in need of treatment" were African American, with a mean age of thirty years.

Following presentation of the statistical data, trainers then "filled in the blanks" of addiction by mapping the "typical" life course of the crime-involved addict and explicating her core "deficits." The "Life Cycle" graphic was particularly noteworthy, as it further solidified imagery of drug, particularly crack, users as hypersexual, violent, immoral, and firmly entrenched in their addictions.

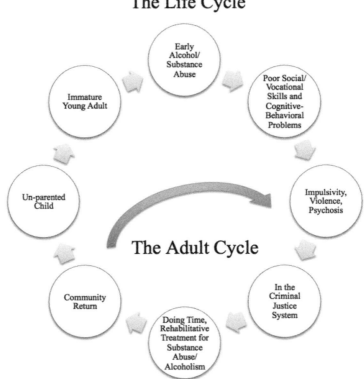

The Life Cycle

Early Alcohol/Substance Abuse

Immature Young Adult

Poor Social/Vocational Skills and Cognitive-Behavioral Problems

Un-parented Child

Impulsivity, Violence, Psychosis

The Adult Cycle

Community Return

Doing Time, Rehabilitative Treatment for Substance Abuse/Alcoholism

In the Criminal Justice System

According to the chart, the drug-involved addict begins life as an "un-par-ented" child and, as a result, becomes an "immature" young adult who exhib-its poor social and vocational skills and "cognitive-behavioral" problems. It is during young adulthood that she begins experimenting with alcohol and ille-gal substances, and experiences problems with "impulsivity," "violence," and "psychosis." In short order, she encounters the criminal justice system, and while doing time she may receive something in the way of treatment (most likely a 12-step, rehabilitation program). Rehabilitation is insufficient because it treats her drug abuse rather than her disordered self. The result is that upon her return to the community, she resumes her drug use and continues to exhibit behaviors that are impulsive, violent, and psychotic. In an unmistak-able nod to the moral panic over "crack babies,"[34] trainers also pointed out that upon her return to the community, she gets pregnant and has a child that she, in turn, fails to adequately parent. Thus the cycle of addiction repeats itself throughout her life and regenerates itself through the lives of her offspring.

The second half of the cross-training sessions was devoted to habilitation and the therapeutic community model. Readers who are familiar with thera-peutic communities will undoubtedly recognize the phrase "drug abuse is a disorder of the whole person" and the term "habilitation." All therapeutic communities share a disease model of addiction, which locates the source of the problem within the self of the addict.[35] Drug abuse is considered a symp-tom of the disorder. Other "symptoms" include criminality, persistent unem-ployment, failed relationships, and poor decision making. Scholarly advo-cates of the therapeutic community vary in their assessments of the cause(s) of addiction and disordered personalities, though most agree that these conditions are the product of a complex of biological, psychological, and social factors.[36] Along with different emphases in the apportioning of causal-ity, there are structural differences among therapeutic communities, which produce considerable variation in the relationship between staff and clients, levels of surveillance and control, and the intensity of confrontations.[37]

Although the Company was operating a therapeutic community for drug offenders in one of the state's prisons for men, most administrators and staff in the women's prison were unfamiliar with the practices associated with "habili-tation therapy," particularly the reliance on harsh and intense confrontations. When prison staff critiqued PHW as "abusive," it was most often in response to confrontation sessions in which counselors could be overheard calling pris-oners names like "dirty dogs" and "crack whores." To assuage their concerns, Company trainers went to a great deal of effort contrasting the more familiar "rehabilitative," medical model of treatment from the therapeutic community's habilitative model, and detailing why "substance-abusing, women offenders" required the latter. According to them, the medical model regards addiction as a "primary disease" and the central problem. In contrast, the therapeutic community model views addiction as one of many "secondary problems," the source of which is the "whole person." In the medical model, treatment is "therapist directed," individually tailored, and occurs in timed sessions. In the therapeutic community, the "community is the primary therapeutic agent" and treatment occurs twenty-four hours a day, seven days a week. Clinical "interventions" occur through group encounters rather than in individualized counseling sessions. The final notable difference is that within the therapeutic community "personal issues are public," while in the medical model such issues remain private between a therapist and a client. After the trainers finished this point-by-point comparison of rehabilitation and habilitation, a Company clinician told the audience that confrontational therapy was the most effective tool for dealing with "criminally involved addicts" because it provided them with "immediate, irrefutable evidence of their flawed thinking patterns, behavior, and emotion states." She then distributed a worksheet that reinforced the link between treatment modality and discrete kinds of subjects:

> TCs [therapeutic communities] are uniquely designed to treat character disorders. These disorders, including addiction, result from backgrounds that are often filled with neglect, physical and emotional abuse, sexual abuse, exposure to criminality and criminal role models, and an absence of socially acceptable morals and values. As a result, many TC residents are unable to identify, label, or express their feelings, and act out on those repressed and unexpressed feelings in negative ways. . . . Through confrontation, the program is uniquely able to help participants who are highly manipulative and dishonest, have minimal impulse control, exhibit an inability to delay gratification, and justify any actions to get what they want, when they want it.

The "medical model" of drug treatment was certainly what a number of prison administrators and staff had in mind when PHW arrived in the facility. The questions they raised about whether PHW was actually providing "rehabilitation" were premised on this model. And, as Company trainers noted, they were right that PHW did not conform to a rehabilitative platform. The medical model provides rehabilitation because it caters to people with "complete" selves. The prisoners deemed in need of treatment, however, did not, in the view of Company clinicians, possess such completeness. By drawing on some of the same themes staff invoked when they talked about "real criminals," Company trainers were able to make the case that the medical model was more effective when directed at populations that needed to "relearn a particular way of life." In contrast, habilitation was best directed at those who never learned "socially acceptable morals," because they were "un-parented" and exposed to "criminal role models." In other words, therapeutic communities were needed to manage and treat "real criminals."

The final theme in the cross-training sessions involved PHW's claim to provide treatment that is "culturally sensitive" and "gender specific." PHW's director routinely made a point of saying that while therapeutic communities are the most effective way to treat addiction among criminal offenders, they require some modification for women prisoners because these techniques were originally designed "by and for white men." These "modifications" primarily involved staffing and "issues requiring confrontation." At any given time, PHW had a total of five counselors, a director, and a secretary who staffed the unit, in addition to designated security personnel from the prison. The Company argued that counselors "should look like" the women they treated, on the premise that they would be familiar with the "unique" issues exhibited by this "particular group of women." Over the course of this study, PHW employed a total of twelve counselors, the majority of whom were African American women.[38] The counseling staff were a mix of what trainers like to refer to as "book educated" and "street smart," meaning that some of the counselors had college-level or higher degrees in social work and related fields, while others had some experience in addictions treatment and other "human service professions" either as caseworkers, clients, or both.[39] The Company justified this mix on the basis that "street addicts" were "highly manipulative" and more than capable of conning counselors who were unfamiliar with the unique "pathologies" of street life. At the same time, "street smart" counselors benefited from the "theoretical knowledge" of social work and psychology that "book smart" counselors possessed.[40] The demographic composition of the counseling staff proved a valuable legitimating device, particularly when some prison staffers challenged Company trainers about the use of confrontational therapy with women who were the victims of abuse. On one occasion, PHW's director retorted, "Who's going to know Black women's issues better than Black women? We're women, just like them, and confronting them on their issues, from one Black woman to another, is not abuse." Statements like this were effective in silencing critics at cross-training sessions and accountability meetings, the most vocal of whom (with the exception of the deputy warden and the senior counselor for the prison) were either men or white.

The irony in the director's statement is that ultimately it was not Black women who structured PHW's thematic content or its control practices—this was set up by executives and clinicians at the Company, the majority of whom are white men. They made the decision to retain surveillance, discipline, accountability, and confrontation as the "four pillars" of habilation, regardless of whether their "clients" were men or women. This was also the case for the issues that were addressed in the confrontation sessions. Although counselors had a great deal of discretion over which prisoners they confronted, when they confronted them, and for what, they did not establish the "major areas" of "disordered personhood" that were deemed worthy of clinical intervention—Company executives and clinicians did. The interventions they pursued were gendered, but they were not based on Black women's articulations of their experiences or their needs—they were based on institutional constructions of "real criminals" and, more broadly, cultural anxieties about single mothers, racial/ethnic minorities, crime, and poverty. This is best exemplified in the following exchange that occurred after the senior counselor from the prison presented a Company executive with data about the percentage of incarcerated women who were victims of violence and sexual abuse. She challenged him on the lack of domestic violence and sexual abuse programming in PHW. He responded:

> These women are clinging to their victimization and not moving on from it. They've adopted a victim role. The men in [therapeutic community in the men's prison] have been victimized, too, but they don't focus on it. Women in there are really weak in this regard, they won't focus on what they need to be focusing on. Instead, they wallow in victimization. That holds them back in their addictions. We move them forward.

His message in conjunction with materials presented at the cross-training sessions was clear. Incoming prisoners were not victims in the sense their predecessors had been. This group "adopted" a victim role and "wallowed" in it. Allowing them to do so doomed prisoners to remain trapped within the "cycle of addiction," and condemned the institution to overcrowding and associated problems. In framing victimization as a choice and an outcome of a disordered self, the Company simultaneously legitimated the use of unorthodox treatment practices in PHW and reinforced racist institutional claims about "real criminals."

Conclusion

In much the way that PHW offered prison administrators a solution to the resource crisis, so too did the program serve as a sort of ideological alternative to the crisis over the meaning of punishment. Both sets of crises were at the center of the institution's break with rehabilitative paternalism.

Rehabilitation, as an ideology of control, might have survived in the face of internal problems like overcrowding so long as the staff's socially constructed beliefs about the subjectivity and needs of women prisoners remained intact. But changes in the racial demographic of the prisoner population, combined with a rise in institutional disorder, prompted staff members to question the core identities of women prisoners: Were they victims or victimizers? Good girls or real criminals?

The Company capitalized on this uncertainty by linking the prison staff's underlying anxieties about race, poverty, and crime to PHW's ideology of addiction. The disease concept offered what appeared to be scientific validation of many of the staff's racist assumptions about incoming prisoners—specifically, that they were immoral, unsocialized, violent, hypersexual, criminogenic, and impervious to traditional mechanisms of social control. The disease concept offered prison administrators a new vocabulary of motive—one that shifted the blame for overcrowding and inmate disciplinary problems off prison staff and squarely onto the shoulders, or more accurately the selves, of women prisoners. Recidivism was no longer a sign of organizational failure; rather, it signaled the rise of an epidemic.

Nowhere was this shift in thinking more evident than in the wake of Alicia's departure from PHW. Prison staff sympathetic to her claims of abuse immediately processed her transfer request on the premise that her identity as a "good girl" and her past history as a victim of violence rendered her too fragile to withstand PHW's confrontational therapy. However, following the warden's accountability meeting in which PHW counselors reviewed her extensive criminal history and multiple incarcerations, prison staff agreed that past efforts to reform her had failed. She was both victim and victimizer, more of a "real criminal" than a "good girl." Staff placed her in restrictive custody as a penalty for failing to complete the program and reported to the sentencing judge that her request for transfer was without merit. The sentencing judge penalized her by requiring that she serve six months more in prison than she would have had she completed the PHW program. The prison's classification committee added to this penalty by refusing to release her on her minimum sentence. All told, Alicia served just under four years in prison on a three to five year sentence for possession of crack cocaine. She later told me, "I got an extra year and a half because they decided that I deserved the abuse [in PHW]."

PART II

The Practice of Habilitation

4

The Eyes Are Watching You

Finding the Real Self

Everywhere you go, everything you do, the eyes are always
watching you.
—Hand-stenciled poster hanging in PHW

Power is in tearing human minds to pieces and putting them
together again in new shapes of your own choosing.
—George Orwell, *Nineteen Eighty-Four*

One of the earliest stops for newly sentenced prisoners as they arrive in
the prison is the classification committee. Prior to PHW's arrival, the classification committee's central tasks were to make housing assignments and
to determine whether an inmate was eligible to earn "good time" credits
through participation in work, educational, or rehabilitative programs.[1] In
the wake of organizational restructuring and PHW, the classification committee's work took on added significance. They were now charged with select-
ing those prisoners who would serve out their sentences in the experimental
program. Classification committee members include prison administrators
and key staff members (including the director of mental health, the senior
prison counselor, and the director of the medical unit), as well as the director
of PHW and two of PHW's counselors. The committee takes its work seriously and its members understand the political and organizational ramifications of their decisions. Ms. Barker, the prison's senior counselor, told me,
"Of course we want to target the hardened cases, the crack addicts, those
who are disordered by addiction, but we've also got to give this habilitation
thing a chance. We can't front-load 'em with the worst cases."

In deciding whether to admit prisoners into PHW, the classification committee endeavors to establish two essential criteria. The first is whether a

given recruit is addicted to drugs and alcohol, and the second is to determine her "suitability" for PHW. The second category, "suitability," is actually of more significance than the first, since the committee regards everyone who has ever used drugs as an addict. Indeed, a prisoner's frequency, duration, and intensity of drug and alcohol use are not necessary conditions for her to qualify as an "addict" from the perspective of the classification committee. Although these categories are often invoked when a prisoner's self-reported use is high, the committee regularly sends women into the program who report only infrequent use of marijuana or alcohol, as well as a handful of others who insist they have never used illegal drugs at all.

At first glance, the committee's failure to make selections based on rather obvious categories such as frequency of drug and alcohol use and other characteristics commonly associated with addiction (e.g., blackouts, overdoses, percentage of income spent on drugs, drug-related crime) seems counterintuitive.[2] After all, PHW's official mandate is to treat addicted women, and since the program can accommodate only fifty women at a time, it might be logical to expect that the committee would employ a screening mechanism to differentiate those with addictions from those whose drug use is more casual. But classification committee members, particularly PHW's counselors, do not trust inmates to tell them the truth about their drug and alcohol usage, much less the conditions that led to their incarceration. Self-report information, then, is regarded as at best unreliable and at worst useless. By discrediting the only major source of information about prisoners drug use, counselors and committee members are left to make their selections largely based on observing behavior and interpreting talk during hour-long, informational interviews with incoming inmates. These "intake" interviews are conducted by PHW counselors, who then distribute a report of the interview and a recommendation regarding the candidate's "suitability" to the classification committee. The committee generally follows these recommendations in deciding which inmates to admit to PHW. Roughly 30% of those screened are ultimately admitted into the program, although this percentage fluctuates based on available bed space.

During the typical intake interview, counselors pay close attention to the inmate, examining everything from her appearance and gestures to the cadence of her speech and the direction of her gaze. Based on these impressions, they decide whether the inmate is an addict and whether she is "suitable" for PHW. If she is both of those things, counselors then endeavor to diagnose the state of her "disordered" self.

As we emerged from one interview with Genie, a woman who had been sentenced to two years in prison for drug trafficking, I asked the PHW counselor why she had decided to recommend her for admission. Bed space in the program was limited and although Genie was a drug offender, she certainly did not seem to have the sort of case history that would make her an obvious candidate for admission into PHW. During the interview, Genie admitted that she "experimented" with marijuana and regularly drank beer on the weekends, but repeatedly denied using "harder" drugs like cocaine and heroin. Her trafficking conviction was premised on several pounds of marijuana that law enforcement officers discovered in the apartment she shared with her boyfriend. Genie claimed that the marijuana belonged to her boyfriend, a man who had a rather lengthy history of drug-related convictions. The counselor confirmed that this was Genie's first time in trouble with the law and that she did not exhibit any "behavioral difficulty" during her first month in the prison. Before responding to my question, the counselor took some time to review the notes she had taken during Genie's interview. When she finally responded, her answer sounded like a judge ticking off multiple counts of offense categories prior to imposing a sentence on a convicted offender:

> First, did you see when I asked her about the boyfriend? She flinched and looked away from me. That's a classic avoidance behavior that you see with addicts. The second thing that I saw was her tapping her foot constantly, all that tapping. I've come to learn that when people have to be moving their bodies all around there is some kind of problem. It could be nerves, but what's she got to be nervous about with me? I'm not one of those crazy girls she's got to be living with in that unit. OK, so that was the second, now I'm really paying attention. The third was how she wouldn't really talk about her family or what *really* [her emphasis] happened the night she got arrested. Again, that's avoidance, and the best addicts are good at making you think it's not, but it is. Look for the nonresponses or the unemotionality. They're clever about the emotions. Which is the fourth thing, it involves the feelings she was giving off, the hostility, and I feel the anger under the surface. It was there and a lot of girls that's abused have that anger in them. It becomes more obvious the longer they're away from their drugs 'cause the drugs mask it, make it sink deeper within them.

During the interview, I did notice Genie flinch at the mention of her boyfriend and she seemed to resent questions asked about her sexual practices (including questions on her sexual orientation, types and frequencies of sex acts performed, age at which she lost her virginity, and whether she was HIV positive or ever had a sexually transmitted disease). Curious about the coun-selor's interpretation that Genie was repressing a deeper anger, I asked her to elaborate on the point she made about hostility:

> COUNSELOR: How can I make you understand this? OK, you know how we're talking now, and you could actually say that I'm being interviewed like [Genie] was being interviewed. I'm answering your questions . . . and everything is casual. Do you feel like I'm hiding something from you?
>
> JM: [shake head negatively]
>
> COUNSELOR: Right, because I don't have anything to hide. Now, what about [Genie]? Didn't you feel that she was hiding, or, um, repressing something?
>
> JM: [shrug]
>
> COUNSELOR: Well, let me again point out to you that we're talking about someone who can really manipulate well. But the signs are there, remember the foot tapping, the avoidance, and the hostility. When we go back to the [PHW], just watch, you'll see the same thing in a lot of the newer ones.

What this exchange reveals is that it is something other than a prisoner's case history, drug use, or overt behavior that is the target of the prison's clas-sification efforts. Indeed, what the PHW counselor was endeavoring to clas-sify in the intake interview was the state of Genie's self. The belief in a "real" self, a coherent entity that resides deep within a person and serves as a sort of inner core on which the rest is built, persists in American culture.[3] It is a baseline assumption of the therapeutic community model that this self is dis-eased and deformed, impairing cognitive, emotional, and moral functions.[4] PHW's appeal was premised on its assertion that perversions of this self were the source of social unruliness and personal disorder. But classifying this self, accessing its inner recesses and darkened corners, presents a formidable challenge to PHW's counselors. As the counselor notes during our interview, this self cannot simply be gleaned from surface appearances. In contrast to the counselor's account of her own self (e.g., "I don't have anything to hide"), she characterizes Genie as "repressing something," "clever," and "manipula-tive." Indeed, while the self is typically thought of as something that is private and subterraneous,[5] the counselor suggests that the remoteness of Genie's self is exacerbated by her drug use. Drugs not only "sink it deeper," they "mask" the real self. The challenge then for the classification committee and the prison writ large is not only to plumb the depths to make that which is hid-den visible, it is also to distinguish the real from the fraud.

The desire to make the internal external not only provides the impetus for new social technologies of control to emerge,[6] it is what distinguishes habilitation from both rehabilitative paternalism and the "get tough" strategies appearing in men's prisons. It also stands in sharp contrast to what criminologist Jennifer Kilty describes as the near-exclusive reliance within Canadian women's prisons on psychopharmacological drugs to govern prisoners behavior.[7] In this chapter, I examine how PHW's control apparatus endeavors both to organize prisoners' behavior and, more crucially, to make the self visible and interpretable. I argue that surveillance is at the heart of this enterprise, but how it is enacted and the ends to which it is put differ markedly from modernist efforts to "normalize" deviant selves.[8]

Encounter Group

Encounter group is the cornerstone of the PHW program and of therapeutic communities more generally. As one counselor explained to me, "If you want to understand habilitation, you've got to sit in on EG. You can see the whole of it in that group." According to the program director, the purpose of the group is simultaneously punitive and therapeutic. On one level, the group is designed to single out and confront "troublemakers." Confrontations are lengthy and dramatic, with counselors and prisoners offering blunt and "raw" indictments regarding the women who have been identified as troublemakers. These sessions leave their targets in varying states of emotional distress, with many women reduced to tears. There is, according to Director Torrence, a therapeutic purpose to the groups as well. First, the indictments are intended to challenge the way the target conceptualizes her "real" self. During one such group, a counselor explained to the women, "If you understood yourself, really saw yourself as we see you, you'd want to change. We're shining the light on your disorder." Second, encounter groups are intended to provoke the women into releasing and then controlling their emotions. Doing so allows the women to "get in touch" with their "real" selves and to learn how to "control their negativity."

Beyond these "therapeutic" goals, however, encounter groups were popular with counselors because they provided a wealth of information about prisoners. Prior to each group, prisoners were encouraged to report one another to the staff for rule violations and displays of "negative" behavior and attitude. From the reports, counselors learned a great deal about the relationships prisoners have with one another and how often program rules were violated and in what contexts. Further, the confrontations were themselves a source of information. One counselor told me, "This is how we really see what's going on inside them, everything just comes up to the surface." Indeed, encounter groups capitalized on PHW's extensive surveillance apparatus and then extended the reach of this apparatus to make the "real" self visible.

The groups are held once or twice a week and are eagerly anticipated by the program's counseling staff and its inmates. The appeal for prisoners is that the group provides them with a forum for expressing their anger, outrage, and hurt feelings in response to the words or deeds of other women in the program. As one woman put it, "EG lets us blow off steam and get everything out in the open." In most cases, the appeal of "blowing off steam" outweighed women's fears that they would be among those who were selected for confrontation and, when they were, the humiliation associated with being the target of such a confrontation.[9]

Encounter groups take a variety of forms, depending on the substance and frequency of rule infractions, and the intensity of the tensions running between and among prisoners and staff. When tensions are high, staff modify the traditional encounter group into a game referred to as "pinball." According to PHW's orientation manual, pinball is a:

> unique and dynamic encounter group where no one is safe from being addressed or allowed to respond to the confrontations. The energy created by this rapid-fire type of encounter commits residents to confront each other in a manner that is both uncensored, and at times verbally hostile. . . . The effect is two-fold. First, the resident is not able to respond and is forced to contain her feelings until she is able to deal with them at a latter [sic] time. Secondly, the random confrontations provoke residents into exposing and breaking negative relationships.

In a pinball session, the target sits alone in the middle of a circle and is confronted in rapid-fire style by staff, as well as by other prisoners whom the staff hand-selects to participate in the confrontation. Pinball differs from traditional encounter group mainly in terms of how much pressure is brought to bear on the target. In the traditional group, the target is not physically singled out and placed in the center of the group, but instead remains seated among her peers. Only prisoners who actually reported the target to the staff for engaging in a rule violation are allowed to participate in the confrontation, and the confrontations themselves are limited to a total of five minutes. In pinball, staff could designate anyone to participate in the confrontation and there is no limit on the duration of the session. Pinball sessions are intended to serve as strong condemnations of the behaviors and attitudes of women deemed "troublemakers." This meant, as several prisoners made a point to tell me, that pinball is "no holds barred." In all, this type of game allows staff to bring considerable social pressure to bear on selected targets.

Although program counselors routinely told me that the type of "troublemakers" they target for pinball sessions are women who had violated a "cardinal rule,"[10] it is more often the case that targets are those who have challenged the staff's authority or women who are thought to be "hiding" something. For example, staff selected Tai for a pinball session after she walked away from a counselor who was in the middle of admonishing her for passing a note to another woman in the program (a rule violation). Such blatant disrespect for the authority of a counselor was infrequent and, according to staff, signaled the potential for widespread disruption. Counselor Tynice explained:

> At this stage of the game, our job is encountering disorder. You can't let them be up in your face because they'll keep pushing it and pushing it until they've got control. That's how they do it on the street and with their families. They take and they push, till they get what they want—drugs, money, whatever. You let one of them do it without answering back and you've put whatever you've accomplished with the rest of them in jeopardy. Deep inside they're still addicts, no matter what they look like on the surface, and they'll take advantage if they can. Part of our job is knowing when it's going on and putting a stop to it.

At exactly ten o'clock on the morning after Tai's initial act of insubordination, Counselor Tynice convened the women in the center of the unit and instructed them to set up the chairs in a circle for a game of pinball. Several women broke into a trot toward the storage area and emerged with dozens of plastic chairs, murmuring to one another all the while. Newcomers to the program asked the more experienced what pinball was, since many had never seen or heard of this particular version of the encounter group, while other prisoners speculated about who among them was "gonna get it" from the counselors. In minutes, all the women in the program were seated and comported in the "ready for treatment" posture (feet on the floor, backs straight, chins set and lifted, faces expressionless, and hands placed palms down on the knees). Standing in the doorway to the staff office with two other counselors, Counselor Tynice looked sternly around the room, taking a moment to look directly into the eyes of the women who faced her. After whispering for a moment or two with the other staff members, Tynice strode into the center of the circle, wheeling behind her an office desk chair. Before taking a seat beside one of the prisoners in the circle, she took great care to place the desk chair in the precise center of the circle, aligned almost directly underneath a glass skylight in the unit's ceiling.

As she moved to take her seat, Tynice called, "[Tai], you can take the seat in the middle. Put your hands on your knees and spin toward me." Tai did as she was told, though breaking with program etiquette by catching the gaze of two other women in the circle and rolling her eyes. She swiveled the office chair so that she was facing Counselor Tynice and, with chin held high, stared directly at the counselor.

"Family,[11] I put you in this circle today to give you some information which you so desperately need about yourself and your emotions. You see, you're not in control like you think you are. You ain't got no control at all. Know how I know that?" At the beginning of the confrontation, Counselor Tynice's voice was low, barely audible. However, by the time she got to the phrase "you ain't got no control," her voice was booming. The other prisoners, who were leaning forward in their chairs to hear her, jumped back almost in tandem as she began to shout.

"[Tai], I asked you a question. Do you know how I know that you're not in control? Dialogue."[12] Tai, her faced flushed, shook her head negatively. "[Tai], I instructed you to dialogue, not gesture. I'm going to ask again and this time I want an answer. You're not going to control me or this session. You can't, you don't have the control you think you do. Now, I asked you twice, and I'm asking you again, and unless you're truly so dumb or so confused as to not know the answer, I want to know why I know, but you don't seem to, that you're not in control."

With her jaw set firmly Tai responded, "I control what I think and how I behave, not you. Isn't that what this program is telling us? That we're responsible for our behaviors—"

"Family, that's enough. That's it, I've had it with your attitude. If you were truly in control, if you had all this power, would you be in here? What kind of woman, what kind of mother, would choose—if she had control—would choose to be in prison? Come on, Family, you're talking shit now and we all know it. Responsibility and control are two different matters. I know you don't got no learning disabilities or other serious mental impairments, so you better believe that you're responsible for what you do. I'm holding you responsible right now for your negative behavior the other day." The onlookers remained riveted on Tai throughout Counselor Tynice's discussion. A bead of sweat slid down Tai's forehead.

"You're saying that I don't have any control and you're asking me how you know that? Well, I guess you know that 'cause you got all them bitches in here monitoring everyone's behavior all the time and we can't make a move without one of them ass kissers all up in your office saying, 'Oh, [Tai] did this and that to this one and said these non-therapeutical things and all that.' I guess you know about me 'cause you is watching me and you think you know me." As Tai spoke, she glared at one of the women in the room whose assigned job as "expediter" required that she act as the "eyes and ears" of the community. In terms of the program's social hierarchy, the expediter was responsible for ensuring that prisoners reported one another for rule violations and forwarding these reports directly to staff members.

"[Tai], I know you're not in control of yourself because I understand the disease of addiction. I know what an addict looks like, feels like, thinks like. I can read the signs, and sister, they're written all over you. Does this sound like you? You can't deal with your emotions and you try to control them by taking your drugs. What was yours? Oh yeah, you was a whore for your crack, I remember. And when you whored around with all those men, you was manipulating all right. But not just them, no, no. You were repressing those emotions, but as you did you let crack rule you. You let those men rule you, you manipulated yourself. A whore is helpless, and that is you."

As Counselor Tynice spoke, Tai's shoulders rolled in toward her chest and she began to cry. Her eyes were cast downward and she appeared to be gazing at the leg of the counselor's chair. Around the room, other prisoners fidgeted in their seats, some looked at Counselor Tynice, others looked blankly at one another. No one, with the exception of Counselor Tynice and the two counselors who stood in the corner of the facility, looked at Tai. The scene was strangely ethereal as a ray of sun streaming into the room from the skylight above cast itself directly onto Tai, who sat slumped in the office chair. Indeed, the setting, the participants, and the image of a lone figure humbled before the sun's rays were eerily reminiscent of Eastern State Penitentiary, the American archetype of Jeremy Bentham's Panopticon, an 18th-century blueprint for the optimization of social control in total institutions.

Penal reformers in the 18th century, interested in rehabilitation rather than vengeful punishment, designed penitentiaries to be therapeutic rather than punitive environments.[13] The origins of correctionalism and modernist penology can be located in the arrangements of the penitentiary, particularly its pursuit of prisoners' minds over and against the enactment of punishment on their bodies. Indeed, the reformers endeavored to create a system of control that would normalize, rather than maim, the deviant and the wicked alike. They relied on architecture to accomplish this task and designed facilities that allowed for continuous, all-encompassing surveillance over inmates in their cells.[14] Consider the architectural design of early American penitentiaries modeled after the Panopticon. Several tiers of cells were arranged in a circular, radial pattern, all of which surrounded a central guard tower or station. The activities occurring at any moment, in any corner of each of the cells, were entirely visible to guards stationed in the tower. In Philadelphia's Eastern State Penitentiary, the ceiling of each cell housed a small window that allowed a single shaft of light to penetrate the room. Inmates were told that the ray of light was the "hand of God" and that during those hours in which the sun shone in their cells, they were to kneel before the light and engage in intense and solemn deliberations about their character and the possibilities of reform while in the "spiritual presence of the Maker."[15] Penal reformers of the day argued that inmates would align their behavior with institutional and social conventions since they knew that doing otherwise would undoubtedly be discovered by either their God or their keepers. As the philosopher and historian Michel Foucault noted of these early penal reformers, "They thought people would become virtuous by the simple fact of being observed."[16]

PHW also mobilizes architecture for the purpose of overseeing and controlling prisoners. This is realized by the arrangement of inmate cells in a two-tiered semicircle along the outside wall of the unit. All the rooms face the guard station and staff offices, and each has a window that is eight inches wide and runs the length of the door, allowing anyone within a few feet of the cell to see the activities taking place inside. But the use of encounter groups and pinball sessions suggest that PHW employs more than architecture to achieve surveillance and control. Indeed, it is unlikely that Counselor Tynice's effort to place the pinball chair in the direct path of the sunlight was a deliberate reference to the architectures of 18th-century penology, nor was it intended to symbolize an omniscient God.[17] On the other hand, the act of placing the intended receiver of one of these confrontations in the direct path of the sun was not unintentional. The counselors did so with too great a frequency and too deliberate a method for it to be merely coincidence. The term "hot seat" as a moniker for the center chair was coined by prisoners to dually refer to the emotional discomfort associated with being the target of a confrontation, as well as the physical discomfort of being forced to sit directly in the sun throughout the duration of the pinball session.

In PHW, the desire to regenerate the wicked is just as intense as it was for the early penal reformers; however, it is not the eyes of God that symbolize the totality of institutional control, nor is it the souls of inmates that mark the target of social control efforts. In fact, it is the self, rather than the soul, that is regarded as befouled, and it is the diagnostic powers of the program's counselors that are celebrated as the higher power from which moral salvation is to be achieved. But the heart of diagnostic power is premised on an overwhelming concern for, and reliance on, a kind of surveillance that can not only observe wickedness and disorder but also penetrate the inner core of the self. This, then, is what is represented with the placing of the desk chair in the sun—the awesome heat and intense brightness of the sun's rays as they shine through the single skylight in the unit's ceiling are at once symbolic of the counselors' omniscience and the denudation of the prisoners selves.

Watching and Being Watched

Toward the end of PHW's first year of operation, handmade posters and signs began to appear on doors and walls around the unit. The posters featured a painting of a large, blue eye with stenciled or handwritten lettering that read, "EVERYWHERE YOU GO, EVERYTHING YOU DO, KNOW THAT SOME-ONE IS WATCHING YOU" or "EVERYWHERE YOU GO, EVERYTHING YOU DO, THE EYES ARE ALWAYS WATCHING YOU." There were also smaller posters depicting the same blue eye with the words "MOST AWARE" written underneath it. Each week, a new name was velcroed to the bottom of the poster and a "MOST AWARE" sticker was placed on the cell door of one of the women in the program. All together, the posters with their looming blue eyes appeared throughout the facility with one notable exception—they did not appear within the environs of the staff's offices. When I asked Latasha, a prisoner who had been in the program since its inception, about the origin of the signs she explained, "Girls in here started dropping out like crazy and they [staff] wanted us to take responsibility for it. Like we're going to watch each other, everyone is a snitch. The posters are to remind us that all of us are supposed to be doing that, watching each other and being watched. Like they say, there are no friends in treatment."

As Latasha's response suggests, PHW's first several months in operation were difficult ones. Many of the women who entered the program dropped out prematurely. Others who had been sentenced directly into PHW petitioned their judges to transfer them to the prison's general population. A few intentionally broke the program's cardinal rule against violence in order to receive an immediate transfer. At one point, after the dropout rate reached 85% and almost half the beds in the program were empty, PHW staff found themselves under considerable pressure from the prison administration, state officials, and their supervisors at the Company to restore order and improve retention efforts. They pursued two sets of strategies. First, staff decided to crack down on "negativity" and "disorder" by placing more stringent demands on behavior, limiting various "privileges" like phone calls, and adding a new set of rules governing prisoners comportment, verbal and non-verbal expressions, privacy, and relationships. This new list of rules included bans on eating certain types of food and restrictions on everything from hairstyles to the content of letters sent to family, friends, and fellow prisoners. During a staff meeting, PHW's director explained that the crackdown was necessary because the women lacked "structure" in their lives. Rules and guidelines for even the most minute behaviors (e.g., when, where, and how to brush one's teeth, and proper cleaning procedure and storage space for the brush) were necessary, she explained, because a lack of structure contributed to "disordered" behavior, including attempts to prematurely leave the program. One counselor was a bit more blunt in response to my question regarding the program's sharpened restrictions on privacy:

> Well, they're addicts. What do you expect? The problem with addicts is if you give them enough rope, they'll hang themselves. It's in their nature. The thing about addiction is that it's a disease of the whole person—that means what they do in every part of their life. I don't care if it's pissing. You let them piss alone and they'll find a way to fuck everything up. That's who they are. It's the nature of the beast.

In order to ensure the new rules were being followed, counselors had to bolster surveillance efforts, and their strategy for doing so became a second mechanism for combating the dropout problem. This strategy called on prisoners to oversee one another and report all rule violations to the "expediter," who, in turn, collected the reports and turned them over to the staff. The failure to report a rule violation was itself a rule violation, often carrying heavier penalties than whatever the infraction was that had initially been committed. Making surveillance the universal responsibility of all prisoners in the program created a system of interpersonal surveillance networks that greatly extended the reach of architectural surveillance mechanisms. The surveillance networks gave rise to an interaction order in which any and all thoughts, feelings, and behaviors were potentially knowable to everyone within the community. Prisoners immediately felt this shift in the program's control apparatus. Latasha described it this way:

> In the beginning there was a lot of confusion and not much control, er, control in terms of them [staff] just watching and waiting for us to do somethin' bad, you know? But I didn't mind it in the beginning, it wasn't bad like it sounds. . . . Now, they's just telling us we're sick and we need some structure. Well, yeah, you know, I'm in here to get some help for my sickness but I didn't think help would be no prison. Yeah, that's it! They watch us more than the COs did in general pop. And all that watching, it

gets to you. . . . It's not like you're necessarily doing something bad, it's just you don't want everything about yourself to be known by everyone. You want to keep some stuff private, even if it ain't stuff that's embarrassing and believe me they know all about the embarrassing stuff. [laughs and discusses how her cell mate reported her to the staff for having a bad case of diarrhea]

Counselors instructed prisoners to make the "eyes" posters to remind themselves that they were both the watchers and the watched, and that everything that took place within the confines of the program was potentially knowable.[18] Like the 18th-century reformers, they believed that the awareness of a pervasive system of surveillance would inhibit prisoners from engaging in deviant acts and disorderly conduct. In the penitentiary, this was accomplished through architecture in that inmates were forced to organize their behavior on the assumption that they were being observed. While the penitentiary controls bodies in the sense that they regulate movement to and from the cells, the body is no longer the *target* of institutional control as it is in the case of corporal punishment and other premodern systems. The target is the mind, as the pervasiveness of surveillance forces the prisoner to adopt the role of the other (in this case the prison) and view herself from the perspective of the institution. In this sense, the institution is quite literally inserted into the minds of prisoners. In a parallel sense, the rhetoric of PHW's staff is quite similar to that of the early penal reformers—constant vigilance is required to prevent deviant persons from engaging in deviant behavior. And while the continuity and visibility of surveillance is not embodied in the form of a guard tower erected in the center of the unit, it is symbolized by the images of eyes that are hung throughout the unit, and it is ritualized in confrontation ceremonies where behaviors thought to be hidden from scrutiny are made the subject of public discussion. The distinction between habilitation and modernist penology is in the embodied mechanisms through which surveillance is accomplished and the ends to which it is put.

Embodied Surveillance

The reach of the interpersonal surveillance networks was in full display during the earlier confrontation between Counselor Tynice and Tai that had precipitated the pinball session described at the top of this chapter. Tai had written two letters to Jamillah indicating that she was having romantic feelings toward her. The counselors officially learned of the letters when Jamillah, after receiving the second letter, reported it to the expediter who, in turn, told the staff that Tai was in violation of the rule against "sexual acting out."[19] After reading the letters and passing them to other staff members, Counselor Tynice waited only a few minutes to call all the prisoners into the large group room. "Family, one of you—maybe more—sure has been up to some sneaky things. Some things you thought maybe you could hide, maybe you thought that something taking place behind closed doors was a secret. FAM-ILY," and at this point Tynice was yelling, "DO WE HAVE SECRETS IN THIS HOUSE?" The women collectively shook their heads negatively and some murmured "no."

"[Tai], get up to the center of the floor." Tai looked at Counselor Tynice and pointed to herself while mouthing the word "me?" When Tynice nodded, Tai rose from where she was sitting and walked to the center of the room.

"What have you been up to behind our backs, [Tai]? What secrets have you been keeping?" Tynice looked disgusted. At first Tai denied keeping any secrets, but after being questioned several more times by Tynice, she divulged that she had smuggled a candy bar into the unit, which she had shared with two other women in the program.

"Well, you're right about that but it ain't no candy bar that I'm concerned with right now. It's that other sweet tooth you got is what I'm concerned with." Tynice waved the letters in the air. "Do you know what these are, [Tai]?" Tai shook her head negatively. "These are letters from you to another woman." Tai stared stonily at Tynice but she was visibly shaking.

"These are letters from you to another woman in here, indicating your romantic interest in this woman." Tynice read from part of the letter and asked, "Did you write these letters, [Tai]?"

"No, no," Tai managed to stammer. Tynice called Jamillah to stand beside Tai on the floor and asked, "[Jamillah], did you receive these letters?" Tai glanced at Jamillah just long enough to see Jamillah nod. Tynice repeated the question, "[Tai], did you write these letters?"

"No, I didn't. I ain't no lesbian, everyone in here knows that." Tynice looked at Jamillah and asked, "Who gave you these letters?"

"[Tai] did, ma'am." Jamillah's head was lowered. Several women in the audience gasped.

"That's a lie, I'm not homosexual and I didn't write no romantic letters to another woman—"

"Come on, [Tai]. You know we were gonna find out sooner or later. I got [Jamillah] saying you did it, and not only that but several people in this house including your roommate remember seeing you write notes during your free time and I got a person that says she saw you pass the note to [Jamillah]." Tai glared at Jamillah who was still standing beside her.

"What does that sign behind you say, [Tai]?" Tai turned to look at one of the posters of the blue eye. She mumbled, "Everywhere you go, everything you do, someone is always watching you."

"We're watching you, [Tai]. Got it? Now admit this so we can move on and those things the addict keeps hidden can come out into the light." Tai shook her head at Tynice and ran off the floor into her cell, slamming the door on the way in.

Such confrontation ceremonies remind prisoners of both the continuity of surveillance (that it is ever present) and the intrusiveness of surveillance (that it has access to behavior that is put on for public display as well as more private thoughts and feelings). But the ceremonies do something more. They emphasize to prisoners that this is an *embodied surveillance*, wherein the observer and the observed are known to one another. It is, in fact, a verifiable form of surveillance although verification may occur after the fact. This is a significant difference from the disembodied method of observation that characterizes the control apparatus of the penitentiary. Unable to discern whether or by whom they were being watched, inmates in the Panopticon were arguably prevented from even the *thought* of revolt. In *Discipline and Punish*, Foucault describes the impact of this for achieving social order:

> He is the object of information, never a subject in communication . . . and this invisibility is a guarantee of social order. [Among convicts] there is no danger or a plot, an attempt at collective escape . . . that this architectural apparatus should be a machine for creating and sustaining a power relation independent of the person who exercises it; in short, that inmates should be caught up in a power situation of which they are themselves are bearers.[20]

In PHW, there was no effort to hide the identities of witnesses from those who stood accused of wrongdoing, nor was there an attempt to render surveillance as anything less than a universal responsibility demanded of every woman in the program. For the designers of the penitentiary system, the ability of the observed to identify their observers creates the potential for disruptions in the social order and thereby threatens to erode the institution's control over inmate behavior. To be sure, verifiability creates problems of order in PHW, but it does so in a way that solidifies the power of the counseling staff over their charges. The situation between Tai and Jamillah is important in this regard. Staff sought to prevent prisoners from becoming friends with one another (one of the most frequent phrases uttered by counselors to prisoners was "There are no friends in treatment") because they regarded the friendship dyad as having the potential to usurp the program's control apparatus. According to the staff's logic, close relations with peers (be they romantically motivated or otherwise) jeopardize surveillance, since friends will be less likely to report one another for subversive thoughts and behaviors. To prevent the formation of friendships and other types of intimate relations, staff went to great lengths to force friends to confront one another for misdeeds. This appeared to be largely successful, as many prisoners reported that they "trusted no one" in the program. With such confrontations, disruptions in order occurred, but order was destabilized only at the bottom, not the top. In the case of Tai and Jamillah in the weeks following the confrontation, Tai stopped talking to Jamillah altogether and took an active role in trying to get her in trouble with staff. Indeed, the challenge Tai's defiance posed for the authority of the counseling staff was not only neutralized, but was used to reify the surveillance mechanism and increase the legitimacy of the staff's claim that they had access to the seemingly private thoughts and feelings of their charges.

In fact, surveillance need not be anonymous as it was in modernist penal arrangements, because surveillance in PHW is intimately related to the process of infiltrating the self, rather than existing simply to prevent the occurrence of behaviors that deviate from institutional guidelines. Indeed, an embodied surveillance where the observer and the observed are known to one another is highly desirable in this setting, because it offers the possibility that internal thoughts and feelings can be externalized and brought under the staff's control. This was the case in the pinball scenario depicted at the beginning of this chapter. Tai, initially confident enough in her own knowledge of self to act defiantly in front of Counselor Tynice during their first confrontation over the letter (first by terminating a confrontation and later by challenging Counselor Tynice's assessment of her as "not in control"), suffered a virtual mental and physical collapse toward the conclusion of the second confrontation in pinball. Her final statement while still on the hot seat in the center of the pinball group indicates a newfound insecurity with respect to her ability to understand herself and her relations with others:

What you said hurts, it does . . . but it's true. It's all true. I did those things, I am those things. I guess I just needed someone else to see it—what I couldn't see myself, about myself. The control is something I want, that I wanted, which I thought I could get at . . . could achieve it [begins to cry]. Today, now, feeling helpless, I know that you've helped me to get in touch with my real feelings. I am helpless against this disease.

What's particularly striking in this statement is that Tai no longer believes she is the source of knowledge about her self. She only discovers who she is ("diseased") through the counselor's vision of her.

In sum, the purpose of embodied surveillance within PHW is threefold. First, as was the case in the early penitentiaries, surveillance is a repressive device in that it is used as a mechanism of control designed to prevent the occurrence of rule-breaking behavior. Given the severity of the penalties associated with violating program norms, staff believe that prisoners are unlikely to engage in rule-breaking behavior if they know they are being watched. The second purpose of embodied surveillance is the production of knowledge. Surveillance yields information about the prisoners that is central to interpreting disorder and uncovering the "real" self. Each of the staff's confrontations with Tai (first over the letter, and later in pinball) illustrates this point well. Counselor Tynice interpreted available information about Tai (e.g., the romantic content of a note, claims to heterosexuality, and walking off the floor in the middle of a confrontation) as an indication of her addiction and the "out of control" character of her self. Further, the information garnered through confrontation operates to further enhance the program's control structure as aggrieved prisoners like Tai vow to report others who engage in rule violations. Third, the embodied nature of the surveillance mechanism functions to legitimate the staff's claims and diagnoses regarding the self. Again, using Tai as an example, the veracity of Counselor Tynice's claim was established not through reference to her own professional competence (e.g., I've been a drug and alcohol counselor for ten years . . .) but through the observations of Tai's behavior by Tynice, Jamillah, and the others. The implication was that counselors possessed privileged knowledge of the self—knowledge that was garnered through surveillance and knowledge that allowed them to apprehend that self and hold it "up to the light."

Bringing Out the Self

On a surface level, counselors use information garnered through surveillance activities to determine if prisoners are conforming with or deviating from program rules. In and of itself, such information does not provide the staff with much knowledge about the self that lies beneath the surface of behavior—what women regard as meaningful, their histories, their identities outside of prison, their dreams, thoughts, and feelings. And although the women frequently break the rules (largely due to the sheer volume of rules regulating even the most minute behaviors), the nature of their rule breaking is often not particularly telling. Indeed, given the fact that counselors spend very little time in private sessions with individual women in the program, how do they gain knowledge of the psychic interiors of their charges? How do they lay claim to the "real" self?

Variations of this question frequently sparked a good bit of explanation and debate among PHW's counselors at their weekly staff meeting. During one such discussion, the senior counselor explained to the other staff members that their job was "reading behavior" and assessing what it meant for the self:

> Addicts don't have the ability to look at themselves critically—they don't understand their behavior and their feelings much less remember any of them. Remember, they use drugs to cover it up, to stuff it. They have to be told where they're at and what's going on with their recovery. By reading their behavior and the stuff they give off, you've got to show them what is the addict and what is the recovering person. When the addict is talking, tell them and make them see how negative that self is, how damaging it is for the person and for everyone around them.

In interviews with the counselors I explored this issue in greater depth. In particular, I was interested in understanding how they differentiated between behavior that revealed something about the self and behavior that did not. Many echoed the senior counselor's response:

> You know by looking, by seeing them and their behavior as they interact in this environment. You know a little of their history, but more importantly, you know they have an addiction. You look at their thinking skills—how they interpret things and events, and you look at emotions because their emotions are really screwed up. They're a window into what's going on. You look for growth. Who's really participating in group, who's follow-ing the rules and reporting others, who's sharing and expressing them-selves. . . . You get a sense of what is being said and whether this is the same as the behavior they're displaying.

In staff meetings, however, it became apparent that surface signifiers such as group participation, conformity, and thinking skills offered less than direct guideposts for understanding the self.[21] For example, counselors bit-terly debated the course of action to take when Tearon, widely considered a model participant in the program, was discovered to be in violation of the rule against "sexual acting out." Tearon had done "everything right" for just over a year in the program when counselors learned that she had had sex in her cell with another prisoner. Violation of a "cardinal rule" typically meant that a prisoner would be immediately expelled from PHW and returned to prison's general population. The stakes were particularly costly for Tearon because she faced an additional two years on her prison sentence if she failed to successfully complete the PHW program. Although Tearon had excelled in treatment, earned her high school diploma while in prison, and had no rule violations in the program, the majority of the counseling staff wanted to throw her out because her "sexual acting out" indicated that her performance in the program was a "sham." One of the counselors in the minority argued on Tearon's behalf, emphasizing that thirteen months was too long for someone to "fake it" and that it was the counselors themselves who had "set her up" by placing her in a cell with a woman rumored to be a "sexual predator." According to Tearon's own account of the incident, as well as the statements of several women in the program, coercion could not be ruled out as an explanation for the situation. The senior counselor challenged this logic on the grounds that Tearon was still thinking and acting like an addict:

> I'm not saying that she's faked us out the entire thirteen months. There may have been moments of sincerity. What I am saying is that if she were really progressing in treatment like she indicated she was, this would have never happened. The fact that it did indicates to me that she is full of shit. It's a shame, but we need to set an example and how are we going to do that if one of the senior residents in here is faking us out and running around behind our backs? . . . They [addicts] don't think like us. I'm sure you would never jeopardize your treatment by having sex in your room, but that's not how she thinks. She didn't think about the consequences. They never do, they don't see them. They see gratification. You have to remember that, if she had progressed she would have thought first. She didn't. It's a sham.

As this example from the staff meeting indicates, counselors believed very little of what prisoners appeared to intentionally communicate about their selves. Since they regarded addicts as persons who were "deceitful" and "manipulative," there was little point in meeting with prisoners privately and discussing their thoughts, experiences, explanations, and rationales. Doing so only created opportunities for prisoners to "fake" it. In this case, counselors voted to expel Tearon from the program without so much as an interview with her to hear her version of what happened in her cell.

It would seem that with so much suspicion directed at their clients, PHW counselors have very little to go on when it comes to actually understanding the self. But this is precisely the reason that confrontations and the heightened emotions they arouse are regarded as *the* constitutive element of habilitation and of therapeutic communities more generally. Encounter groups, pinball, and other forms of ritualized confrontations provoke behavior, utterances, and expressions that appear to be outside their bearer's control. It is these seemingly unintentional forms of communication that counselors take as signals from the "real" self. As the PHW orientation manual notes of the encounter group, it is an "ideal setting where one can look exactly as you are and concede telling the truth BELOW AWARENESS" (caps in original). For this reason, counselors are instructed to regard emotional displays as a relatively robust marker of the self. They do, of course, recognize that emotional performances are manipulable and have on more than one occasion sent a sobbing prisoner to her room after claiming that she faked her tears for sympathy. In endeavoring to solve the problem of how to make the internal external, however, they came to regard emotions—particularly emotional outbursts—as a direct connection to the "real" self.[22]

PHW counselors draw their assumptions about psychology from the therapeutic community model. It asserts that all people have basic, "gut-level" feelings that are composed of anger, hurt, fear, and loneliness.[23] These feelings serve as guideposts to the inner self. Within PHW specifically, counselors regard two types of emotional displays as unintentionally produced and thus more reliable guides to the self: anger (particularly that which is enacted through violent behavior) and sadness/hurt (enacted through sobbing). Of the two, anger is considered the truest representation of the self.

Anger

Staff meetings are occasions for planning confrontations designed to elicit anger from targeted prisoners as well as to interpret the meaning of anger and other emotional displays that emerge during the confrontations. During one such meeting, counselors decided to engineer a confrontation with Sam, newly arrived in the program, because they thought she was too placid and unrevealing. The mechanism they elected to provoke her with is called an "injust." An "injust," according to the senior counselor, is a "lie that reveals the truth." In this case, the counselors decided to have another prisoner falsely accuse Sam of failing to keep up with her assigned laundry duties (a rule violation). Initially, Sam calmly denied the charge. But when one of the counselors informed her that she would lose her phone privileges and be required to perform additional hours of cleaning, Sam went ballistic. She screamed that the other prisoner was a "liar" and strode toward her as if she was going to strike her. Other women in the program placed their bodies between the two and pushed Sam back, at which point Sam hurled a plastic chair across the room and screamed expletives at the counselors.

According to PHW's manual, prisoners who engage in violent or threatening behavior are subject to immediate expulsion from the program. In this case, however, counselors were pleased. In the staff meeting that followed, one counselor speculated that Sam's outburst indicated that she had been "beaten up pretty badly" in her life, and that her display of hostility toward the other prisoner was really sublimated anger she held toward an abusive parent. Another counselor suggested that Sam's "insides were rotting out from that anger" and that this prevented her from being able to "relate positively" to others. As their discussion concluded, they decided to have Counselor Belle meet with Sam to reveal the true purpose of the injust. Belle would then bring Sam back to the large group room where she was to "get in touch" with her self by discussing her thoughts and feelings "out in the open."

While the counselors may have been right about the source and consequences of Sam's anger, they never managed to validate their interpretations. Sam refused to speak with any of the counselors and requested that she be transferred immediately from the unit. The counseling staff approved the request and urged prison administrators to expedite it; they theorized that once Sam realized that the program was the only place where she had actually experienced "real" feelings, she would return. Approximately one week after the incident, the prison classification committee processed Sam's request and she was returned to the general population, where she served out the remainder of her sentence. Sam never asked to come back.

Curiously, staff regarded the departure of Sam and others like her as an indicator of PHW's effectiveness. In a group meeting following Sam's transfer, the senior counselor explained to the prisoners that anger like Sam's, even when it led to an early exit from the program, is a sign that the self is overcoming addiction and "rising to the surface":

· Of course you're going to get angry when you get an injust but that is what you want. You want to get in touch with your anger and be happy that you can feel something inside yourself for a change. We want you to be angry, just not to act on it. Acting on it means your addiction is in control. Feeling it means your real self is finally rising to the surface.

The senior counselor's sentiments regarding the productive uses of anger were echoed in a meeting between Company executives and prison administrators over the program's high dropout rate. Dr. Nesbitt explained to concerned administrators that limited retention is a "good thing" because it demonstrates that the program staff are "doing their job" by really "getting to" prisoners. In this formulation, emotional discomfort, particularly anger, is an unmediated message from the self, one that has not been diluted by drugs or contrived by the bearer. Anger, even anger that results in violence, suggests that the "real" self has been captured and revealed.

Sadness

The other emotion that confrontations were designed to elicit was sadness. Counselors regard crying, particularly sobbing, as an indicator of sadness and a signal from the "moral self." The program director explained to me, "When a woman in here expresses sadness, deep sadness, sorrow, we know that we've got hold of the moral self—that part that hasn't adequately developed or matured. You can begin to understand and manage their disorder then, when you expose this."

Staff gauge the sincerity of tears according to the context in which they emerge. For example, tears that emerge during the course of a confrontation are often regarded as impulsive and unintentional. Following Tynice's pinball confrontation with Tai, for example, she remarked to the other counselors that although she did not yet accept at face value Tai's admission that she was "out of control," she did feel that the pinball session "got to her." The other counselors agreed, with one counselor remarking that Tai's sobs at the end of the session proved just that. The same counselor later pulled me aside and explained:

> These women are tough, they don't crack easy [she begins to laugh at the reference to crack and assures me that she doesn't mean to joke about addiction to crack cocaine]. . . . Remember they was out there on the streets victimizing people, not just helpless victims. We're talking about people who committed armed robbery. Survival on the street means not appearing weak and these women have mastered that. I take any display of weakness [like crying] in here to indicate that treatment is working. They'd never let themselves be seen like that otherwise.

This counselor's explanation raises another important point regarding the failure or inability to express sadness. If tears are a signal of the moral self, then the failure to cry or "appear weak" suggests that prisoners lack such a self or are continuing to mask it. As in the case of anger, counselors engineer confrontations designed to elicit the display of sadness. In "branch groups," counselors selected one or two women to stand in front of the group and recount painful and traumatic events in their lives. Often, branch groups are devoted to accounts of rape, childhood molestation, abuse, and the loss of loved ones. By their nature, branch groups do not have the kind of hostile back-and-forth exchanges that characterize encounter groups. However, they are confrontational in that counselors press women to provide gritty details and share feelings, particularly when they believe a speaker is not being "real." In these groups, crying is expected and, in some cases, demanded in order to demonstrate one's "realness." Several women in the program confided to me their concern that counselors did not understand how painful certain events in their lives were because they were unable to cry about them during group sessions. Vonda, who had recently given birth to a daughter addicted to crack cocaine, recalled:

> They kept confronting me and confronting me about it. How did I feel I caused my child to be like that, and all that. Well, how the hell do you think I feel? It makes me sick, I feel really fucking sick . . . but we keep going over it and going over it 'cause they don't think I'm processing it right. Well, how the hell do you process something like that? It's not about just getting up there and sobbing and crying about it. I can't do that, I just can't do that in front of people [she is crying as we talk about her daughter]. . . . A lot of girls will just cry to get them off their backs, but I feel like that's humiliating. They don't care nothing about me or my daughter so why should I put myself out there other than it's probably the only way I'll get out of this place.

As Vonda's comment indicates, emotional displays, even impromptu outbursts, are potentially contrived. This creates a conundrum for PHW staff whose job is not only to control behavior and to guide perception, but also to actually get inside the selves of their charges. Since they regard most of what prisoners say about themselves as unreliable or intentionally deceptive, they endeavor to interpret a set of signs from the self as well as to create opportunities to render the "real" self visible and knowable.

Conclusion

The key question occupying a good many scholars and prison workers alike these days is what purpose the contemporary prison serves. It is an 18th-century institution that has become an increasingly prominent feature of our postindustrial age, albeit one whose purpose seems more remote than ever. While the penitentiary was designed with the intent of disciplining and normalizing the criminal classes, mass incarceration appears as little more than an end in itself. This has prompted some scholars to suggest, in the case of men's prisons at least, that the new penology bears a closer relation to premodern efforts to brutalize the body than modernist attempts to salvage the soul. As Lorna Rhodes' ethnographic study of maximum security prisons for men suggests, there is now a willingness not only to incarcerate more, but to implicate the body more directly in carceral practices.[24] In men's prisons, architecture and new technologies of restraint and control serve as the bottom-line guarantors of social order. This is not the case in PHW, however, where architecture and electronic devices play second fiddle to social technologies of control. Here, surveillance is intimately linked to processes of self-construction and takes a visible and embodied form.

The reason social technologies are in play in PHW is, of course, because the purpose of punishment has already been worked out. The source of the problem is the "disordered" and "unruly" self, and so this self becomes the object of control efforts. But the self as an object of control in habilitation is quite distinct from how the self was implicated in rehabilitative, "modernist" regimes. Consider again the Panopticon as the blueprint of correctionalism. Normalizing the self is accomplished through an architecture of surveillance that alters the perception of prisoners. The institution quite literally becomes a "generalized other" from which prisoners normatively reflect on their actions.[25] This is also clearly the case with rehabilitative paternalism, the system of control that predated the arrival of PHW in the women's prison. In this case, the institution is inserted into the minds of prisoners through embodied purveyors—the "Warden Daddy" and the staff who serve as parental role models. In both instances, the goal of punishment and control efforts is discipline and normalization. The self is implicated in this endeavor though not necessarily reconstituted by it.

Reconstituting the self demands a system of control well beyond what grew out of 18th-century penitentiaries or 19th-century reformatories. Herein lies the significance of embodied surveillance and elaborate confrontation ceremonies like those found in my study, as well as in other recent studies of correctional programming for women.[26] PHW's staff require an instrument that allows them access to the "real" self. Since this self is both "hidden" and "deceptive," counselors cannot rely solely on what prisoners say and do. They must also know what they think and feel. To learn this, they must collect information from other prisoners and create, in effect, a universal system of "eyes and ears." But power is exercised not only through social and architectural webs of surveillance, but also in highly charged confrontation sessions designed to provoke their targets into exposing something they might otherwise endeavor to repress. Emotional displays become a primary source of information about the self, an instance where what is believed to be internal is brought to the surface and made visible to all.

Externalizing the internal self provides a source of knowledge, but it also is a key mechanism for exercising control over this self and reconstituting it. In PHW, what is inserted into the minds of inmates are not only institutional norms guiding conduct and behavior, but also institutional claims over the "real" self.

5

Diseased Women

Crack Whores, Bad Mothers, and Welfare Queens

Substance-abusing offenders do not gain insights or behavior change from a single, calm, insight-oriented psychotherapy session. Change is effected best by monotonously and consistently repeated feedback, strong emotional responses, and predictable and immediate consequences.
—Excerpt from PHW's training manual for counselors

You let someone name you, you give them power over you.
—Prisoner, on why she objected to counselors calling her a crack whore

On any given day, someone passing by the PHW unit may overhear counselors addressing prisoners as "crack hos," "lowdown addicts," and "dirty old dogs," and admonishing them to "tighten the fuck up." When prisoners recount their initial impressions of PHW, they speak first of language, particularly the use of derogatory names. Visitors to the program as well as prison staff who work outside it make a similar set of observations. For each of these groups, what primarily distinguishes PHW from other units in the prison is not the visual imagery of cells arranged in a semicircle or the brooding posters of eyes that hang from the walls. Rather, it is the vivid and repetitious use of disparaging and often degrading language.

Although rules restrict the kinds of language prisoners may employ in response to being called "hos," "addicts," and "dogs," many risk sanction in order to tell counselors and other prisoners to "fuck off" or "go to hell." The ubiquitous use of profanity by counselors and prisoners alike is part of the lyrical content of the program, but it is not what draws complaints from prisoners and the attention of prison workers. Vonda, a prisoner who spent nearly eighteen months in the program, explained to me, "When they [counselors] cuss you out, they for real. They getting your attention and most of us, you know we from the street, can respect that. It's when they strap you down.

That's what everyone reacts to when they come here, getting strapped down." Getting "strapped down" is a phrase that prisoners use to refer to a specific kind of language game, one that takes pointed aim at the self.

Counselors, like prisoners, distinguish language that serves to hold a prisoner accountable for rule-breaking behavior ("cussing out") from language that lays claim to the self. Counselors refer to the latter as "breaking down the addict." It is worth noting that the prisoners' phrase, "strapping down," places emphasis on the coercive elements of this discourse, recalling images of shock treatment and other dark practices associated with psychiatry and asylums. In contrast, the staff's phrase, "breaking down addiction," underscores the forceful character of the language but does so while simultaneously referencing its target—the drug addict.

All the counselors tell me this is the essence of their work. The senior counselor explained to me why it is necessary to break prisoners down:

> To heal the addict, you have to get rid of all the stuff, the negative thoughts and asocial behaviors, inside them that makes them an addict. It's like a disease that you've got to remove from inside them. I guess you could say that we are here to break them down, to break down the addict so a new person can emerge.

When I asked the program director why counselors use terms like "crack ho" and "dirty dog" to refer to some of the prisoners, she referred me to a passage in her dog-eared copy of PHW's counselor training manual. The manual draws its core philosophy from the therapeutic community model.[1] The highlighted passage read that substance-abusing offenders "do not gain insights or behavior change from a single, calm, insight-oriented psychotherapy session." The manual goes on to explain that although "calm, insight-oriented" interactions may work in other sorts of counseling situations, addicts lack an "external source of self-awareness" and a "conscience," and this prevents them from adequately conceptualizing and understanding the self. Counselors are to act as the prisoner's external source of "self-awareness, conscience, and super ego." When I finished reading, I asked one of the counselors in the room how they accomplished this. "We get up in their face. We're their mirror," she said. "Through us they see who they are and what they have become."

In this chapter, I take up two interrelated questions. First, what is it that counselors see when they gaze at the selves of their charges? Habilitation relies extensively on surveillance for rendering the private territories of the self visible and knowable. Here, I inventory the contents of that knowledge and examine the diagnostic claims that are refracted from counselors to prisoners. This raises a second question, and that is how the particular language game of "strapping" or "breaking down" is implicated in the management of addiction and disorder. Language, as strategy, is a constitutive element of habilitation. I argue that just as surveillance is the mechanism through which the internal self is apprehended and brought into view, language is the medium through which counselors endeavor to "break down" the self. Like surveillance, the use of language reflects and reinforces the race, class, and gender regime of the new penology. The images of internal disorder that counselors "mirror" back to prisoners directly implicate their identities as women, mothers, lovers, and workers.

Breaking Down the Addict

During the first summer PHW was in operation at the prison, the warden received a letter from a prisoner complaining that over the course of a week in PHW, counselors had called her "a dog, a baby, a crack ho, dirty, crazy, ill, uncaring, selfish, mean, lazy, and diseased." The letter generated a good bit of gossip and speculation among supervisory and line staff, with some correctional officers adding that they had heard stories from prisoners suggesting that the program required women to "bark like dogs" and "cry like babies." At the subsequent meeting between PHW counselors and prison administrators regarding this issue, the program director denied rumors about barking and crying but acknowledged that counselors did indeed refer to prisoners as, among other things, "babies" and "dogs." She emphasized that in this respect, PHW was no different from well-respected and long-standing treatment programs like Alcoholics Anonymous (hereafter AA).

It is a relevant point of comparison. The use of derogatory, even outrageous forms of address in treatment programs for addicts and alcoholics is present across a range of treatment modalities, from self-help groups to highly structured residential programs.[2] In Norman Denzin's ethnographic study of AA, he argues that the program's unique discourse provides drinkers with a new moral and symbolic frame from which to re-evaluate their relationship to alcohol and with which to conceive of their "alcoholic self."[3] This is evident in an interview excerpt with one of his subjects who remarked how the AA phrase "his majesty the baby" changed the way she viewed herself: "That's me. I'm a spoiled brat. I want my things my way and I want it now. . . . The *Big Book* and the *Twelve and Twelve* talk about me—I prefer her majesty the baby!"[4]

The language of AA is encapsulated in the themes of powerlessness, personal shortcomings, wrongs, and surrender that run through the *Big Book*.

It is from this language that members acquire the idioms, vocabularies, and grammars of speaking from which to describe their experiences, assemble their biographies, and narrate the self. According to AA philosophy, this language is crucial because excessive and problematic drinking stems from a disease that inhabits the self. In this sense, the Twelve Step process is primarily narrative in that members learn to tell stories about the self that are consistent in both structure and content with AA ideology. Recovery, according to this formulation, is a process of restorying the self.[5]

When PHW counselors endeavor to "break down the addict" they are putting language to similar use. That is, they aim to change the self by regulating the linguistic and discursive resources available for self-representation. To do so they utilize all the mechanisms that are common across AA and other self-help groups in the form of unique program vocabularies and philosophies of addiction, rituals for confrontation and disclosure, and rules regulating who talks, when, in what form, and about what subjects. But beyond this and at the heart of what it means for counselors to "break down an addict" and for prisoners to be "strapped down," are the searing and very often mortifying appraisals counselors make about prisoners' selves.

Before I turn to the content of such appraisals, it bears emphasizing that the scale of coercion is considerably greater in PHW than in AA. This is intentional. Charles E. Dederich, the man who is widely credited with developing Synanon, the first therapeutic community for drug addicts, was active in the AA movement throughout the 1950s. However, he felt that the AA model was largely ineffective for dealing with drug addicts. He argued that a more coercive response was needed, and subsequently he developed a confrontation group called "the game" that serves as a blueprint for contemporary methods of habilitation, including the encounter groups used in PHW.[6] While philosophies of addiction and confrontation therapy are in many respects complementary across the two modalities,[7] PHW subjects its clientele to at least two levels of coercion that AA does not. First, as prisoners, none of the women in PHW is there by choice. Many have been sentenced directly into the program, while most of the others went in the hopes of obtaining a sentence reduction. Less than 10% reported going for the sole purpose of obtaining treatment for their drug problem.[8] In contrast, all of the research subjects in Denzin's study went to AA on their own, interested in modifying or abandoning their patterns of alcohol use. While it is surely the case that many AA members are pressured or forced into the program by employers, family members, or as a condition of probation or parole, AA retains elements of voluntarism that PHW does not. Beyond this, AA does not demand anything of its members, not even that they stop drinking.[9]

Second, PHW "happens" in a total institution, so much so that prisoners often refer to it as "a prison within a prison." Habilitation, given that it is so dependent on surveillance in all its guises, could not happen in another type of institutional setting. For this reason, the control of language, imagery, speech, and expression takes on a weight far greater than that which exists in AA. Prisoners cannot establish alternate identities outside the program because their lives are lived entirely within the confines of PHW. In contrast to AA, which encourages the formation of friendships and broader social networks among members, PHW reminds prisoners that "there are no friends in treatment." As such, there are no opportunities for prisoners to engage in alternate discourses or to switch linguistic gears because virtually every interaction is surveilled, structured, and circumscribed by the program. Sociologist Erving Goffman, who famously coined the term "total institution," referred to such structures as "forcing houses" for changing persons. They are, as he described, "natural experiments on what can be done to the self."[10]

In contrast to AA, PHW's reliance on charged and humiliating claims about the self, *coupled* with the institutional arena in which they are set, make this akin to what the sociologist Harold Garfinkel famously described as a "status degradation ceremony"[11]—in this case, one that is extended in both duration and intensity. Status degradation ceremonies involve considerably more than affixing a negative label like "addict" or "criminal" to an individual's public identity. Instead, they claim to reveal something about the self lurking behind the public identity. To paraphrase Garfinkel, such ceremonies get at "motivational" features of the self and the "ultimate grounds" for why the individual acts, thinks, and feels the way he or she does. Erving Goffman makes a similar observation: "Built right into the social arrangements of an organization, then, is a thoroughly embracing conception of the member—not merely a conception of him *qua* member, but behind this a conception of him *qua* human being."[12]

In PHW, the person is the disorder. PHW's mission statement explains it thusly:

> Drug abuse is a disorder of the whole person. The problem is the *person* and not the drug, and addiction is a *symptom* and not the essence of the disorder. [emphasis in original]

The task of "breaking down" disorder requires counselors to reveal the motivational features of the self back to its owner. This involves something more than calling them addicts or identifying bad choices associated with drug

use and criminal lifestyles, though they surely do this. Instead, their training manual directs them to use "shame," "honesty," and "discomfort" in order
that the target of a confrontation achieve the requisite amount of "emotional
pain" to help her "break through the fear of change and immobilization." The
language and imagery they use to do so takes aim at women's participation
across the overlapping terrains of family, state, and market.

Motherhood

Just over three-quarters of the prisoners in PHW are mothers. A few were
pregnant with their first child during the period of incarceration, while many
more had two or more children under the age of eighteen. The overwhelming majority of mothers have regular contact with their children through letters, phone calls, and personal visits. Most of the women eagerly anticipated
visits with their children, many spent their designated "free periods" writing
letters or making crafts for their kids, and all made a point to post photographs of their children in their cells. There were only a few women who did
not have any contact with their children, and fewer still who had a criminal
charge of child abuse or neglect in their files. Indeed, during the period when
I had access to prisoners' files, only two women out of 170 had a criminal
record of child abuse and neglect.[13]

Despite this, motherhood, particularly their failure as mothers, is the
most frequent theme emerging during confrontations that are intended
to "break" the women down.[14] Counselors make two sorts of claims about
motherhood and the self. The first and most prevalent set of claims involves
the victimization of children. Counselors routinely report to the women that
their "worst" crime, and the one that reveals the most about their diseased
selves, is the harm they inflict on their children through their "lifestyles" and
poor choices. The second set of claims builds on the first by challenging prisoners' assertion of motherhood as an authentic identity.

Children were always an important legitimating symbol for the PHW program. Company executives used children to persuade prison administrators
that traditional rehabilitation programs were inadequate for women who had
the capacity to "victimize" their children. At the same time, executives used
the plight of prisoners' children to convince the Department of Correction,
and by extension state politicians, that spending money on a drug treatment
program amid the "get tough" era was a worthwhile endeavor. In administrative meetings and press conferences, PHW's director routinely emphasized
that public funds spent on PHW would ultimately work to "save the children." Underlying this claim was the specter of children who were neglected

and abused by their drug-addicted mothers. As if to underscore the point, PHW staff hung a poster near the entrance to the unit that depicted a photograph of a tiny, sobbing, African American infant accompanied by the caption "BEAT YOUR DRUG PROBLEM INSTEAD." It was a powerful image, one that made explicit the connection among incarcerated mothers, the nationwide panic over "crack babies," and fertility rates among young, low-income, African American and Latina women.[15]

Child-saving rhetoric was not just political theater—it was inscribed into confrontation sessions between counselors and prisoners. Rinda explained to me that she dropped out of PHW after staff insisted not only that she had victimized her child by being in the street, but also that she was *still* victimizing him from prison:

> It happened after I had my visit with my son and [the counselor] called me to the floor, almost as soon as he left, telling me I was acting fucked up during the visit 'cause I was being emotionless. The truth was, if they would've let me talk, the truth was I was going through something real bad when I saw my son because I hadn't seen him since I've been in here and I was choking up just looking at him. My son, he's a strong little boy, I didn't want to let him down 'cause I know he gets down and how do you say you're sorry about all the things that have happened without crying? I didn't want him to think it was his fault, 'cause you know how little kids his age think about stuff, they just blame themselves so I didn't want him to feel bad and I just kinda, like, held back, I guess, emotionally. And, um, she just hauled me up to the front of the room and was yelling at me, telling me how bad I hurt my son with my drug use and asking me did I know that the real victim of my crimes was my son? Well, I couldn't talk, you can't say nothing, you know? And she just kept on going about how fucked up I am and how I'm still victimizing him even though I'm not on the streets because I'm withholding from him emotionally and that's just like physical abuse because it scars. And she's telling me that I'm unfit because I've abused my son.

Rinda's account is consistent with the exchanges I observed between counselors and prisoners during encounter sessions and branch groups.[16] In these sessions, the point is not only to demonstrate the numerous ways that mothers' drug use contributes to neglect, poor parenting, and a host of additional problems for kids and families, but also to emphasize that the problem is, as PHW's literature emphasizes, "the person, not the drug." Since drug use is not "the essence" of the problem, the termination of use should not be taken to imply that the women are now better mothers. Quite the contrary.

In Rinda's case, the counselor argued that her decision not to cry in front of her son is another form of victimization, one that is as consequential as "physical abuse." As is consistent with all confrontation sessions, prisoners are denied an opportunity to challenge these interpretations, so Rinda's own logic shaping the interaction with her son went unheard.

The claim that mothers in prison are victimizing their children extends beyond the counselors' observations about face-to-face interactions with children. It also includes the strategies women pursue as they do time. Consider, for example, the following confrontation between a counselor and Terra. Terra graduated from PHW six months earlier but had been sentenced by a judge to return to the program a second time, following her escape from a work-release facility. Upon her return, Terra confessed during a group session that she left the work-release facility out of concern that her four-year-old daughter was "in some kind of trouble." Prior to serving her first term in prison, Terra had no relatives or friends willing to take her daughter, so she left her in the care of her boyfriend. While she was incarcerated, Terra's boyfriend broke up with her and informed her that his new girlfriend would be moving into their house. He agreed to continue to care for Terra's daughter and he regularly brought her daughter to the prison and work-release center for visits. He also sent Terra checks so she could buy cigarettes, cosmetics, and other small items from the prison commissary. His attentiveness led Terra to believe that she could trust him. Following a visit with her daughter, however, she became concerned that the new girlfriend was abusing and neglecting her daughter during the day when her ex-boyfriend was at work. Distrustful of social services and desperate to make sure her daughter was not being harmed, Terra "escaped" from the work-release facility (she was given a pass to leave the facility to go on job interviews and never returned). During her escape, Terra retrieved her daughter from the ex-boyfriend's house and took her to a friend's apartment, where Terra and her daughter remained until a parole officer discovered them.

Two days after the group session, the counseling staff called Terra to the center of the facility for a confrontation. One counselor asked why Terra had decided to escape from work release when she had only three months remaining on her sentence. Before Terra could respond the counselor asked a second question: "What kind of mother fails her child like that?" Terra shrugged. The counselor moved closer to Terra so that she was standing just a few feet away from her and said, "I'll tell you what kind of mother, a bad mother. You're victimizing that little girl of yours. What do you think happens to her when you're gone?" Terra shrugged again. The counselor shouted, "Dialogue," a command that gave permission for Terra to speak.

"I saw her when she came to my Friday visit." Terry's face reddened and she looked as though she was about to cry. "Something was wrong with her." The counselor sighed and asked what was wrong. Terra said that she could not identify exactly what was wrong, just that something was different.

"Do you think you would know if you weren't sitting here in prison?" the counselor asked. Once more, Terra shrugged and then mumbled, "Maybe, but I was trying to get to her in case something was going on at the house where she was staying." The counselor turned her back on Terra, walked back to the desk where the correctional officer was stationed, and conferred quietly with the senior counselor. The counselor walked forward, toward Terra, and said, "I just learned that social services has your daughter, so there you go! Your worst fear came true. Talk about self-fulfilling prophecies, you guys have a way of making them happen. Whatever happened to your daughter—and I hope it was nothing like the trauma you caused her by making her hide out like a criminal—but whatever happened, you caused it. Do you see that? You're responsible for what happens to that little girl because you had choices and you chose to neglect her and leave her—"

"Fuck you! Fuck you for saying that! Who the fuck do you think you are? You don't fucking know me! I hate you, I hate this fucking place!" Terra's face was bright red, her fists were clenched into tight balls and, breaking from the program's rules governing comportment, she paced back and forth across the front of the room. Several prisoners seated in the first few rows got up and scurried to chairs toward the back of the room. In low tones, the counselor told Terra to calm down and direct her anger "inward," and use the anger to get rid of the "bad self." Terra screamed another expletive, ran to her cell, and slammed the door.

As this episode reveals, at the core of counselors' claims that prisoners have victimized their children is the notion that the women are both autonomous actors, with access to choices and options, and, at the same time, that they consistently make the *wrong* choices. In both Rinda's and Terry's cases, counselors frame their criminal activity and subsequent incarceration as choices whose ultimate victim is their children. In these sessions, counselors make clear that regardless of what motivated women to engage in criminal activity, the logical outcome of crime is punishment, which, of course, prevents mothers from adequately caring for their children. And since counselors regard prison as a *logical*, unavoidable outcome, they see mothers' crimes as revealing something very bad about mothers themselves. In fact, what makes the women, in the words of the counselors, "unfit," is that they are incapable or unable to make rational, responsible decisions that enhance rather than detract from the well-being of their children.[17] In Rinda's case, a counselor equates her failure to adequately emote with "physical abuse." In Terra's case, it is her inability to keep her child out of social services. In both scenarios, counselors regard bad choices as evidence that something is wrong with the self. The irony, particularly in Terra's case, is that she is evidencing the kind of self-sacrificing behaviors that are consistent with white, middle-class norms of mothering.[18] However, because this self-sacrifice occurs within the tangled web of poverty and correctional supervision, she literally cannot win. A key part of why women like Terra cannot win is in their claim to motherhood as an authentic identity.

In Dorothy Roberts's important study of race and state regulation of reproduction, *Killing the Black Body*, she devotes an entire chapter to detailing how the War on Drugs effectively criminalized motherhood for poor, African American women.[19] She argues that media-hyped images of the pregnant crack addict fueled aggressive, criminal prosecutions of African American mothers who used or were suspected of using drugs during their pregnancies.[20] In these cases, pregnant drug users were prosecuted when they carried their pregnancies to term as well as when they choose to remain fertile. It was, as Roberts describes, one of the most extreme examples of state regulation of pregnancy and motherhood, and one that was legitimated by the iconography of the bad, Black mother.

Aggressive regulation of pregnancy and motherhood carried over into the prison system as well. Indeed, one hallmark of the new penology as it unfolds in women's prisons is enhanced restrictions on reproductive rights. This includes limitations on prisoners' access to abortion and adequate prenatal care, as well as restrictions on parental rights, including termination of those rights.[21] As the "get tough" movement played out in East State, women's parental rights were increasingly subject to challenge. Indeed, state officials moved to permanently terminate the parental rights of incarcerated mothers who delivered their babies while serving time for a drug-related crime. Later, prosecutions became more aggressive, targeting children that had been born well before the start of the mother's prison sentence.[22] Although little is known about these cases (because records are sealed), research done by reproductive rights scholars suggest that drug use and poverty serve as thresholds for a charge of child abuse and neglect.[23]

The challenge to motherhood is also evident in the social technologies of habilitation, particularly counselors' efforts to "break down" the self. This was pronounced in instances where prisoners asserted their identities as mothers. Toomi, for example, was a thirty-year-old mother of two, and one of the first women in the program to have her parental rights to her youngest child terminated following a second conviction for drug trafficking. The process had taken months, not years, and left many women, most notably

Toomi, in a state of shock and disbelief. PHW counselors immediately called a branch session so that Toomi could "get in touch with" and "correctly process" her feelings. Toomi brought a binder to the session that was full of official-looking documents and handwritten pages filled with drafts and copies of letters she wrote to social workers, lawyers, prison officials, and her son. When asked by a counselor to describe what happened, Toomi rifled through the pages of documents. After several minutes, she looked up at the counselor and said, "I don't know what happened."

The counselor clarified, "I don't mean the legal procedure. Just tell the group what happened in terms of the process, the process of getting a new family for your son."

"They took him," Toomi began to cry, "the office for—God, I can't even find the name—took him away from me. But they can't do that, I still don't see how they can do that. If I get a lawyer, I mean if I hire a real lawyer that—I didn't never abuse my kids. I'm their *mother*. How can they do that? I'm his *mother*" (her emphasis).

The counselor walked over to Toomi, handed her a tissue, and rubbed her back. "Honey," she said, "it's gonna be OK. He's gonna be OK and you're gonna be OK. But this is the reality of addiction. This is what it does. It's ugly, it's painful. It destroys families, it destroys relationships. It takes whatever else you are and makes it secondary. You can't be a mother, a real mother, when you're an addict. It destroys that."

The counselor's point, that Toomi cannot be a "real" mother because of her drug use, echoes media coverage of the crack baby crisis, in which health care professionals were periodically quoted making inflammatory statements like "crack cocaine seems to be undermining the maternal instinct."[24] But counselors not only challenged the authenticity of prisoners' motherhood claims based on their drug use, they also emphasized that the circumstances in which prisoners became mothers and the ways they used their motherhood discredited the authenticity of their claims to be "real" mothers.

During a group that was devoted to parenting issues, counselors told prisoners that "babies should be born out of love, not addiction." Following a confrontation with a counselor who had demanded to know whether her third child was born out of "love or addiction," Vonda acknowledged that she had been using crack cocaine during her pregnancy but explained that she really "wanted" her child because it was a girl and all her other children were boys. Later, during a parenting session, Vonda again emphasized that she had wanted all of her children. The same counselor responded that just because she "wanted" her children did not mean they were born from love. To clarify her meaning, Vonda said that her children were born from love, which, she emphasized, was obvious because she treated her eight- and twelve-year-old sons just like "friends." Smirking, the counselor told Vonda that that was an entirely inappropriate way to deal with "young children," and was indicative of both her "inability to make responsible decisions" as well as her "lack of parenting skills."

In addition to claiming that many of their pregnancies took place in the context of drug addiction, counselors asserted that the women used their pregnancies and motherhood itself as a form of overt manipulation. Here the most frequent charge was that the women intentionally became pregnant in the interest of snaring a man. In a confrontation session between a counselor and three prisoners regarding an upsurge in petty rule violations, the counselor accused all three of being more focused on their boyfriends and husbands than in "getting in touch" with their selves. As the confrontation wore on, the counselor told one of the women that she would not put it past her to "fake a pregnancy" just to get the attention of her boyfriend. When another of the women being confronted giggled, the counselor told her that such a response was inappropriate and indicated that she could identify with giving birth for "selfish" and "greedy" reasons.

Counselors also accused prisoners of using their identities as mothers to generate sympathy and to elicit special treatment in prison. Nallie, for example, began crying during a group session in which one of the counseling staff inquired about the disciplinary trouble her daughter had gotten into at school. One of the counselors remarked that Nallie was not one to "let her guard down," and another asked, "What's really going on? You're not using your daughter to get some sympathy for your own troubles are you?" Although counselors generally approved of overt emotional displays, in Nallie's case they contended that the tears were a contrivance. Nallie's reaction to having her identity as a real mother challenged by the staff was typical:

It's like I don't have the right to deal with things in my own way, you know? If I don't handle it like they would handle it, then I'm a bad mother or shouldn't even be a mother. I keep a lot of my feelings to myself, you know, especially about my kids, but sometimes I can't hide it and it comes out. They say that I must want something by crying about my daughter's trouble in school. Well, it's fucked up, 'cause if I'd have cried when they wanted me to, they'd call it growth and say I was getting to be a better type of person. Instead, I do it when they don't expect it and now I'm like insincere.

In each of these cases, counselors told prisoners that their attitudes and behavior indicated that they were not "real" mothers, in the sense of motherhood being an authentic reflection of the self. Real mothers are in love when they get pregnant, prioritize their children's needs, and do not use their status as mothers to satisfy their own wants and desires. Unfit mothers are those for whom motherhood is rendered inauthentic by their drug addiction. Motherhood is a contrivance, something done to manipulate others for selfish and ulterior purposes. It is precisely because prisoners are not "real" mothers that they engage in "abusive" behavior that "victimizes" their children.

Sexuality

While motherhood was thematized more than any other component of selfhood during the confrontation sessions, sexuality ran a close second. Not surprisingly, discussions of motherhood and sexuality often went hand in hand. Counselors regarded unplanned pregnancies as an unfortunate outcome of either a prisoner's unrestrained sexuality or her manipulative nature. But counselors also used sexuality, particularly the terrain of practice and desire, as another grid on which to decode the self and to showcase the perversity of addiction. They focused primarily on sexual practices, with a particular emphasis on promiscuity and selling sexual services. Sexual desires, particularly those deemed "unhealthy" and "compulsive," were a second area of concern.

Although only a few women are serving time on prostitution convictions, just under 90% of prisoners in PHW admitted during their intake interviews that they had engaged in sex-for-drugs or sex-for-money exchanges at some point in their lives.[25] Of those, just over a third reported regular participation in prostitution. For counselors, prostitution and other kinds of sex hustles represented a clear break with "healthy," "normal" sexual behavior. It did not matter what circumstances a woman found herself in or what goal her hustle was intended to accomplish, selling sex was a sign of disease. Many prisoners challenged this construction on the premise that sex hustles were a rational response to grim economic conditions. They did not gain any traction with counselors when they made this argument. A counselor's response to a prisoner who observed that there was more money to be had in prostitution than in low-paying service work was typical: "Fast food workers don't degrade themselves. They do not hate themselves with such venom that they let themselves be used and thrown out like trash. What you did made you garbage, human waste."

The message to the women regarding sex-based hustles was unabashedly clear—"healthy" women do not engage in such sorts of behavior. Diseased women do. In confrontations, counselors focused both on the sale of sexual services on the street and on promiscuity in general as indications that the self was flawed. In the case of the latter, they endeavored to convince women that most of their sexual liaisons were problematic, even those that women described as freely given and an outgrowth of mutual desire. This generated a significant amount of confusion among prisoners, most of whom were willing to accept that prostitution was morally wrong, but were baffled as to why counselors condemned sex that was mutual and pleasurable. This is demonstrated in the following exchange between a counselor and Jenna, an admitted prostitute-turned-madam:

> COUNSELOR: It's sick, it's a sickness. Women don't do that to themselves. They value their bodies. Your body is yours, not to be sold and used. There's something awful in that. Do you see what I'm saying? It's not right, it's not normal for someone to do that. There's something very wrong inside. That's what I'm saying. Do you see? Dialogue.
> JENNA: That I'm sick? Yeah, OK. But that's sex-for-money or what? What about when I do it for free, for myself? That can't be sick. I'm saying this is what I want and this is what I'm going to do.
> COUNSELOR: Healthy women value their bodies. You can't value your body and then sell it, and it doesn't matter if what you're getting for it is money or popularity, or some sense of accomplishment. I doubt very much that you're getting pleasure from it—I think you're still selling when you "give it away" as you say. That's self-hatred. You need to get in touch with what the message is in here [points to her chest]. There's a reason for that dislike, it's a sign something's very wrong.

While counselors went to great lengths to catalog the various practices that constituted unhealthy sexuality, it was unclear what healthy practices actually looked like beyond allusions to traditional marriage or to a long-term, monogamous relationship. In the above example, the counselor suggests that to be healthy is to value one's body. In the same exchange, however, she dismisses Jenna's comments about "doing it for herself" as evidence of "self-hatred."

Prisoners frequently sought clarification on what constituted healthy sexual practices, and they periodically challenged certain counselors as having a "double standard" when it came to sex. For example, during a confrontation between Counselor Tynice and a prisoner nicknamed Star, Tynice informed Star that she occupied the lowest position in society because she was a "crack whore." Although she was not given permission to speak, Star countered, "Well, if I'm a whore, you're a cock sucker parading around like you is *somebody*! At least I don't hide what I do to earn my way" (her emphasis). Star was referring to the fact that before Tynice was a PHW counselor, she worked as a prostitute, sold drugs, and smoked crack on the same streets as several PHW prisoners, including Star. Counselor Tynice never made a point to hide her past, and although she never discussed her experiences on the street in any detail, she would often remind prisoners that if she could succeed in drug treatment so could they. In response to Star's explicit indictment of her former lifestyle, Counselor Tynice retorted:

> I've sucked a lot of dick in my life and it's not something I'm proud of, Family. It feels real fucking dirty and every last one of you in here knows what I'm talking about. It took me a lot of years and a lot of hard work to get that dirt out from under my skin and out of my self. But I'm clean, my soul is clean today. Y'all can't say that yet if you can't admit who you are. Confront who you are, otherwise it'll never leave you no matter how much you rub it in or try to cover it up. [Star], you're a crack whore and a dirty one at that. I can see the real you, that inner you, better than anybody.

This is closest any of the staff came to describing what the path to healthy sexuality would be. Through these exchanges, prisoners were taught that sexuality is a marker for the self. The two are linked such that sexual practices both reflect and reinforce the state of "hatred," "sickness," and "dirtiness" that plague the diseased self.

Among themselves, counselors agreed that there was more to women's sexuality than their drug addictions. Most were well aware of research literature that demonstrates a relationship among sexual abuse, promiscuity, and prostitution.[26] Yet they were hesitant to say that the sexual behaviors they regarded as problematic were an outgrowth of sexual victimization. As the senior counselor noted during an interview, "Where does victimization stop and self-directed behaviors begin? I don't know, I can't begin to sort it all out. We're here to handle addiction, not the other stuff."

The second theme that emerged during confrontations over sexuality involved desire, particularly same-sex desire. The staff's focus was almost exclusively on this as it was expressed in the context of the prison. Although PHW prohibited sexual activity of any sort, counselors directed most of their surveillance and their sanctions toward sexual acts and romantic relations between women, rather than toward autoerotic behaviors (although the latter were undertaken with considerably more regularity than the former).[27]

Counselors, like many inmates, evaluated and weighted the significance of sexual desire according to the sexual identities of the participants. When women who identified as heterosexual had romantic or sexual relationships with other women while in prison, they were said by inmates to be "jailing" and by counselors to be "sexually acting out." For both inmates and staff, the terms were pejorative. Both heterosexual and lesbian prisoners were suspicious of heterosexual women who entered prison, got involved in a sexual relationship with another prisoner, and later denied such involvements to their family and friends. Among prisoners, the principle objection to these "fake dykes" was not so much the expression of same-sex desire as it was the appearance of deception. Veronica explained:

> What it tells me is somebody's up to no good. I've been in and out of institutions for close to twenty years and I've learned a lot about people and how to read them. In here stuff that goes on out there that's maybe no big deal is important 'cause you watch your back. Things are more serious, or they can be, if somebody fucks with you here. So, when I see these straight women come in here, get it on with some woman and, you know, they could be having a full-on relationship like they running around in love. And nine times out of ten the women they're all wrapped up with in here isn't another straight woman looking to pass the time or experiment or whatever, but a gay woman. Anyway, they go out and they deny it. They leave that other woman, the one they was all in love with, they leave her hanging. Now I don't have a problem with the ones who don't deny it or whatever. But the ones who is straight, running around acting like the biggest dykes in the institution, they is lying about who they really are, misrepresenting to everyone, including that person they said they were in love with. I don't have no respect for that shit, they the lowest on the pecking order around prison.

Like most of the inmates, PHW counselors reserved some of their harshest criticisms for heterosexual women who had sexual relations with other women during their incarceration. What was problematized among counselors, however, was not interpersonal deception per se, but the expression of "inauthentic" sexual desire. There was no other bit of information about prisoners that drew the attention and focus of the counselors more than reports of sexual relations or romantic overtures between women. In the privacy of staff offices and during get-togethers outside the institution, such information was always met with one or more expressions of disgust and disapproval (e.g., "That's disgusting," "These women are crazy," "Don't leave me alone with her—she may jump me," "It gives me the creeps to know what they're doing").[28]

When staff learned of liaisons or romances between prisoners, they staged fairly lengthy, public confrontations of the sort described previously.

Over the course of my participation in the setting, there was no other behavior or rule violation, including violence, that drew so much attention and intervention from staff. During the confrontations, counselors cultivated expressions of outrage and condemnation from other prisoners to drive home the point that expressions of same-sex desire were, from the perspective of program ideology, inauthentic and deviant representations of the self. The following exchange occurred after counselors caught a prisoner named Tracy kissing another PHW prisoner. In this confrontation, counselors showcase how the "inauthentic" expression of desire reveals something "wrong" about the self:

COUNSELOR #1: What's going on, you gay now? Dialogue.

TRACY: No, I ain't gay.

COUNSELOR #1: What'd you call making it with another woman? I've been around a long time. In my book, that's gay. [Counselor #2], how would you call it?

COUNSELOR #2: I'd say she's wrestling with some feelings and issues deep down inside. Better get in touch with that. Women just don't get those feelings for women, something's going on, right Family?

PRISONER #1: Hell yes!

PRISONER #2: She's a lesbian, she's gay for doing that.

PRISONER #3: I don't want no gay stuff going on around me! That's sick!

PRISONER #4: She's jailing and faking it in here. She's not being honest.

COUNSELOR #1: OK, enough, hold up, Family! [Tracy] you need to deal with this. If you're not gay or you're not wrestling with feelings about your sexual identity there's something real bad going on, you see? I ain't never had no feelings for no woman—you see what I'm saying? I'm not saying it's wrong if you a lesbian, but you either are or aren't! You just don't get feelings for a woman and act on them in a sexual way. I understand you reaching out for another person, we want you to feel safe emotionally, physically, and spiritually in here. But you crossed the line and made it sexual. Something inside took you there, that's part of what's wrong in here, inside you.

Although counselors usually made a statement to the effect that the confrontation was not intended to be discriminatory or pejorative toward lesbians, stigmatizing statements about such relationships being "deviant," "wrong," and "bad" suggest otherwise. Further, while counselors generally reserved their strongest criticisms for heterosexual prisoners, they frequently voiced their suspicions about the motives underlying the behaviors of lesbians. Prisoners who were "out" in PHW reported having to be careful about offers to lend support to other women for fear their actions would be misinterpreted by staff. Yvonne commented:

> Well, they say it's not a gay thing, it's a behavior thing, but I don't believe it. If I so much as pat someone on the shoulder or hug someone who's crying, they [counselors] look at me funny. What's crazy is they think I'm just after everything that moves. I made a point to out myself when I first came in here and talk about my girlfriend who I've been living with for the last five years, but it doesn't seem to matter. I feel like I get scrutinized more than the others and I've been called on the floor several times for what they say is "instigating." That means, if somebody in here writes me a note or asks me about being gay—and that's happened a couple times—I get in trouble because they think I encouraged it! That's crazy, I definitely think they [staff] have issues about gay women. Like they think we're all out to turn out a bunch of straight women.

In sum, there was little about the prisoners' sexual practices and desires that were not problematized by staff during confrontation sessions. In this sense, "breaking down" prisoners through the regulation of their sexuality does not so much represent a break with the gendered control practices of the past but a continuance of them. Surveillance in women's prisons, regardless of historical era, has been deployed primarily to observe, catalog, and regulate women's sexuality.[29] As the sociologists Candace Kruttschnitt and Rosemary Gartner observe in their comparative study of women's prisons in California, the purposes to which this surveillance is put vary over time, but the fact of the surveillance does not.[30] The twist that the habilitative apparatus puts on sexuality is diagnostic. Whether prisoners identified as gay or straight, staff frequently told them that their sexual practices and desires were not consistent with what it meant to be a "healthy" or "real" woman.[31] Instead, such behaviors, particularly promiscuity and same-sex relations, were indicative of turmoil and "sickness" within the self.

(Co)dependency Queens

The third theme that emerged during confrontation sessions was dependency, primarily as it related to how prisoners were situated at the nexus of the labor market and the state. As a topic of confrontations, dependency ran a distant third behind discussions of motherhood and sexuality. This was somewhat ironic given that the "get tough" platform was animated by racist constructions of African American women as welfare queens and crack whores.[32] Indeed, a good bit of rhetoric in the state about the "new offender" centered not only on her criminal involvement but also on her dependency on state subsidies, especially welfare.[33] Studies of community-based alternative to prison programs have demonstrated how constructions of women offenders as overly dependent gave rise to a set of "empowerment" policies aimed at encouraging economic independence.[34] In most cases, these programs offered a combination of educational, vocational, and therapeutic interventions.

In contrast, PHW did little in the practical sense to counter women's "dependence" on the state. There were two reasons for this. First, the reality was that few of the women in PHW were welfare clients. In some cases, they relied on support from "baby daddies" and men with whom they were romantically involved. More often, they were unable or unwilling to go through the various hoops and hurdles necessary to receive public assistance.[35] Most of these women considered themselves "hustlers," in that they engaged in a host of licit and illicit entrepreneurial activities designed to generate steady income.[36] Although they did not have regular jobs, it was difficult for counselors to make the case that this particular group of women was economically dependent on anyone other than themselves to provide food, shelter, and clothing for their families. As Jenna told me of her life before she became a well-known madam, "Are you kidding me? I was poor but I was never busted. Hell no would I ever go on welfare. Hell no, that's for people with no hustle. I'd sold my butt before that." Most of the women that I talked to in PHW were as removed from the world of welfare as they were from the legal labor market.

The second reason dependency did not get as much play as motherhood or sexuality was that PHW did little to counter structural sources of dependency. In its first year, the program barred prisoners from participating in any programs outside of PHW. This meant they could not take GED or high school equivalency classes, vocational training, or apply for jobs within the institution. In later years, the policy was modified to allow prisoners to take GED courses, but they still were barred from vocational training as a matter of course.[37] The reason for this was that program ideology held that addiction was at the center of everything. Prisoners were expected to prioritize dealing with their addictions over their education and job training because, as the PHW director put it, "without habilitation there is nothing. You cannot educate or train an addict and expect that it will pay off in terms of economic independence."[38]

When PHW counselors confronted prisoners over dependency they framed it as a psychological, rather than a structural, condition. Counselors used information garnered in intake interviews to diagnose the majority of prisoners as "codependent." It was of little relevance to the staff what it was that prisoners were dependent on (men, criminal pursuits, state subsidies, families, "fast living," etc.) because they conceptualized it as yet another manifestation of the diseased self. The diagnosis of "codependence" was premised on the staff's belief that prisoners were "excessively" reliant on someone or something outside of themselves for happiness, material sustenance, or psychological survival. Although most prisoners were not welfare recipients, counselors often drew on neoconservative constructions of the welfare queen to make the case that codependency rendered prisoners simultaneously lazy and greedy. For example, a counselor told Ann, who returned to PHW a second time after being arrested with drugs:

> You may not be a welfare queen like some of the others who sit around in here but you're a queen, all right. You're dependent just like them, you're committed to the money. We gave you the tools last time you were here to go out and get yourself some legitimate work, but it don't pay as much, right? You are not as independent as you like to think of yourself, you need to get in touch with why you're sacrificing yourself for dirty money 'cause you are. You're somebody's slave, don't kid yourself.

Although many of the prisoners in the program were from poor families, were poor themselves, and had little or no means of securing stable work that could support their families, counselors regarded their dependence on criminal income, state subsidies, and men as a trigger for their drug addictions. As one counselor lectured to prisoners in a seminar on addiction, "Dependency will kill you. For most of you, it's what got your addiction to drugs started in the first place. We break that shit down and kick it out! We make independent women in here, we don't want no queens when we're done!"

Staff told prisoners their goal should be to become independent and self-reliant, but they framed independence as a mental state as opposed to an economic condition. During the final moments of a graduation ceremony, the staff warned Toni of her "psychological tendency toward codependency":

COUNSELOR #1: You know your trigger, watch it. You gravitate toward being lazy, toward letting others do for you. Fight it or it will take you right back to addiction and you'll be back in here.

COUNSELOR #2: We've all got stuff in ourselves. You've got to watch the welfare queen in there—you worked hard in here, you can do it!

COUNSELOR #1: Yeah, your inner self can get the best of you, watch the psychological tendency toward codependency. Don't let others do for you, don't depend on anyone else. Make your own path and you'll see that part of you will be less and less tempting. You won't face the same obstacles, you'll find that good-paying job, a good man, and the right place to raise your kids. If you give into the queen, she'll take you right back down, Family. Successful people are not dependent people!

Although the staff positioned "independent women" as the polar opposite of "queens," prisoners were often confused by this juxtaposition. Prisoners like Ann assumed that they were independent because they did not rely on either men or welfare to make ends meet. Counselors, of course, argued that crime was not a viable pathway toward independence and, in fact, was yet another source of dependence. The senior counselor explained to me in an interview, "It's possible for someone to be *criminally dependent*. . . . Most of them in here are" (my emphasis).

In contrast to sexuality, PHW's treatment of dependency represented a radical break from rehabilitative paternalism. In the case of the latter, dependence was not the problem—victimization was. Prison staff did not encourage the "girls" to be independent so much as they directed them to become dependent on the "right" people who would serve as role models and caretakers.[39] In contrast, habilitation sought to counter the psychological condition of codependency, but this was realized through making women into something less than autonomous, self-governing actors.

Addiction and the Diseasing of the Self

If motherhood, sexuality, and dependency are all vectors for diagnosing the self as diseased, what of the thing itself? That is, what is it at the core of the self that renders it so flawed and incomplete as to be incapable of "authentic" mothering, "healthy" sexuality, and labor market independence? I have previously indicated that PHW is premised on a therapeutic community model of addiction in which substance abuse is framed as a symptom of a "disordered" and "diseased" person, in which the "problem" is "the person, not the drug."[40] According to the disease model, addicts suffer from a range of cognitive, emotional, and behavioral deficits that manifest in "confused" values and the pursuit of "unconventional" lifestyles.[41] But what does all this actually mean to counselors as they go about their day surveilling, diagnosing, confronting, and sanctioning prisoners? How do they interpret the disease model in the course of their day-to-day interactions with prisoners?

When I asked counselors how they interpreted program philosophy, particularly the phrase "disorder of the person," most responded in somewhat tautological terms by invoking concepts like "addictive personalities" and "diseased minds." For staff, these were morally loaded categories. In an interview, one counselor elaborated her conception of addiction:

> They are deprived of basic social, cognitive, and feeling abilities. It is a problem inside of them. A lot of people drink, I drink, but not everyone becomes an alcoholic. I'm not of the mind that just because you drink regularly you are addicted. Addiction involves a loss or even the absence of moral reasoning and serious psychological problems.

Another counselor said there is a "type" of person who becomes an addict:

> In here, it shows pretty well that the type that get addicted are those with, um, addictive and criminal personalities. They think like addicts whether they're using or not. They constantly think about how to manipulate people to get what they want. They don't go out on their own and set goals for themselves, earn their way. They con their families, go on welfare, con the government, they get over on people around them! They've got a psychology that is different from the rest of us, one that is, I don't want to say this, well, just that what they do is evil. I'm not saying that they're evil, but what is inside of them, the addiction, it's evil.

Morality anchored their explanations and it played a crucial role in their diagnoses of prisoners. This is distinct from both a medical model of addiction in which biochemical vulnerability separates "addicts" from "normals," as well as from early AA frameworks which held that alcoholism was caused by an "allergy."[42] In essence, counselors did not believe that addiction strikes individuals arbitrarily; rather, they considered it a disease brought on by the choices and actions of those it afflicted—choices that both reflected and reinforced a flawed, incomplete, and unruly self.[43] During an interview, one counselor referred to the "typical" prisoner as a "spiritual wasteland":

> These are women without souls. . . . You can't do what some of these women do to earn a buck or get a hit and still have a soul. When you lose your morals, your self-respect, you lose your soul. You have no conscience, you victimize. They want to blame others for their condition, but they had choices. When you get addicted, you lose your ability to choose, but the fault is ultimately your own.

While this particular counselor was unique in her charge that prisoners were "without souls," all the counselors identified the prisoners as women who were lacking in conscience and morality. Indeed, while they acknowledged that prisoners could potentially be physiologically predisposed to substance abuse, they identified immorality as that which activated the condition of addiction. Director Torrence's discussion of the "latent aspects" of addiction is telling in this regard:

> DIRECTOR: For them the possibility of addiction is always there unless they are treated at some point in their lives. It is usually brought out in the course of lifestyle pursuits which could generally be seen as deviant and unhealthy.
>
> JM: So in your mind, addiction is sparked by a combination of drug use and other factors?
>
> DIRECTOR: Not just in my mind, that's basic clinical knowledge, yes, that a variety of events get the ball rolling. Early alcohol and drug use, combined with antisocial behavior, say in school, dropping out of school, hanging out with the wrong crowd, stealing. For addicts, these things are a slippery slope because they initiate a commitment to a deviant lifestyle, one which results in pathological dependence on drugs and criminal activities. I'm not saying if they don't do these things they won't ultimately end up addicted to something or another, but in here, most of our women exhibited criminogenic tendencies before their serious drug use began and it made it that much worse.

The staff's conceptualization of addiction as both disease and moral failure led to two distinct, seemingly contradictory representations of the "type" of women who become addicts. Among themselves, counselors spoke of addicts in moral terms and differentiated them from "normal" people. Counselors frequently reminded one another that addicts were a fundamentally different sort of person because they were "immoral," "needy," and "manipulative." Difference rhetoric, as I will refer to such statements, served to distinguish the counselors and other "normals" from addicts based on moral and psychological deficits. On the other hand, when counselors interacted with prisoners they often downplayed differences between addicts and others. Sameness rhetoric included phrases like "addicts are not special" and "addiction doesn't discriminate," and was used by counselors to inform the prisoners that "anybody" could become an addict. Although each of the rhetorics appears to contradict the other, they are held together by the internal logic of the staff's conception of addiction as disease and moral failure. Below I present brief vignettes demonstrating how each type of rhetoric is used during the course of a day in the program, and explicate how each is an outgrowth of the staff's ad hoc interpretation of the disease model.

Difference Rhetoric

Staff meetings were held every Friday after the prisoners left the facility to eat lunch in the prison cafeteria. Beginning at eleven o'clock, the counselors on duty convened in a large corner office, prepared their lunches, and reviewed paperwork and handwritten notes that prisoners put in their mailboxes. If prisoners desired to speak privately with a counselor, they were required to write a request explaining the reason for the meeting and why they could not deal with their problem in group therapy sessions.[44] During one such staff meeting, a new counselor in the program shared a note from Elena requesting to speak privately about an emergency involving her three-year-old daughter, Ana. Elena had arranged for her younger brother to care for her daughter during her incarceration. Four days before submitting the request, Elena learned that social services had visited the apartment where Elena's brother lived with his girlfriend and Ana. Following the visit, a social worker contacted Elena and informed her that they would be removing her daughter from her brother's care. No one else from Elena's family was able to take her daughter and Elena was terrified that they would put her daughter in foster care. Additionally, Elena was worried that her brother, who was a heroin addict undergoing methadone treatment, would relapse if Ana were removed from his care. Elena did not want to bring the issue to group because she wanted to protect both her daughter's and her brother's privacy.

The new counselor was sympathetic to Elena's situation and wanted to hold a private session with her immediately following the conclusion of the staff meeting. Other counselors asked how long Elena had been in treatment. When the new counselor indicated that Elena had been in treatment only a month, the senior counselor launched into a lengthy discussion regarding the "neediness" and "codependency" addicts exhibit upon arrival. She said that under no circumstance should new prisoners be allowed to break the rules and talk privately with staff, since doing so would only aggravate their tendency to "repress" and "hide" their issues in group. The new counselor indicated that she understood the staff's concerns regarding "codependency issues among addicts," but was vehement in her assertion that an exception should be granted in emergencies. At that point, the program director slammed her notebook on the desk behind her and leaned over so that she was speaking directly to the new counselor:

We have a philosophy of addiction that is based on years of research and therapeutic practice. This group of women are addicts, they are in need of treatment. As addicts, these women are superb manipulators. They will say and do anything to get what they want when they want it. They use and manipulate others, others whom they love and who love them. Those people are enablers. We are not. They fuel the addiction by giving in to what the addict demands. We treat addiction by breaking them down, by preventing them from manipulating, by healing the sickness, and breaking the dependency cycle. Our policies prevent us from being conned and from becoming enablers.

When the meeting was over the new counselor commented to me, "It's not that I am making exceptions for Elena . . . it's just that my heart goes out to her for the situation she's in. She's a mother worried about her kid." Overhearing this, another counselor walked over to us and said:

One day you'll thank [the director] after you've been conned by one of them. They're not just like any old worried mother. They're addicts, all of them. Sometimes our judgment is clouded, that's when we're most likely to get the wool pulled over our eyes. I think your compassion is admirable, I really do. Just don't let it get in the way of your judgment.

Sameness Rhetoric

Later that day, Counselor Tynice was holding an "addiction education" seminar for the prisoners. These seminars were structured according to categories of drugs, focusing on the pharmacological properties of the drug, and the psychological and physical dangers associated with its ingestion. On this particular day the topic was crack cocaine. The prisoners were more lively than usual during the lecture, frequently interrupting Tynice to make comments about their observations of "heavy" crack users, different highs they had personally experienced while using crack, their cravings after "coming down," and different objects (e.g., cans, bottles, pipes) they had used or had seen other people use to smoke it. During the question-and-answer session a debate broke out among prisoners about how widespread crack use was, with a few prisoners saying they had never tried it because they regarded it as "addictive" and less "pure" than drugs like cocaine, heroin, and marijuana. Tynice interrupted them and said that any substance could be "addictive." Sedra raised her hand in protest. When Counselor Tynice called on her, she countered that her experience on the street as a dealer and a "dope fiend" convinced her that crack was more addictive than other drugs. Tynice retorted that Sedra's claims lacked "scientific proof" and added that "anything" could be addictive because "addiction is about the person, not the drug."

"Bullshit," Sedra said under her breath. There was a moment of silence as Tynice erased the blackboard and wrote the word "addiction" in large, capital letters across it. In that moment, Sedra spun around in her chair so that she caught my eye and asked if college students from my university smoked crack. I told her that I was sure a few did, but that alcohol and marijuana use were likely the most widely and frequently used drugs on campus. "I just wondered 'cause I've been to three drug treatment programs including this one and I have never seen a college kid in treatment." She paused and asked Tynice, "Did you hear that, Counselor?" Tynice shrugged and asked Sedra what her point was.

"Those kids are using drugs and if addiction is about the person not the drug, how come you don't see them in treatment programs? It's cause the drugs they're using aren't as addictive as what some of us have used." Several prisoners who were doodling on their notebooks stopped what they were doing and looked back and forth from Counselor Tynice to Sedra to me. A few women commented that they sold drugs to college kids, attended parties in the nearby university town, and had heard stories from friends and relatives about drug use in "white boys' fraternities." Tynice sighed loudly and said, "Addiction doesn't discriminate. Anyone can be an addict. Black, white, yellow, or blue! I don't care if they're rich or poor, addiction doesn't discriminate!" A chorus of voices shouted back in protest, "So why they not in treatment?"

"Most of those kids come from money. They go to private facilities that cost their parents a lot of money, isn't that right, Jill?" Tynice asked. All eyes in the room turned to me. I shrugged and said that was probably the case, although I had known only one person from my undergraduate institution that had ever gone to a residential drug treatment program. Just then, Counselor Elizabeth walked across the living room area toward the staff bathroom.

Tynice called out to her, "These women are telling me they think they're some kind of special people 'cause they're addicts! They think some kinds of people can't be addicts!" Elizabeth strode over to the front of the blackboard, put her hands on her hips, and demanded to know who had made such allegations. Tynice pointed to Sedra and the prisoners who sat near her in the circle of chairs. After a lengthy tirade about the disease of addiction and a comparison of the arbitrary manner in which both addiction and cancer strike individuals, Elizabeth conferred with Tynice and they agreed that all the prisoners needed to write "I am not special because I am an addict. Addiction is a disease that does not discriminate on the basis of color, creed, ethnicity, gender, or money" five hundred times in their best penmanship. All the women groaned and a few remarked, "We're not the ones who said we're special." Tynice laughed and said, "I don't want to single anybody out. Addiction doesn't discriminate and neither do I!"

* * *

I have reproduced each of these two scenes from a single day in PHW to present what appears to be two contradictory views of addicts. On the one hand, counselors told prisoners during the seminar that "addiction doesn't discriminate" and that "addicts aren't special." Earlier in the day, however, a good portion of the staff meeting was spent reinforcing the belief that addicts were different from "normal" people. That a contradiction exists between what was said among the counselors in the privacy of staff meetings and what counselors said to prisoners during the course of therapy is not, in and of itself, problematic. Certainly this could be described as an enduring characteristic of the formal interactions occurring between laypersons and professionals of all stripes (e.g., teachers and students, lawyers and clients, doctors and patients). Withholding information can potentially be a beneficial component of interaction in cases where such information is stigmatizing or devastating to the recipient's self-image.[45]

Protecting PHW prisoners from being stigmatized, however, did not appear to be the counselors' intention in withholding their view of prisoners as "special" and "different." Instead, the tension between sameness rhetoric (e.g., "addicts aren't special," "addiction doesn't discriminate") and difference rhetoric (e.g., "they aren't like us") is resolvable when one examines the juxtaposition between moral and therapeutic frameworks. Staff regarded addicts as "special" in the sense that their "disordered" and "addictive" personalities can be differentiated from "normal," healthy personalities. Addicts exhibit "criminal" thought patterns, "codependency" in their relationships, inappropriate desires, and "manipulative" behavior. Further, staff believed that addiction is a latent condition activated by bad choices and immorality. Indeed, staff believed that immoral acts are of greater consequence for the addict than for the "normal" person, in the same way that drinking a beer is of greater consequence for the alcoholic than for the social drinker. For the alcoholic as for the addictive-prone personality, the initial act promises to snowball into something much more serious. In this sense, addicts are fundamentally different from "normal" people.

At the same time, counselors employed sameness rhetoric to downplay the significance that social factors such as race, class, and gender play in drugs, crime, and incarceration. During the debate over whether crack was more addictive than other drugs, both counselors and prisoners acknowledged that college students are socially privileged relative to the prisoners. Counselors, however, hastened to emphasize that their privilege did not protect them from becoming addicts ("anybody can be an addict . . . it's the person, not the drug"). Rather, social privilege changed the venue where college students went for treatment ("private facilities . . . that cost money"). The belief that "anybody" can be an addict was an outgrowth of the counselors' interpretation of the disease concept. According to the staff's philosophy, anybody has the potential to be an addict since "disordered" and "addictive" selves are latent and often unverifiable—thus the counselor's comparison of addiction and cancer. She told the prisoners that some individuals are predisposed to cancer and others are not, and in much the same way, some individuals are more "at risk" for addiction. Although predispositions vary among individuals, cancer occurs across all race, class, and gender subgroupings, as does addiction. Addiction, like cancer, appears to strike arbitrarily since none of us knows whether we have an "addictive prone" personality until we engage in practices that activate it. As one counselor commented to me privately:

> Hey, I could be in their [prisoners] shoes just like you. Either of us or both of us could have the potential to be addicts. But you and I aren't going to go out and take that risk and do the kinds of things that trigger it.

In this sense, then, we all could potentially be addicts ("addiction doesn't discriminate"). Not all of us, however, engage in the immoral behaviors that counselors allege that women in the program engaged in ("addicts are different").

It is important to emphasize that although PHW's own grant application mentions that social factors such as poverty and violence give rise to drug use and criminal behavior, the staff's causal explanation of addiction is constituted along psychological and moral grounds. In part, their tendency to psychologize addiction is attributable to their interpretation of the therapeutic community literature the Company made available to them during their training, but it is also a part of formal, clinical training seminars. Over the course of my fieldwork, I attended a variety of training sessions but I never, with one exception, heard the trainers reference social conditions as an explanation for crime and addiction. The exception occurred at a prison drug treatment conference in Chicago organized by the granting agency. The conference featured a clinical workshop on a "new" area of treatment dubbed "criminal thinking." The session was designed to show how drug-using offenders exhibit patterns of thinking that predispose them to criminal behavior. Toward the conclusion of the session, the featured speaker mentioned that criminal thinking could be considered a "rational" response to a "socially disorganized" environment. There was widespread murmuring among the audience and one attendee asked how the consultant could consider "deviant," "self-destructive," and "law breaking" behavior rational. The consultant reiterated much of what he had mentioned earlier, stating that criminality was a "reasonable" and "logical" means of survival in the face of poverty, violence, and limited institutional supports. Several hours later at dinner, two counselors and the director of PHW were still talking about the session, expressing disbelief that the consultant had equated immorality with rationality. The director of the Committee attempted to explain the speaker's remarks and to show how immorality, specifically in the form of criminal behavior, might be a rational response to certain circumstances. The counselors appeared unpersuaded. They listened politely until she was finished and then one counselor responded, "I'm not dismissing what you're saying but you haven't seen what I've seen. There's lots of poor people living in disorganized communities, but only some of them are criminals. It's personality, not environment."

Subsequently, in day-to-day interactions within PHW, sameness rhetoric reinforces the counselors' contention that prisoners are responsible for their condition and are not "innocent" victims of a disease that strikes arbitrarily. Had they not engaged in immoral behavior and "deviant" lifestyles, they may never have become addicts. Difference rhetoric reminds counselors that as addicts, the prisoners do not have the same moral standards and commitment to conventionality that "normal" people do. Further, the sameness/difference rhetoric serves to decouple the conceptual linkage between "disease" and "victim." Addicts are not "special" in the sense that they do not deserve the special (read: empathetic) treatment reserved for victims of other diseases. As a sign hanging in the interior entranceway of the PHW facility proclaims, "THE CRIMINAL IS A VICTIMIZER, NOT A VICTIM."

Conclusion

As a system of control, habilitation relies on surveillance, confrontation, and language games not only to render the diseased self visible and knowable, but also to act on that self. In the previous chapter, I demonstrated how surveillance, deprivation, humiliation, and confrontations, particularly "encounter" groups, allowed the counseling staff to diagnose the self and make a series of claims about the state of the disease. In this chapter, I explored the contents of the knowledge generated within the habilitative apparatus. The three dominant sets of claims emerging during the confrontation sessions involved motherhood, sexuality, and dependency. In this sense, PHW is not much different from modernist structures that aimed to "reform" women prisoners, nor is it distinct from contemporary, community-based programs designed to "empower" them. In each of these cases, motherhood, sexuality, and women's situatedness relative to both the state and the labor market stand at the core of a gendered punishment regime. Subsequently, it is not the themes that PHW counselors draw on that make habilitation distinct from other modalities of control—rather, it is the ends to which these themes are put. Habilitation is distinct from modernist efforts to "reform" and "rehabilitate" the self, because in this model the self is regarded as incomplete. It is the incompleteness of this self that is the core of the problem, not victimization or a lack of adequate socialization to parenting, intimacy, or labor market norms. As Company executives were fond of saying, "rehabilitation implies a fully formed self." In habilitation, no such self exists. Counselors "break down" addiction by showcasing how women's performance as mothers, lovers, and workers is perverted and undermined by a self that is, at its core, diseased.

Habilitation is also distinct from contemporary efforts to "empower" women through responsibilization schemes. Responsibilization refers to state efforts aimed at making individuals self-governing and self-regulating.[46] So, for example, in Hannah Moffat's study of "woman centered reforms" in the Canadian prison system, prisoners were encouraged to deal with structural issues like poverty and violence by taking responsibility for their own choices and actions and, ultimately, their own reform.[47] Such efforts are compatible with neoliberalism in that the state divests responsibility for social problems like poverty, violence, and inequality. In habilitation, however, there is no hope that prisoners will become self-governing, rational, and autonomous subjects. This is evident in the staff's formulation of "real criminals" as women who are plagued by a pathology that, at best, can be held at bay and, at worst, can be activated by a single bad decision. In much the same way that the staff provides no guidelines for how to achieve authentic motherhood or healthy sexuality, they also offer no cure for addiction. As we will see in the chapter that follows, habilitation offers only one path out, and it is not in the direction of self-governance, but of self-surrender.

PART III

Contesting the Boundaries of Self

6

Rentin' Out Your Head

Navigating Claims about the Self

It is not very practical to try to sustain solid claims about one's self.
—Ervin Goffman, *Asylums*

Rentin' out your head—it's when you let somebody else tell you who you are.
—PHW prisoner

For its first five years of operation, PHW held an annual press conference to celebrate the date the program first opened its doors at the prison. Among the guests regularly in attendance were a number of politicians (including a U.S. senator and East State's governor), local judges, representatives from the Committee, university researchers, news reporters from three local papers, and two television crews—one from a large, regional news station and the other from a small, local station. All the press conferences followed a similar format. PHW's director, Joanne Torrence, would welcome everyone to the facility, and then several invited speakers would give a short speech lasting between five and ten minutes. Generally, Torrence spoke first, followed by the governor, the senator, a drug court judge, a Company executive, and then a professor from a nearby state university. The press conference concluded with a testimonial given by a current prisoner in PHW about how the drug treatment program had changed both her identity and her life.[1]

This year, the counseling staff selected Carla, a "senior resident" of the program, to present her testimonial at the press conference. Being selected to tell one's story was considered an honor by the staff, although many prisoners told me privately that they dreaded speaking before an audience of "suit and tie guys."[2] Director Torrence explained that the staff collectively decided to select Carla because she had a good speaking voice, had overcome a "tragic" life history, and was a model participant throughout her entire two years in the program. Carla spent nearly a month writing the speech, which she submitted and resubmitted six times to the staff for their review. After the senior counselor modified the speech for the sixth time and the other counselors approved it, she returned it to Carla and told her she could have a three-day respite from treatment so that she could rehearse. Carla spent her days and nights memorizing the five-minute speech and reciting it to anyone who would listen. One day before the big event, she told me that although she was proud of her progress in the program and all that she had survived in her life, she was apprehensive speaking before the "suit and tie guys" because, as she put it:

> Those kinda people, the suits, you know, it's like they sit there and clap at all of us and all that but it's like they look down on us, you know? Like I get the impression I won't be getting no invitation to dinner in their big houses, you know, no matter what I would do—I doubt they'd even let me *serve* it! They just make me nervous, you know, 'cause it's like they looking at me with no respect 'cause of who they *think* I am. [her emphasis]

For the press conference, PHW's large group room was re-arranged to accommodate a long table filled with pastries and coffee, a podium, and approximately eighty chairs. The podium was placed at the front of the room, by the guard station, and facing it were three sections of chairs in the middle of the room. The handful of cushioned seats to the left of the podium were reserved for the speakers, and the two sections in the center of the room comprised seven or eight rows, with six or seven hard, plastic chairs in each row. The group of chairs located to the left, nearest the speakers' section, was designated for media, family and friends of prisoners, counselors, prison personnel, and others whose work brought them in contact with prisoners (e.g., clergy, probation officers, social service workers). The group of chairs located to the far right was reserved for PHW prisoners. Although there were several seats available in that section and almost none in the section of chairs to the left, no one with the exception of a university professor, four graduates of the program, and myself took a seat with PHW prisoners.

I sat directly behind Carla, who quietly rehearsed her speech while several of the outside speakers informed the prisoners of how "lucky" they were to be in PHW, warned them against "wasting" opportunities, and congratulated them for "doing something positive" for themselves. Carla periodically looked up from her notes to check which speaker was up to determine how much time she had before being called to the podium. The last speaker was a professor from the state university, who reminded the prisoners of the importance of research and emphasized that they should be honest in interviews with university researchers because their answers were "very important" to the university and would "make a difference" for "other people" like them.[3] In her closing statements she turned away from the prisoners and, looking toward the other speakers, said:

> I think these women should also be congratulated for trying to turn their lives around. This is a very difficult thing to do. Addiction is like—imagine if someone told you that you could never, ever eat another piece of chocolate cake in your life again, ever! I mean, wow. That would be awful for us, no more chocolate. I don't know if I could do it, it's so hard. I really give them credit.

When the professor concluded her talk, several of the prisoners sitting near me snickered. I overheard one woman comment, "You don't go to prison for buying, selling, and eating chocolate cake!" As Director Torrence announced Carla's name as the next speaker, Carla turned and whispered to a few of us in the row behind her, "Did you hear that? Addiction is like chocolate cake. Who is she, Dr. Forrest Gump?"[4] As several of us giggled, she threw her speech down on the floor and strode to the podium. Along with a few of the prisoners sitting near me, I expected Carla to abandon her carefully scripted remarks and tell the audience precisely how drug addiction carried with it far more devastating consequences than did a propensity for chocolate cake. In fact, Carla told me that morning that she felt "disrespected" by the "suit and tie guys" at past press conferences. In particular, she pointed out that prisoners were not allowed to approach the food table, much less eat the pastries, while "the suits" were in the facility. Her criticism was echoed by a number of prisoners who confided in me that they objected to the strategic physical and symbolic separation of the suits and the prisoners. For many of the women, the chocolate cake remark validated their concerns that they would never be accepted by "the suits," and that the press conference was not so much a celebration of their achievements but a patronizing public relations effort. One prisoner sitting near me commented after the professor's talk:

> They don't want to know about what it's like out there on the street. They already got their own ideas about it. Shit, they comparing it to chocolate cake! They just parading us in front of everybody for display. It ain't got

no depth to it, nobody's going to really sit down and interview me on the news. They'll interview her [nods at the professor] or him [nods in the direction of the governor].

This same prisoner predicted that Carla was going to "break it down" for the audience. Carla did not.

Shifting from foot to foot, Carla gripped the microphone attached to the podium and began hesitantly:

Hi, everybody. I know that some of you sitting over there [points to the section of PHW prisoners] know me, but a lot of you over here don't, so here goes. I'm a drug addict and being in this program has made me see that. I didn't always think that about myself but I do now. I guess the reason I wouldn't have called myself that before is 'cause I was blinded by my own negative attitudes and behavior. I thought everything was about me and getting what I wanted. That caused me to do some real crazy things. I sold drugs, a lot of drugs, I stole, I sold my body. I was a criminal thinker, just trying to find the easy way out of situations. . . . I want to apologize to you for that. I want to apologize to the people I victimized, especially my family. This program has made me take responsibility for the things I've done in my life. I no longer call myself a victim, because I had choices and I chose to lie, steal, and manipulate. Now I don't blame others for my situation, I blame myself. . . . But I'm working on myself today and I thank you for giving me this opportunity to be in this program and to become a productive member of society. It's truly, truly changed my life. I'm a better person today, I'm a positive person because this program showed me how.

Carla's speech before the audience was exactly as she and the staff had written it, and was similar to the testimonials given by prisoners at previous press conferences.[5] Toward the end of her speech, tears rolled down her cheeks but she continued to speak in a clear voice. At the conclusion, the audience loudly applauded and the governor approached the microphone and asked if he could hug her. Wiping tears from her eyes, she nodded, and he gave her a brief hug as the shutters from several cameras clicked open and bright lights from the flashes illuminated their faces. The senator came up and shook her hand, as did the drug court judge. Carla, still standing near the podium, smiled broadly at the audience and waved to the prisoners. The senior counselor tapped Joanne Torrence on the arm and pointed to Carla. Torrence strode over to Carla, and patting her on the back, pointed her in the direction of her chair among the prisoners. Carla nodded and quickly took her seat as if embarrassed. The formal part of the press conference concluded with Torrence thanking the guests for coming and inviting everyone to take a tour of the facility.

"Ah shit, she didn't say nothing," one prisoner near me commented to no one in particular. "Yeah," said another, "she's just rentin' out her head." That was the first time I heard the phrase "rentin' out her head." According to Veronica, a prisoner who had served two years in PHW, the phrase refers to a person who allows someone else to define her. She explained:

> The counselors tell you to surrender to the process. Some of us inmates in here call that rentin' out your head. It's when you let somebody else tell you who you are—as a person and as a woman. Nobody knows you in here [points to her chest] but you—I mean really knows you, deep inside. It's OK when people tell you how you're affecting them or whatever, but when you let them define you, you just sold your, your self. Not your body, but your self. If you surrender, they tell you who you are and what you are supposed to become, you know?

When I asked Jen, one of the women who clucked in dismay after Carla's speech, about the phrase, she elaborated:

> She's bought into it. She keeps letting them live in her head rent-free! She wants to make it in here so badly, she'll just let them disrespect her like that. I thought with the way she was acting before her speech she was really going to express herself. You know, break it down to 'em. I was disappointed she didn't, but I understand. We all renting our heads in here to some degree or another. Some just don't want to admit it.

The phrase "renting out your head" refers to a specific pain of imprisonment that is unique to PHW and its control structure—the prison's invasion into the private territories of the self. All prisoners experience pains associated with the loss of autonomy, security, and liberty, and each of these pains carries with it important implications for identity and the self.[6] Incarceration in general constitutes an assault on the self in the sense that it strips prisoners of the material and symbolic markers of their pre-prison identities.[7] Habilitation, with its emphasis on embodied surveillance and narrative control, intensifies this, but it does something more—it aims to destroy the "diseased" self and replace it with something else. In contrast, the core self was not the target of control efforts in rehabilitative paternalism. The "girls" were the victims not of "flawed" selves but of external forces (e.g., men, poverty, sexual violence). The efforts of the staff were rehabilitative in a modernist sense, aimed at resocializing prisoners rather than remaking them.

When PHW prisoners invoke the phrase "rentin' out your head," they are referencing this shift in institutional control and, concomitantly, the ensuing struggle to preserve the integrity of the self. Indeed, the phrase describes, with tremendous insight, the replacement of one's own conceptualization of self with an institutional definition. Instead of challenging PHW's definition of her as diseased and flawed (symbolically conveyed with the physical separation of the prisoners and the suits, as well as by the patronizing tone of many of the speeches), Carla went along with it. She told the story of her life in a manner that was entirely consistent with program narratives (e.g., her own personal deficiencies caused many of the problems she experienced and led her to victimize others). Although Carla was aware of the discrepancies embodied in PHW's claims about who she was as a person, such awareness did not prevent her from using the disease narrative to describe herself and her life to the audience. She defined herself as the institution defined her, and in doing so she "rented out her head" to the institution. She became a vessel through which the institution's definition of the kind of woman who becomes a drug offender was realized.

In this chapter and the next I examine the effects of habilitation from the perspective of those who were its targets—predominantly young, poor, African American women who found themselves incarcerated for fairly petty sorts of drug offenses. For them, habilitation presented a new dilemma that moved well beyond their concerns over when they would be released. They were now confronted with the question of what it meant to "rent out their heads" to a total institution.[8] As Jen said to me of her experience in PHW, "So much humiliation and then to break a person down. What happens if that person can't pick theirself up? Who is she then? Where does her old self go?" This question dominated all my interviews and conversations with PHW prisoners. They were convinced that the program would irrevocably alter their sense of self, and many believed this would be for the worst. All wondered who they would become at the end of their time in prison.

Strategizing the Self

In *Asylums*, Erving Goffman devotes a chapter to exploring the "moral careers" of patients in a mental hospital. The term "moral career" refers to the relationship between intersubjectivity (e.g., individual consciousness, self-awareness, self-definition) and an individual's participation in an organization (e.g., position, status, experiences).[9] Goffman was interested in the process of institutionalization and, in particular, the consequences of identity mortification in total institutions like mental hospitals and prisons. His analysis tracks changes in how patients conceptualize the self as they are processed by and through the mental hospital. He reports that after undergoing a series of abasements, degradations, and profanations of self, mental patients experience a variety of changes with respect to the beliefs they hold about themselves and others around them. Patients learn that defending a respectable vision of the self and making alternate claims about who they "really" are is pointless in the total institution. Every counterclaim and effort to distance oneself from the status of mental patient is widely discredited by institutional staff. Goffman argues that this inability to put forth a respectable image of self leads to a unique adaptation with respect to self-identity:

> Having one's past mistakes and present progress under constant moral review seems to make for a special adaptation consisting of a less than moral attitude to ego ideals. . . . It is not very practicable to try to sustain solid claims about oneself. The setting, then, seems to engender a kind of . . . civic apathy. . . . In the hospital, then, the inmate can learn that the self is not a fortress, but rather a small open city; he can become weary of having to show pleasure when held by troops of his own, and weary of having to show displeasure when held by the enemy.[10]

He concludes that inmates in total institutions develop, over time, an apathy and a numbness toward the self. They undergo a sort of psychic withdrawal in which they are no longer devastated, as they once were, by their degraded status in the institution, nor do they bother to engage in a protracted battle to construct a "respectable" self.[11]

Although Goffman's conclusions are based on his study of patients in a mental hospital, social scientists have frequently made use of them to analyze how institutionalization affects the selves of prisoners.[12] Sociologists Thomas Schmid and Richard Jones, for example, argue that the intensity of new identity demands and the loss of resources like money and one's personal wardrobe constitute a "massive assault" on the selves of all prisoners.[13] In the case of PHW, Goffman's observations about patients' inability to put forth "solid claims" regarding their selves are certainly consistent with prisoners who say they feel as if they are "renting out their heads" to the program. Nonetheless, most women in PHW did not simply divest in the self in the manner of Goffman's mental patients. Consider the tension present in Carla's behavior at the press conference. It is clear from her critical remarks regarding the suits that she did not entirely embrace the institution's view of her self. In other words, she had not succumbed to the institution's claims regarding her identity. At the same time, Carla could hardly be considered to have rejected those identity claims out of hand. She was, as PHW's counselors noted in her file, a model prisoner in the program—one who rarely broke rules and who consistently used addiction rhetoric to describe past experiences in her life, particularly her involvement in criminal activity and drug use. In Carla's case, her expressions of dread and nervousness in anticipation of being "disrespected" by the suits indicate that she was far from ambivalent about her self. The expression of moral feelings such as dread and embarrassment suggest that Carla was engaged in an extended process of self-reflection in which the discrepancy between how she defined herself and how she imagined the suits defined her generated an emotional response.[14] In contrast, Goffman's subjects abandon such self-reflection in favor of "the amoral arts of shamelessness," for they no longer "seek a new robe and a new audience before which to cower."[15]

I argue that habilitation generates a more complex set of responses among prisoners than analytic terms like "civic apathy" or "psychic withdrawal" would suggest. The tension that Carla faced emerged from her conflicting desires to be accepted by the suits and to express a self that was both authentic and respectable. The catch, of course, is that PHW's rules for self-expression are so narrow and limited that counselors interpret any departure from the script as a sign of one's failure in treatment. This generates even greater stigma because prisoners who fail to progress receive demotions in standing within the program and are the targets of an increasing number of staged confrontations. Within the structure of PHW, the only path to respectability is through embracing and "owning" the claims counselors make about the self. To demonstrate that she owns these identity claims, a prisoner must publicly castigate her "diseased" self and narrate her life experiences in a way that emphasizes her own moral blameworthiness. Doing so, however, does not confer respectability in the sense of being accepted as a "normal" or "equal" by the suits. No matter how much progress she makes in treatment and how "conventional" her behavior and actions become, the PHW prisoner will always bear the mark of a diseased self. In the words of counselors, "Addiction is either active or in remission—it's never cured."

Subsequently the dilemma faced by all the prisoners who were "renting out their heads" was how to manage a self that was under siege. Early in my fieldwork, prisoners and counselors told me that habilitation forced prisoners to respond in one of two ways. They either "surrendered to the process," meaning they adopted a definition of the self as diseased, or they "walked with the dead," meaning they refused to accept the program's claims and were subsequently returned to the general prison population. As time wore on, prisoners confided that there were actually three ways to navigate habilitation's demands on the self. As one prisoner explained, "staff will say you have two choices: surrender or die. But there's another way: you can fake it to make it."

The first two strategies, "surrender" and "walking with the dead," can be considered institutionalized in that they are built into the formal structure of the program. PHW is organized to coerce prisoners into abandoning their earlier definitions of self and accepting that the self is flawed and diseased. The prisoners who surrender and embrace the program's claims are following the "official" path that PHW has laid out for them. At the same time, PHW is also organized to handle women who reject and resist these claims. There is, in other words, a contingency path for those who rebel. Prisoners refer to this strategy as "ripping and running." Counselors characterize the women who pursue it as the "walking dead" and subject them to a series of degradations in program standing and increasingly harsh and intense confrontations. For those who continue to rebel despite the sanctions, their career path ends where it began—in the general prison population.

The third strategy stands outside of PHW's formal structure. "Faking it to make it" is designed to circumvent the dilemmas posed by surrender (loss of self) and outright rebellion (additional deprivations). In the remainder of this chapter, I explore the first of these strategies—surrender. In the next, I examine each of the resistance strategies and consider the implications of resistance for prisoners' self-identities. It is important to emphasize that the focus of this chapter is not toward getting at who a person "really" is or whether the prisoners in PHW are the type of people staff say they are. Determining the extent to which the self is at all discoverable is, as Goffman insists, a dubious undertaking.[16] Subsequently, the point is not to gauge the accuracy of the claims staff make about the self; rather, it is to understand how prisoners interpret those claims and their impact on prisoners' articulations of their self-identity.

Surrendering to Habilitation

The vast majority of prisoners who enter PHW (even those who go on to successfully complete the program) are not looking to experience a transformation of self or even to stop using drugs. Most women enter the program for more pragmatic reasons. Many are repeat offenders who face lengthy prison sentences. They volunteer for PHW in the hopes of persuading their sentencing judge or the parole committee to release them on their minimum sentences. Others are directly sentenced into PHW by drug courts and risk a resentencing hearing (and additional prison time) if they fail to complete the program. During the period of this study, 80–90% of the inmates who entered PHW did so for reasons relating to their prison sentence. This is not to suggest that women prisoners in East State are apathetic or unaware of the problems posed by their drug use. Many of the women entering PHW, even those looking for a reduction or modification in time served in prison, desired insight regarding their drug use and criminal activity. Many sought ways to control their drug use or, in the words of several women, to find a "cure" that would allow them to use drugs in moderation.

Of the seventy-four prisoners I interviewed for this study, thirteen reported that they "surrendered" to habilitation. Each of these women went on to complete all five stages of PHW's program. It is important to emphasize that to graduate from the program does not in and of itself imply that one has surrendered to it. Thirty of my respondents graduated from PHW,[17] but just over half told me that they rejected the program's philosophy or its definitions of the self as diseased. Their ability to succeed in the program while simultaneously resisting its claims on the self was based on their strategic efforts to "fake it."

Those who surrendered not only embraced the disease concept and "clean living" philosophy (e.g., avoid people, places, and things associated with drugs, crime, and other "negative" behaviors), they also framed their experiences and self-identities in a manner consistent with the claims put forth by the PHW staff. In interviews and informal conversations, all of these women described themselves as "plugged into the process," "walking the walk," "walking with the living," and "in recovery"—terms that were synonymous with behavioral conformity and identity conversion. Indeed, these were the same phrases used by the counselors to refer to prisoners who were "transformed" by habilitation. In an interview, the senior counselor explained that phrases like "plugged into the process" referred only to those prisoners who wholeheartedly embraced PHW's rules and philosophy:

> [They are] . . . working on their issues, making stuff public in group and listening to what others tell them about it. Holding themselves accountable and taking responsibility for their negative attitudes and behaviors. In other words, surrendering to the process. Fulfilling their job functions without fuss and excessive direction from others, following orders from those above them, taking what is said in confrontation without reacting, and just generally being a good role model to others in the community. In all, they surrender to the therapeutic process, meaning they apply what we tell them to their lives and make changes accordingly.

In other words, women who "surrender" and who are "in recovery" are those who are actively in the process of being transformed. They behave, express themselves, and define themselves and their life experiences differently. The direction of the difference, of course, is in accordance with PHW's normative order. They act, think, and feel in ways that are consistent with program guidelines. On occasion, some of their more critical peers and a handful of prison staff members referred to them as "brainwashed."

In describing their experiences in PHW, women who surrendered often drew sharp contrasts between what they regarded as their old and new selves. Shawna, for example, clarified in an interview what she meant when she referred to herself as "plugged into the program" and "walking the walk":

> When I say that I'm plugged in, or I'm walking the walk, I mean that I've surrendered to the program. I've given it up—all the negativity, the criminality or, I mean, criminal thought patterns, the addictive behaviors, I let it go. I let go of the person who wanted to represent [Shawna] that way. I do what I'm told, I listen to what others are telling me and I think about it. I think about what they're saying 'cause they're helping me see who I really am. I'm a positive person now. I'm not that old, played-out self anymore. I'm doing it in here and I've gained respect for myself that I didn't have before. I thought you didn't let someone tell you what to do or you was letting them disrespect you. Now I know that disrespect comes from degrading yourself whether that's on the street, with a man, using drugs, or whatever.

There is little that appears to differentiate women who ultimately surrendered to habilitation from those who did not. In my interviews with women who surrendered, most admitted entering PHW for reasons other than personal transformation. Four were directly sentenced into PHW and had no choice but to participate or face additional prison time. An additional five had lengthy sentences and hoped their participation would persuade the sentencing judge to modify their prison term. They ranged in age from nineteen to forty-two years, with a median age of thirty-one, which was just one year older than the median age of all PHW prisoners. Their discussions of the regularity and intensity of their drug use, as well as their experiences on the street, were generally consistent with how other respondents described their drug use and street activity. All admitted to using drugs one or more times a week, particularly crack, cocaine, and heroin. Eleven of the women had been in a drug treatment program before and had relapsed at least once, and all referred to themselves as "addicts," although in most cases they did not use that term prior to entering PHW. In fact, eight of the thirteen respondents recalled that they did not apply the term "addict" to themselves prior to entering the program, while five respondents were unclear with respect to when they began to define themselves in this way. Sheila's ambiguous response to the question of when she first began calling herself an addict was consistent with answers given by the other four women:

> When? I don't know, I've always *been* an addict [her emphasis]. You are what you are, you know? It's like the counselors say, you know, I was using at age fifteen but I was an addict long before that. I just hadn't picked up yet but I had all the elements of an addict then. . . . It's like they say, there's something wrong with the person long before they pick up the drug. It's like if you find out you got HIV, it don't matter when you found it—it's been there you just didn't know it. You was HIV positive before you started thinking about yourself like that. That's like addiction, I don't know when I said it, but I've always been it.

There is a marked tendency among the women who surrendered to forget the interpretative frames they used to understand their experiences and their worlds prior to entering PHW. The tendency to confound the present with the past is exemplified in Sheila's failure to identify the point at which she actively began using the term "addict" to describe herself. In the sections that follow I will explore the reasons why they, more so than other prisoners, are prone to conflate present and past. The point here is to demonstrate that they are not much different from other women who come to the program in terms of their identity as drug users. They did not come to the program calling themselves addicts, nor were they motivated to enter PHW solely for drug treatment.

The one quality that did distinguish them involved their feelings about drug use *prior* to entering PHW. They, more so than other prisoners, described themselves as feeling tremendously "tired" from drugs and associated components of the drug-using lifestyle (most notably, extensive contact with the criminal justice system). Most had served several prison and probation terms, and many had been in and out of rehabilitation programs. They blamed their recidivism on drug relapses. Although Dallas was sentenced to PHW by the courts, she explained she was willing to try treatment because she was "exhausted" from her drug use:

> I had been in treatment before and relapsed. Two times. I went to a twenty-eight-day program, stayed clean eight months, and then relapsed. Then I went to a six-month program . . . stayed clean nineteen months and

then relapsed. And I was out, out using again for like eight months and I got incarcerated for violation of probation.[18] I was tired when I went in there [PHW], I just wanted to get back into treatment so I could get myself together. I don't want to relapse no more. I'm done with that deal.

Melissa described her life outside her prison stints as frantic:

In and out, in and out. I'm just so tired. I come here [prison] for a rest. I would rest while I'm here and then I would be back out and start using drugs again, within the first hour. And now I'm looking differently at things. I can't keep it up, it's killing me—that's how tired I feel with the whole thing. It's not even pleasurable anymore. I've got two kids I have to raise, and I haven't been employed and that really bothers me.

It bears repeating that other prisoners in the program have also been in and out of prison, probation, and various treatment programs. What differentiates prisoners who surrender is not their recidivism or the intensity of their drug use, but their feelings about their use. All expressed feeling "tired," "worn out," "beat," and "downed" by their drug use and lifestyles. Unlike many of their peers, they entered PHW with an increasingly negative view of drugs. Indeed, upon entering prison, these women reported that they did not look forward to their next opportunity to get high or "party," but instead spent a great deal of time worrying about their next relapse.

It is worth noting that the exhaustion with drugs that the women who surrender experience is distinct from alcoholics' narrative of "hitting bottom."[19] Hitting bottom involves losing important aspects of one's public identity (e.g., job, home, family, personal appearance) as the result substance abuse.[20] The experience serves to profoundly destabilize the way alcoholics and addicts conceptualize their use of alcohol and other drugs. For example, the subjects in Denzin's ethnography of Alcoholics Anonymous report that hitting bottom causes them to problematize, often for the first time, their drinking and to seek out new frameworks with which to understand it.[21] The women who surrender to habilitation were also in search of new ways to think about their drug use, although they did not account for this in terms of "hitting bottom" or the loss of social standing. Indeed, for nearly all the prisoners in PHW, the absence of steady employment, the experience of being arrested, losing one's home, having a family member or loved one break off a relationship or die unexpectedly, surviving physical and sexual violence, street hustling, and struggling with chronic medical conditions were recurring patterns in their lives. They did not characterize these experiences as "hitting bottom" or describe them as turning points in the way they interpreted their drug use. Instead, women who surrendered spoke of recurring tragedies as events that added weight to their weariness. In many respects, poverty made these women considerably more resilient than Denzin's subjects. They were not overwhelmed by any one particular experience, but struggled to survive them all. The shift in their thinking about drug use was gradual. They initially regarded drugs as an important part of their survival because drugs provided momentary relief from emotional pain, were a source of income and personal esteem, and provided a vital force around which social ties were created and maintained. Ultimately, however, the weight of the struggle to survive in communities marked by poverty, crime, declining institutional supports, and violence outstripped the momentary relief and pleasure that drugs afforded. As they considered their situations, women who surrendered began to modify their thinking about drugs. As they saw it, it was necessary to gain control over their drug use so that they could maintain families, relationships, and income, and avoid further prosecution.[22] As one prisoner who surrendered recalled:

> I was a cashier for a parking garage and I used to stand there and pray for help to get off drugs, 'cause I knew that I was spending too much money on cocaine. That's all I knew, that's how my life was a mess. I was spending too much money and I was praying to get off, and when I went to jail, and when I woke up in prison, I got on my knees and I prayed and I said, "Thank you." 'Cause I knew why I was there. I knew that that was my help to get off drugs, but I didn't think I was a real addict. I just needed some help to get off cocaine.

Their desire to reinterpret and control their drug use set the foundation for how they reacted to the disease concept and the demands it placed on the self. Using Goffman's concept of a moral career, we can trace the impact of habilitation on their self-identities in terms of three distinct stages.[23] The first stage occurs prior to their entry into PHW and involves, as I've described above, a new, decidedly more critical perspective on drug use. Although most women did not consider themselves addicts, nor did they want to quit using altogether, they did express a sincere desire to reinterpret and reconfigure their drug use. This made them decidedly more open to learning about the disease concept, and paved the way for stage two, in which they practiced narrating their life experiences solely in terms of their drug use and addiction. In the third stage of their moral careers, they were so thoroughly invested in the narratives of the disease that they could not think of their life in other terms. It is here that they surrender the self.

Centering Addiction

During PHW's mandatory thirty-day orientation period for incoming prisoners, counselors spent a great deal of time explaining that drug use of any kind, including the use of legal drugs such as alcohol and prescription tranquilizers, was wrong.[24] Prisoners were told that any type of drug use, no matter how much or how little, was problematic because it contributed to immoral behavior, criminality, poverty, and contact with criminal justice agencies. Unlike many of their peers, the women who went on to surrender embraced this new normative framework from the start. They accepted that drug use of any kind was wrong. Many went so far as to give up smoking cigarettes and a few stopped placing requests with the medical office for over-the-counter pain medications such as Midol. When I asked Shawna, who was literally doubled over with pain from menstrual cramps, why she did not take an aspirin she explained:

> The one thing I've learned so far in here and something which I truly believe is that there is no good drugs, not even legal ones. You can get addicted to anything, any substance, if you use it to cure your problems and too much of any substance is bad. And I've learned that using drugs will only cause more problems for you and your problems will always be there. They'll take away your pain, but you'll still have pain the next day.

Their willingness to not only accept but also embrace the staff's critical perspective on drugs set them apart from other PHW prisoners, the vast majority of whom continued to smoke cigarettes and use over-the-counter medications throughout their time in the program.[25]

In communicating that drug use was wrong, staff introduced new prisoners to the disease model and their theory of addiction. Through confrontations, counselors demonstrated how addiction was causally linked to traumatic events in the prisoners' lives, as well as to their current thoughts, feelings, and behaviors. The content of these confrontations has been discussed fairly extensively in earlier chapters, however, it is important to add here that counselors spent a great deal of time eliciting information from prisoners about traumatic experiences and then demonstrating how addiction was directly or indirectly implicated in them. For example, Leda (known in the program for being shy and unemotional) broke down during a group session after one of the counselors repeatedly asked her why she hated herself so much. With tears rolling slowly down her cheeks, Leda told a heart-wrenching story of how, as a small child, she had been badly burned after a dress she was wearing caught fire when she came in contact with a coal-burning stove. Her legs and lower torso were horribly scarred and she spent her childhood being tormented by other kids who called her, among other things, "retard," "freak," and "monster." She concluded her story by revealing that even her mother acted ashamed of her and had allowed her siblings to make fun of her. When she finished, the senior counselor told her that she should never feel ashamed of her body and then went on to link the experience to addiction:

> Your addiction has kept this alive in you. Instead of being able to pro-
> cess those things that took place in your childhood, you've held it and it's
> become this thing inside eating away at you. You can't blame them now,
> it's your addiction. You used to numb the pain, but the drugs kept it alive.
> Your inability to process it or even to talk about it is part of your addiction.
> The addiction finds ways to keep us in pain because that's how it feeds
> itself. It knows as long as you're in pain, you'll keep using and that's what
> it wants—the drugs, the self-destruction, the immorality. It feeds on that.

As this example demonstrates, even when painful experiences could not be directly linked to drug use (e.g., she did not use drugs until much later in her life), counselors still found ways to implicate addiction in the experience. In this case, as in many other sessions dealing with childhood traumas, staff informed prisoners that it was their addiction that fueled feelings of self-hatred rather than the torture they suffered from others.

Subsequently, during orientation prisoners learn to regard drug use not just under a new set of normative guidelines (e.g., drugs are bad) but also in terms of a particular interpretative structure (e.g., addiction is a disease of the self). Within this framework, drug use is regarded as an outgrowth of the disease of addiction, the symptoms of which involve patterns of living, as well as current states of thinking and behaving. Beyond this, they learn a new vocabulary for describing experiences and a new discourse for expressing the self. Following the thirty-day orientation period, prisoners were not allowed to express themselves without using PHW vocabulary and discourse. The vast majority of PHW prisoners, even those who were resistant to the program's ideology, learned to use the vocabulary and to link experiences in their life to drugs and addiction. What differentiated women who surrendered to habilation is not only that they become exceedingly adept at casting their life history in terms of disease rhetoric (so much so that their stories are virtually identical to one another), but that they become incapable of conceptualizing their lives in any other terms. Consider the similarity of each of the following stories from life history interviews I conducted with two women, Red and Ice, both of whom described themselves as having surrendered:

I started drinking when I was nine or ten, and the first time I smoked pot I was thirteen. My brother was an alcoholic, always in trouble with the cops—actually he's serving a life term right now, but anyway he smoked a lot, and a friend and I got a hold of his bong one day and smoked it, or I should say tried to smoke 'cause I didn't really know how to use it. Anyway, after that I partied with friends and stuff on the weekends and my dad was so pissed, he basically ended up kicking me out—well, I ran away and I started hanging out with my cousin who shot up, you know, and I told her I had done it before so she would give me some and she did. . . . When my mom found the needle and shit she wanted me to shoot her up, that's real crazy I know, so it's like in my addiction I turned my mom on to heroin and like my addiction didn't just want me, it wanted her, too. Well, I was still hanging with my cousin and I didn't know it but she was prostituting for the money for the drugs and after a while I started up with that, too, 'cause I didn't want her to always have to do it. . . . The addict took over when I was little, I was always bad, a real disrespectful creep. I can remember that much. I showed a lot of disrespect to my dad, even when he would take me out back with the switch. I'd be scared to death, but I didn't always listen. Now, I can see he was trying to hold me accountable, but I didn't want none of that. . . . So, it's like eventually I did a lot of prostituting, selling my body, and when I got sick of that I started robbing . . . holding up convenience stores and stuff, but I never hurt nobody doing it, I mean physically. I did hurt a lot of people by victimizing them. I just wanted what I wanted when I wanted it and that's how I lived my life. (Red, twenty-seven years old, white)

My life up till now has been basically about my drugs and my needs, you know, trying to get what I wanted when I wanted it. I didn't know I was an addict for a long time, but now that I see that, everything kinda makes sense. Everything that I didn't understand before, like why I was so tired when I come in here [prison]. I couldn't get a grip on it till now, but it's that I have the disease of addiction. The signs were there when I was little, like I had problems with my parents when I was little, I used to get in so much trouble and be so disrespectful, but it's like I couldn't stop myself. And I started hanging out with the wrong crowd, you know, and experimenting with marijuana, then speed, then crack, and like there weren't no good reason for doing none of it except that I had this pain and need to get high. I always wanted the next rush, you know? The pain is from the disease trying to get me all keyed up. . . . Addiction really caused me to disrespect myself, I mean I started doing a lot of drugs when I was prostituting, you know, to cover up the feelings about that and I would steal stuff from the men 'cause I was mad at them. Can you imagine that! I'm the one out there selling myself and I'm mad at them and stealing their wallets and their car phones while I'm giving them blow jobs. I was really fucked up. I'm lucky I didn't get my ass kicked for being such a creep. But anyway, it just continued like that with me using every day or every other day, and prostituting, and selling rock on the side sometimes. I was a real fucking mess. (Ice, thirty-six years old, African American)

Each of these narratives is configured so that drug use is the central focus in the women's life histories. The experiences in their lives can all be neatly organized around a single category: addiction. When I asked women who surrendered to tell me about their lives, a few asked if I meant about their drug histories. Most assumed that is what I meant and began their stories with the first time they used drugs or alcohol. Their narratives follow a similar pattern, one that was apparent in Carla's testimonial at the press conference. Women who identified as having surrendered began their stories with a description of the first time they used, and then they rattled off the various types of drugs they tried and how they were introduced to them. They explained their drug use in terms of impulsive needs and cravings for the high, and emphasized their own moral accountability. Indeed, the theme of accountability figures prominently, as does disrespect, when they discussed their crimes, painful relationships, and traumatic experiences. Strained relations with family members, for example, were the result of their "disrespectful" behavior toward an authority figure when that individual attempted to hold them "accountable" for their actions. They explained their drug use and criminal activity by referring to characteristics of their "addictive" personality ("I want what I want when I want it"). The similar format of the stories is not necessarily because these women have lived the same sorts of lives,[26] but because they are required to speak about their lives using a very specific narrative format. The structure of the narrative is nicely captured in the lyrics of a rap song one prisoner wrote about her experiences in PHW:

We didn't love ourselves and we didn't know what for,
Until we walked through the [PHW] door,
We got into groups to recoup. To let go the guilt, and the pain.
We were so strung out that we were insane.
We found our higher power, he was by our side.
And then we realized we didn't have no pride.
We had to learn our thoughts on our own,
Getting pulled to the floor is making us strong.
[PHW, PHW]
[PHW, PHW]
Making us aware of a lot of pain,
Using drugs has slowed down our brain.
We made a truce to get our lives back,
We made a decision not to smoke no more crack.
[PHW] opened up our eyes, now we see,
Life isn't easy so why should recovery be?

This format is similar to the narrative structure reported in previous studies of therapeutic communities, and has been referred to as a "programmed" or "mechanical" style of interaction.[27] In discussing their lives, these women described virtually everything in terms of drug use and addiction metaphors, emphasized their own blameworthiness in the events that had transpired, and categorized various feelings, thoughts, and actions in terms of "positive" and "negative" valences. The prevalence of this sort of talk (referred to by counselors as "recovery talk") is, as I have noted elsewhere, a product of the program structure.[28] Subsequently, control in PHW creates a tightly organized interaction order in which prisoners express themselves using only the official vocabulary and approved styles of talking. All prisoners, at one point or another, described their lives according to this narrative format, and most prisoners used this format quite frequently. What distinguishes women who surrender from the others is that this format assumes a hegemonic status in their repertoire, such that they become incapable of conceptualizing their lives in terms that depart from the disease concept. This creates the memory problem I mentioned earlier. The women I interviewed could not remember how they conceptualized their lives before they entered PHW. When asked about the first time they referred to themselves as "addicts," several respondents could not remember and instead indicated that they were "always" addicts. For example, I interviewed Red twice: once when she had been in the program for less than a month, and again a year later (portions of this later interview are included at the beginning of this section). In the earlier interview, she talked extensively about her father's frequent use of amphetamines and alcohol, and the aggression and violence that followed his drug use. He beat Red, her mother, and her brother frequently when he was high, so much so that her mother began regularly using prescription pain relievers and later, after she discovered Red's "works" (i.e., drug paraphernalia), she began injecting heroin. After one episode when her father discovered that Red was smoking marijuana, he beat her with a tree branch and told her to get out of the house. She left and moved in with her cousin.

After being in PHW for a year, Red recounted the same events but did so in a way that emphasized her own moral blameworthiness. In the second interview, for example, she minimized her father's violence and suggested that she encouraged it through her "disrespectful" behavior. Further, she corrected herself when she began to say he kicked her out of the house, and instead framed the episode in terms of her own actions ("I ran away"). Finally, Red suggested that she was responsible for her mother's heroin use ("I turned my mom on to heroin"). During the second interview, she volunteered that PHW made her "see" her life in a "whole new way" but could not remember how she had previously accounted for her experiences. After I showed her sections of the transcript from the previous interview, she commented:

RED: It's weird, I can't even remember some of those things anymore. My dad, I just hadn't thought about it that way in so long. I'm not sure, I mean, I feel like this is what happened, how it happened, what I'm saying to you today, you know? I just can't really remember, I mean I remember parts of it, like how angry he got, I'm thinking about that—

JM: Why do you think you forgot some of this stuff?

RED: I don't know, I mean it seemed that for a lot of my life I couldn't understand things that other people did and I didn't think I had a brain that I couldn't, you know, that I couldn't comprehend things but it was probably because I was doing drugs. That's why I couldn't comprehend things and now that I haven't had nothing in my system it's like I catch on to things so fast. . . . The counselors call it PAW. Like post–acute withdrawal, I had that when I first came in the program. Like for my first seven months I couldn't remember nothing. Seven, eight, maybe even nine months. But like these past few months, you know, I read something and I can remember the next day and a week from now. That's my best guess what happened, everything was so clouded then,

> I understand things much better now in terms of my own life and stuff
> that I learn in here about, you know, like the medical aspects of addic-
> tion or different drugs.

What women like Red remembered most clearly were those events and circumstances in which their drug use was directly implicated, experiences that made sense in terms of the new interpretative frame they had acquired in the program. Without a linguistic structure in which to constitute other experiences (most notably, those not directly linked to drug use), those experiences fall away and fade from memory. Over time as the prisoners became increasingly fluent in therapeutic discourse, their narratives began to mirror the narratives the counselors used when they discussed the life of a particular prisoner. Prisoners who surrendered consistently emphasized the centrality of drugs in their lives, their moral blameworthiness, and various personality deficits associated with the program's disease concept of addiction. That they did so is critical because it laid the foundation for the final stage in their moral careers—the reformulation of their self-identities.

Surrendering the Self

A number of prisoners in PHW developed critical perspectives on drug use and became adept at narrating their lives in a manner consistent with the disease concept. The majority, however, stopped short of surrendering their selves. The women who did replaced their earlier definitions of self with the definitions supplied by PHW. In other words, these prisoners became who counselors told them they were. This third stage of their moral career is more tenuous than the previous two. Prior to entering PHW, these women had already decided that they were interested in finding new ways to think about and control their drug use. In PHW they learned that drug use is part of a disease process that affects all major areas of their lives. For the most part, they made the behavioral, cognitive, and emotional changes that counselors demanded of them without protest. They observed the program's rules for behavior, learned the vocabulary, and revised their ways of thinking in accordance with the staff's philosophy of addiction. They offered little, if any, criticism of the suitability of that philosophy for explicating the events that shaped their lives. Very few problems emerged during their first few months in the program. Of those that did, the most serious involved their trouble remembering certain experiences and ways of thinking and feeling. But this, too, was thematized as part of their addiction and was used by the staff to show how insidious the disease of addiction can be to the self.

The goals of habilitation, however, require more than temporary invest-ment in a particular discursive framework—they require a transformation of self. It is the self of women drug offenders, after all, that is problematized by everyone from line staff to administrators, state officials, and Company executives. It is at this stage that many women who are making satisfactory progress in treatment, and who accept the disease concept of addiction, stop short of meeting the program's expectations. For many women, accepting PHW's claims about who they "really" are is problematic and considerably more difficult than simply referring to themselves as addicts. This raises the question of how the women who surrendered the self were able to do so, given that many did not enter PHW thinking they were addicts. Dallas, for example, reports being offended by counselors calling her a "junkie" during her first day in the program:

> Oh, I remember how insulting I thought it all was, you know, being called names, silly names, by the counseling staff and them telling me that I'm just another junkie. You know, saying real insulting things and I was real offended. I was thinking to myself, what kind of treatment program breaks people down like this, you know? Why you got to be tearing us down?

All thirteen of the women who surrendered recounted similar experiences in reaction to some of the imputations staff made about their selves during early confrontation sessions. In response, the women would often challenge staff members or walk away from the confrontation session. In an interview, Red recalled her reaction when a counselor called her a "dingbat" after she had failed to file some paperwork on time:

> I did not like nobody calling me a "one-day dingbat" because it made me feel like they were telling me I was stupid or something because I forgot. You know what I mean? And I ended up cussing them out for the first time, you know, and going to my room.

Counselors called Sedra a "damn dingbat" and a "disrespectful creep" during a confrontation session. She reacted differently than did Red but expressed a similar level of frustration:

> The first time they put me on the floor, I stayed there. I took it. I think it wasn't until the second or third time that I, um, she [counselor] started hollering at me real, real loud and what happened was . . . I don't like peo-ple to holler at me 'cause if you holler at me I won't listen to you. And, um,

I got so frustrated that I couldn't say nothing back to her and I started crying 'cause I just wanted to cuss her ass out. I didn't allow people to disrespect me and say what they wanted to say to me when I was on the street and I'm definitely not going to do it when I come to jail, that's what I was thinking.

In fact, a number of the women went from being model newcomers to unruly prisoners in a relatively short amount of time (usually in the first two or three weeks following their completion of the orientation phase) and they did so in response to the confrontation sessions. Toward the end of their second or third month in the program, however, these women went back to being model prisoners again. They were rarely subject to confrontation and when they were, they verbally acknowledged the legitimacy of the claims made by staff about their selves. For example, after Sedra had been in PHW for five months, she told me that she accepted claims the counselors made about her irresponsible parenting:

Now I see that not only have I fucked my life up, I caused a lot of hurt, too, in my family. Like my father and my kids, you know what I mean? I caused—I did a lot of crazy, crazy shit to people that really do love me, you know what I mean? I started thinking about, like, my son was three the first time I ever came to jail and he's fourteen now. . . . I did a lot of crazy shit and what I need to do is change my life and get myself together. . . . Yeah, I'm like on the outside now looking in. That was real fucked up to do that crime, that was real fucked up to do that.

They had not only become adept at using disease rhetoric to express themselves, but had fully incorporated this rhetoric into their self-conceptualizations. Red, after thirteen months in the program, described her new sense of self:

Once I realized that, that I was an addict and I was always going to be an addict—that there wasn't going to be a cure, because I was basically looking for a little cure [laughing]. . . . OK, I can't be cured and just go on and do anything else I want to do. . . . It did change how I felt about myself. Because I had, like I said I had no skills when I came in here and when I looked back at—when I looked at myself and they [counselors] asked me a question, you know, "What have you accomplished while you was on drugs?" And I was like, "How to do a crime a different way." That was the first thing, you know what I mean, and still get caught at it!! [laughing]

> That's the first thing I thought and, um, I was like I could not think of nothing positive. You know, and I was like, you know, do I want to be an addict in my addiction or do I want to be a recovering addict with some things under my belt and, you know, some kind of civility.

I interviewed Mikki two months after she graduated from PHW. She reported still having to work hard every day to embrace the staff's claims about her self and to accept this definition as her own:

> I do a moral inventory of myself every day. I sit there and allow myself to be disintegrated 'cause that's what it [cocaine] did.[29] I mean, just like, a vacuum cleaner, that's how I allowed cocaine to do me. I hate it, I do. But it was a drug that I loved. *I hate the things it caused me—I hated the things that I allowed it to do 'cause nobody didn't do it but me.* Nobody forced me to use. [my emphasis]

Although my interview with Mikki took place after she was released from prison, she still remembered to correct herself when she departed from PHW's narrative script. In this excerpt, she began to say that drug use caused her to do certain things but midway through she corrected herself and emphasized her own blameworthiness ("I hated the things I allowed it to do").

The adoption of a new discourse combined with high levels of surveillance and intense confrontation sessions proved overwhelming for women who already entered the program weary from their drug use. The excerpt from Red's interview is useful in demonstrating this point. During her first few months in the program, Red learned to talk about her life according to the program's addiction narrative. She focused on her drug use and the criminal activities that coincided with that use and began to re-evaluate her understanding of traumatic life events that were seemingly unrelated to her drug use (such as her father's violence). She adopted this new narrative structure willingly because she was tired of her drug use and seeking a way to control it. As the confrontation sessions with staff grew more intense and counselors attempted to "break her down" by revealing what her addiction had caused her to become, Red balked and "cussed" at the staff. For violating the program's rules of interaction during the confrontation, the counseling staff punished her with sixty hours of cleaning. Her second infraction, which came after she protested being referred to as a "whore" and a "crackhead," resulted in forty-three hours of cleaning, loss of phone privileges, three days in an isolation cell, and an hour-long seminar in which she had to detail the history of her drug use before an audience of staff and prisoners. Her third infraction resulted in another sixty hours of cleaning and additional restrictions. For Red, challenging the claims staff made about her self no longer seemed worth it:

> I did that last sixty hours and I just, I got tired of cleaning. I don't know, it was just real, it was hard. It was hard for me when I first came in this program. I thought they were disrespecting me and I was defending myself, but what do I know, I mean I'm sitting here in prison for robbery.

In this sense, women like Red did not so much choose to acquire a new definition of self. Rather, they quite literally surrendered to the claims the staff made. They abandoned their efforts to defend the self in order to avoid additional sanctions. The result is that the self is transformed in the sense that the staff's claims supplant any understanding the prisoner may have previously maintained. When a counselor asked Red what she accomplished during the years she used drugs, she was unable to think of anything beyond her criminal activity. This is not because Red had no accomplishments—she had, during those years, returned to school and completed high school equivalency classes and was awarded a diploma, raised her son, worked three jobs at a time to support him, and successfully enrolled her mother into a counseling program for her heroin use. None of these things occurred to her during the confrontation because she had learned to frame her life according to the program's narrative structure. When she looked back over her life, she saw the same things that staff did—drug use, prostitution, robbery, and incarceration.

Subsequently, the final stage in the moral career of these women comes with the acknowledgment that the imputations the program makes about the self are correct. In interviews, they said that the confrontations ultimately "opened their eyes" and caused something in them to "click," which made them realize that staff were "right all along." What "clicked," of course, was a particular discursive strategy they were forced to use on a daily basis for months at a time. As they adopted a new frame for viewing their lives, the claims staff made about their selves became more plausible. The staff's claims that they were unfit mothers, for example, took on greater legitimacy as prisoners were required to emphasize the selfish motives underlying their criminal activity. In framing income from criminal pursuits as an example of one's greedy nature ("I want what I want when I want it") instead of as a logical response to material deprivation, prisoners came to regard their actions as "crazy" and "fucked up" since such behaviors resulted in incarceration—which, in turn, affected their children. Seen from this perspective, women surrendered to the staff's claims that they were "unfit mothers" because they had become accustomed to thinking about their actions as indirectly victimizing their children.

With a new perspective on their self-identity, the women reported feeling "shocked," "horrified," and "disgusted" by the behaviors they engaged in on the street and the "kind of person" they felt themselves to be. Their choice, as Red framed it in an earlier quote, was either to reject habilation and remain an "addict in addiction," or to surrender to it and become a "recovering addict." Either choice carries with it an acknowledgment of one's enduring stigma since it is, according to the staff, a flawed self that encourages addiction in the first place. There were no opportunities in PHW for the flawed self to become normal or whole again. However, by embracing the identity of "recovering addict" prisoners could distance themselves from the more egregious qualities of their addict selves (e.g., selfishness, immorality) and gain, again to quote Red, "some kind of civility."

Conclusion

Counselors and prison administrators regarded the women who surrendered as shining examples of PHW's success. These women increasingly relied on addiction narratives not only to make sense of the contradictions in their lives, but also to resolve contradictions in their self-identities. For them, surrender meant that the locus of identity construction shifted from the individual to the institution such that they became entirely dependent on the institution to supply the narratives around which they fitted their lives. They became what they were told they were. Of all the prisoners I interviewed for this project, these women most closely conformed to Goffman's claim that total institutions engender among patients a civic apathy toward the self.[30] For them, habilation "worked" in the sense that it brought about the destruction of their old selves.

But habilation "worked" only on a comparatively small scale and, as we will see, its usefulness in helping women navigate the complexities of their lives following their release from prison was limited. It bears repeating that women who surrendered constituted less than a quarter of the entire population of prisoners in PHW. Among the overwhelming majority, habilation generated something less than a total shift in the management and construction of self-identity.

7

Unruly Selves

Forms of Prisoner Resistance

I can see this program for what it is—it's just like jail only they want
to fuck with your head. Why would anyone surrender to that?
—Prisoner, on why she chose to "rip and run" from PHW

Our ability to resist control, or our submission to it, has to be
assessed at the level of our every move.
—Gilles Deleuze, *Negotiations*

One summer afternoon, a prisoner I did not know passed me a note as I
walked down the long corridor to the PHW unit. It turned out that the note
was from Meesha, an African American prisoner in her early twenties who
had recently been kicked out of the program. In it, she indicated that she
had been placed in the prison's maximum security housing unit and that she
urgently needed to speak with me. I received permission from the deputy
warden to visit her later that week. As we spoke, she recounted a long list
of flagrant rule violations she had engaged in at PHW, a list that included
refusing to participate in treatment activities, fighting with another prisoner,
and threatening to harm a member of the counseling staff. When I initially
heard that Meesha had been kicked out for fighting, I was shocked. She did
not have a reputation in prison as a fighter and, in fact, was anxious to get
home as quickly as possible because she had recently been accepted into a
community college. As we talked more, I pressed her about why she engaged
in activities that she knew would jeopardize her early release and, potentially,
her admission to college. She was firm in her response: "I refuse to surrender
my head to them. I did what I had to do, they wouldn't have let me out [of
PHW] otherwise." Meesha's defiance came at a significant cost. She had to
serve an additional fifteen months in prison and she lost her spot among the

incoming freshman class at the community college. But she was not alone in making a dramatic exit from PHW. A number of women engaged in similar acts of violence and rebellion in the hopes of being kicked out of the program. Indeed, during the program's first two years of operation, the dropout rate ranged from 60% to 90%.

In its original guise, PHW was to house up to a quarter of the prison's most drug-involved inmates during the final twelve to fifteen months of their level-five sentence.[1] Prison administrators and Company executives initially stipulated that prisoners should enter the program voluntarily, on the premise that those who chose habilitation would be more open to its ideology and techniques. Optimally, they hoped that most who entered would be like the women profiled in the previous chapter—weary from drugs and willing to entertain a new way of thinking about themselves and their drug use and criminal involvement. Of course, PHW's philosophy of addiction tempered much of this optimism. Addicts, according to the program's ideology, could hardly be expected to pursue a course of action that did not immediately gratify some need. To that end, representatives from the Company and the Committee encouraged prison administrators to provide incentives to prisoners who successfully completed PHW, most notably good-time credit and sentence modification. Almost immediately, this presented a number of problems. Chief among them was the fact that the structure of prisoners' sentences varied. In most cases it was judges and parole boards, not prison administrators, who had the final say in when a prisoner would be released.[2] In the case of mandatory sentences, there was nothing anyone could do to release a prisoner prior to the expiration of her minimum. Exacerbating this issue was the fact that neither prison authorities, Company executives, nor Committee members had initiated any formal arrangements with sentencing authorities regarding the proposed incentive system. As a result, there was a tremendous amount of confusion among prisoners and prison staff regarding what participation in PHW would mean in terms of overall length of stay in prison.

The consequences of that confusion within the prison were significant. Nearly half the prisoners who entered PHW in those first few months dropped out, complaining that they had been lied to by prison administrators about sentence modifications and good-time credit. A number of women entered the program only to find out that their mandatory sentences made them ineligible for early release. Others were granted early release but did not actually get it because of a lack of bed space for women in the state's halfway houses. Although none of these prisoners exited the program in as dramatic a fashion as Alicia (whose infamous departure generated a round of applause among an audience of general population inmates and correctional officers), the stories of their grievances against PHW circulated widely throughout the prison. Many general population inmates were already suspicious of PHW because of persistent rumors that the program made women "bark like dogs" for medication and forced them to wear diapers and carry baby bottles as a form of punishment.[3] As a result, the staff's efforts to recruit new prisoners into PHW stalled at the very moment the attrition rate began to soar.

Under pressure from the granting agency, state officials, and prison administrators to get their numbers up, PHW implemented a number of modifications designed both to liberalize admission policies and to make exit from the program more difficult. First, criteria for admission became less stringent. Previously, PHW admitted only those prisoners with "serious" drug and alcohol histories. Generally, these were women who had previously served time in prison on drug charges or those whose drug use was so extreme that they appeared unable to survive on the street. While this latter group did indeed symbolize to many in the state the problem of women's drug use, they constituted a minority of those incarcerated. The majority of inmates could be described as "drug involved." Drug-involved women are capable of street survival but they regularly use illicit substances, their lives are at least partially structured by the acquisition, intake, and sales of such substances, and they have been admitted to prison because they violated the terms of probation, usually for a positive drug test. Under the modified policy, PHW counselors requested that the prison classification committee forward the names of all newly admitted inmates who reported *any* history of regular drug or alcohol use. Counselors then met with these prisoners and encouraged them to seek treatment in PHW.

The second and most controversial change to the admission policy involved a reversal of the program's commitment to inmate volunteerism. The Committee and the sentencing commission engineered a deal that allowed judges, at their own discretion, to sentence prisoners directly into PHW.[4] Dr. Nesbitt, vice president of the Company, explained the break in the program's stance toward volunteerism this way:

Voluntary entrance is an ambiguous notion to begin with. . . . Can we really say who enters treatment on their own, versus those who are doing it for a family member or spouse? There is at least one study which I'm aware of showing coercion into treatment is more than just the court ordering someone to go there, it's the family members. Anyway, they [researchers] haven't found that there is any difference in success between those who are [court-ordered] into treatment and those who enter voluntarily. We did this because we think it will get more women into treatment who need to be here, women who might not otherwise get into treatment because they don't think they have a problem, or because an abusive spouse might prevent them from getting treatment. We see it as helping clients.

At the same time that PHW was broadening its eligibility requirements, it also sought to make dropping out more difficult. Among the changes made to the exit policy was a mandatory waiting period that required all prisoners (those who had been sentenced into the program as well as those who had entered voluntarily) to wait thirty days before petitioning either the classification committee or the judge to be removed from PHW. Previously, women who desired to leave PHW could write a letter to the classification board, which would, with the recommendation of PHW staff, reclassify them to another unit in the prison. The process usually took no more than two weeks and was often resolved in three to four days. The new restriction prevented women from initiating this process until they had completed thirty days in the program.[5] It also stipulated that before being classified to a new unit in the prison, dropouts would serve an unspecified amount of time in the prison's maximum security housing unit, which was notorious for inmate fights, "crazy" behavior, and conditions that resembled solitary confinement. Women who absolutely refused to participate in the treatment program during the mandatory thirty days were locked in an isolation cell within the PHW unit.

Both Joanne Torrence and Dr. Nesbitt justified these changes by suggesting that incoming prisoners were "still in their addiction" and were unable to make sound judgments with respect to habilitation. By forcing them to remain in the program, the PHW staff felt that they could work on the prisoners' "negative thinking patterns" and encourage them to see that participation in the program would help them overcome their "disease." In one meeting with administrators and state officials, Torrence claimed:

> Research shows that once they're in for thirty days, they're less likely to drop out. If we can get them over that hump, I'm sure we can reduce the attrition rate. The best way to do it is work on them while they're here, get them to see how messed up they are, and make leaving look less attractive.

Policies that liberalized the admission process, as well as those that made exit from the program more difficult, did serve to increase referrals to PHW and reduce the attrition rate. The addition of coercive measures to prevent prisoners from leaving, however, did not take effect in a particularly smooth manner. The only way prisoners could leave the program prior to the expiration of the thirty-day waiting period was to violate one of the three "cardinal rules" (violence, drug use, or sexual relations), which all but guaranteed immediate expulsion. Anxious, but unable to leave, many women like Meesha engaged in behaviors, such as fighting and other forms of violence, in an effort to be expelled back to general population. Their rebellion was motivated by an intense desire to defend the self.[6]

Ripping and Running

"Ripping and running" is a phrase commonly used by all PHW prisoners, as well as general population inmates, to refer to a variety of experiences on the street and within the criminal justice system. The phrase typically describes situations in which an actor got over on the system. The "system" could refer to the criminal justice system (e.g., eluding police capture), the welfare system (e.g., receiving checks despite violating terms of eligibility), business organizations (e.g., shoplifting from a store), or a male-dominated crime ring (e.g., underreporting earnings to a pimp or drug boss). Within PHW, the phrase was used exclusively by prisoners to refer to overt forms of defiance that challenged the program's rules, ideology, and claims about the self. In this context, it means getting over on habilitation. Meesha, for example, described her remaining days in PHW after engaging in a series of rule violations that would surely result in her expulsion:

> The last few days I was just ripping and running in here. Nobody couldn't do nothing to stop me. I told 'em [counselors] they is full of shit, I told the other women in here to get out, and I just did my own thing. I didn't care what they did to me, I knew I was getting up and out of here and I wasn't going to stand for the bullshit no more.

As a group, the women who "ripped and ran" rejected the disease concept and its claims about the self. Their rebellion was primarily designed to accomplish two objectives. First, they objected to systemic forms of "disrespect" and they used their defiance as a means of defending the self against pejorative claims made by program staff. One prisoner explained her rejection of PHW this way:

> Don't believe the hype, you know, the hype they telling you. That's my motto. I don't have no problem with no drug treatment, but when they start disrespecting me and then trying to make me disrespect my self, no way! You know what I'm saying? I'm not playing that 'cause that's disrespecting your self and all you got in this world is your self.

Second, they sought to provoke staff into immediately expelling them from the program. In interviews with me and in conversations with their peers, women who pursued a strategy of "ripping and running" made a point to emphasize that they had not "surrendered to the process," nor had they been "broken down" by the staff. Rather, they left PHW with their sense of self intact.

Staff rarely, if ever, used the phrase "ripping and running," nor did they regard violating program rules as a kind of strategy for navigating institutional life. Instead, they spoke of a *type* of woman who persistently defied program rules.[7] They referred to her as "walking with the dead" (or "dead" for short), and as a "hard-core addict," "career criminal," and "bad seed." They explained her recalcitrance in terms of profound psychiatric disorder (which they often characterized as "dual diagnosis"), impaired intellect, violent tendencies, and an inexplicable commitment to deviance. Such explanations are neither accurate nor adequate.

Other prisoners, using approved program vocabulary, referred to these women as "dead" and "walking with the dead." For their part, prisoners who ripped and ran referred to themselves in terms of what they were not.[8] Alicia, the prisoner profiled earlier who caused quite a stir after she left PHW claiming she was "abused," described her strategy for navigating habilation by comparing it to the strategies of other prisoners:

> Some of them, you know, are just brainwashed. They buy into anything the staff tell 'em after a while. They the ones that gets broken down. Most of the other ones are just fakin' it to make it in there, you know. When you be telling people, you know, "Surrender, break you down," and all this and you got people facing three, four, or five years in prison they gonna do what they have to do even if they get lost in the process and end up, like, brainwashed. Then there's some of us, you know, like me and [names seven other women] who just not like that. I'm not going to let you disrespect me for any reason, even if I gotta serve more time.

For the purposes of this analysis, I am using the category "ripping and running" to refer only to those prisoners who overtly rejected PHW's philosophy of addiction *and* who left the program prematurely (either because they were kicked out by staff or because they petitioned the prison classification board to transfer them back to the prison's general population). While they periodically conformed to the program's behavioral guidelines, prisoners who ripped and ran made their opposition to habilation (particularly claims about the self) well-known to other prisoners and to staff.[9]

Twenty-two women interviewed for this study self-identified as having pursued a strategy of ripping and running during their time in PHW.[10]
None of them went on to complete the program. They were as likely to petition for transfer out of the program as they were to be kicked out by staff.
Compared to their peers, prisoners who ripped and ran had a short career
in the program. While women who surrendered averaged twelve months in
PHW, the women who ripped and ran averaged three months. None stayed
in the program longer than five months. Among those I interviewed, thirteen were directly sentenced into the program and nine entered voluntary.
Of these nine, all but two said they entered the program because one or more
members of the prison classification committee told them that they would
receive a sentence modification if they successfully completed the program.
Several agreed to enter PHW "voluntarily" because they were facing prison
sentences of three or more years.

As a group, they maintained three different sets of outlooks (positive,
neutral, and negative) regarding drugs. The majority maintained a fairly
positive outlook with respect to their involvement with drugs. Most often,
their regard for drugs was a function of income potential. A number were
either drug dealers themselves, had a drug-dealing partner or boyfriend, or
sold drugs on a part-time basis, usually in conjunction with prostitution.
This group also mentioned enjoying the highs associated with drug ingestion
and the social interactions afforded by "partying" with drugs, although these
responses were nearly always secondary to the pleasure they derived from
the additional income.

A smaller number of prisoners who ripped and ran had what could be
described as a neutral outlook with respect to drugs. That is, they regarded
drugs as a relatively unremarkable aspect of their lives. They were not seeking
to control their use, nor were their lives organized around it. They reported
that they did not use "hard" drugs of any kind (e.g., heroin, powder cocaine,
crack) and engaged only in recreational use of alcohol or marijuana. They
certainly did not regard themselves as addicts or in need of drug treatment,
although they did not disparage drug treatment or the concept of addiction
at the outset. All of these women reported being encouraged by a prison staff
member to enter PHW and believed that by doing so, they would receive a
reduction in the amount of time they were serving. None was incarcerated as
the direct result of a drug-related crime.[11]

Finally, only two of the women who ripped and ran expressed a negative perspective on drug use—one that was similar to the view expressed
by women who surrendered. They reported feeling "tired," "burned out,"
and "overwhelmed" by their drug use. Although neither of these women

regarded themselves as addicts, they entered PHW with an interest in getting their drug use under control.

In sum, women who ripped and ran were distinct at the outset from women who surrendered. The majority did not regard drug use or their involvement in drug-related crime as problematic. And although the majority of both groups of prisoners entered PHW for reasons relating to their prison sentences, women who surrendered expressed at least some interest in learning how to control their use. With few exceptions, women who ripped and ran did not. They spent less than half the amount of time in PHW that women who surrendered did and, as a result, their moral careers consisted of just two stages.[12]

She's Not Me: Rejection of the Addict Label

While the majority of all the prisoners who entered PHW did not regard themselves as addicts, many were willing to entertain the notion upon entering the program because they were interested in conceptualizing their drug use in a different way. Early in their moral careers they may not have believed they were addicts, but they allowed themselves to be referred to as "having an addiction" and as "addicts," and occasionally referred to themselves using these labels. This was not the case for women who pursued a strategy of ripping and running. The first step in their moral careers involved their stalwart rejection of either term as an applicable label to describe their identities, their drug use, or their life histories. For example, Jenna was in charge of a local prostitution ring and admitted to selling drugs through the women who worked for her, and occasionally using cocaine, marijuana, and alcohol herself. She explained her reasons for entering PHW and her reaction to being called an "addict" upon her admission to the program:

> I wouldn't refuse any other treatment, 'cause I do do drugs. But I was never caught with drugs, and drugs was never my charge. . . . I never even had a dirty urine 'cause I knew when to stop doing it. It's not like I did it every single day, which I didn't. A lot of these girls were out there selling their butts for five dollars. I wasn't out there selling my butt for five dollars. I just don't see it, how they could even think I'm an addict. . . . I'm not an addict and I'm not going to say I am.

Betty was fifty-two years old when she received an eighteen-month prison sentence for possession of cocaine after police searched her apartment on a tip that her grandson was dealing drugs out of the home. She had no previous charges and was emphatic in stating that she knew nothing about the drug sales and was never a user herself:

> It's ridiculous I'm in here at this age, on a drug charge, and I've got to sit in some drug treatment program that's telling me I done slipped through the cracks all these years! I never, I tell you I never mess with that stuff, never! I sure as hell can't be an addict if I ain't never tried none of it! I'm not an addict and I ain't got no drug disease and that's not denial, that's the truth!

PHW staff responded to statements like these by telling prisoners that they were "in denial" and that their unwillingness to accept the label "addict" was indicative of how deeply entrenched the disease of addiction was in their selves. When the women continued to challenge the applicability of the label, they were forced to endure repeated confrontations with staff members, multiple hours of required cleaning, and the loss of coveted privileges such as phone calls, visits with family members, and unrestricted commissary purchases. Most women who initially rejected the claims gave up and began referring to themselves as addicts. Prisoners who ripped and ran, however, continued to defy the staff. In Jenna's case, the staff had imposed so many punishments on her for her adamant refusal to identify herself as an addict that they literally ran out of sanctions. By her eighth week in the program, Jenna spent all of her weekends, a significant portion of her evenings, and most of her days cleaning. She had lost all her privileges at the commissary, and could not use the phone, have visitors, or visit the law library. When she again refused to call herself an addict despite the sanctions, the staff created what they thought would be the ultimate punishment—loss of her long, blonde hair. First, they told her she was no longer allowed to curl it. When this did not stop her, they told her she could not wear it in a ponytail. Finally, two of the counselors took Jenna in the office and cut at least five inches off. The haircut did not work. Jenna continued to reject the label. After four months in the program, Jenna was transferred out of PHW after she told a prison psychiatrist on three separate occasions that she would commit suicide or hurt another inmate if they did not remove her from the program.[13]

I found that there were two reasons why women who ripped and ran refused to define themselves as addicts. The first involved a dispute over the working definition of the term "addict." The second reason was based on their suspicions that staff were using the term in an effort to promote class and status distinctions between themselves and prisoners. In the first case, women who ripped and ran came into PHW with their own working definition of what an addict was. Specifically, they regarded addicts as people who could not control their drug use, and this lack of control spilled over into other areas of their life. In their framework, addiction is not based on the kind of substances that one ingests or the amount, but on whether the person is capable of "getting herself together" when situations in her life demanded her to be sober and productive. This is reflected in an earlier quote from Jenna, who commented that she never had a "dirty urine" (i.e., tested positive for drugs on a urine test) because she was capable of terminating her drug use when under legal surveillance. Alicia drew on the same concept when she explained to me why she did not consider herself an addict:

> Addicts is like the people you see out on the street, you know, just can't get themselves together, you know? They dirty, I mean physically unkept and a wreck and they begging for money, stealing from anybody— not even thinking about getting caught or nothing. They out of control is what it is, so messed up on the drug they can't get themselves together. . . . That's not me, I used but not a lot, I worked for [local beauty salon], sold drugs on the side, had a real nice apartment. I didn't have as much as I wanted money-wise, but my children were never in want of anything important.

This group of prisoners did not regard the use of drugs or the pursuit of illicit drug work as indicative of drug addiction. In contrast, PHW's addiction ideology held that criminal activity and the use of any illegal substance were clear indicators of addiction. Women who ripped and ran, however, differentiated between their use of drugs (which may roughly be compared to alcohol use among "social drinkers") and other drug users they had known on the street. They emphasized their ability to maintain a household and a stable source of income, as well as being able to terminate drug use when situations (particularly those involving law enforcement) demanded it. Their objection to the term "addict" derived, in part, from their experiences on the street and their awareness that drug use is a complex, multifaceted phenomenon that cannot be reduced to a single interpretative framework. Carmen, who had four prior convictions for trafficking narcotics, commented:

> I don't buy what they're [counselors] saying. I'll be the first to admit I have a drug problem—but my problem is not from using too much and getting out of hand—I don't do that shit. My problem is the money, I make so much damn money but my luck's been running out . . . I'd break it down like this if they'd let me. There's women in here that can't control their drug

use, they're addicts, I got no problem with that. But look at them and look at me. I sold drugs 'cause of the money, not 'cause I was looking to use cheap. Most of them who've tried to sell blow it, 'cause it all goes up their nose! They sell their butts on the street real cheap, you know, to men they don't know nothing about. They addicts! I'm not an addict, there's nothing I've ever done that looks like that. You see what I'm saying? She's not me. You can't call us the same, we're different. One label don't apply to both— she's not me!

The second reason women who ripped and ran rejected the label "addict" was based on their beliefs about what the term *actually* meant to staff members. This was related, in part, to the staff's failure to distinguish those who were casual drug users from those who were "out of control." Indeed, the staff's apparent inability to differentiate among types of drug users indicated to this group of prisoners that the staff lacked "street smarts" and had a troubling naiveté about life on the street. Their apparent lack of knowledge about the street made these prisoners doubt the accuracy of the therapeutic gaze. Sony complained to me about a counselor known among prisoners as the "porcelain doll" because of her perceived fragility and naiveté:

She be saying this and that about who am I and all that. I'm an addict, I'm in denial, I'm really sick—I'm a sick addict in denial!! [laughing] But what the fuck does she know, she's never been out on the street. She doesn't know shit about hustling or anything else. And that, her ignorance, isn't something I would have a problem with if I didn't have to sit here 24/7[14] and listen to her tell me all about me, you know?

This group of prisoners also took issue with the claims staff made during confrontation sessions—in particular, the staff's frequent and liberal use of degrading terms to refer to women in the program. For example, although Alicia used words like "dirty," "unkept," and "out of control" to describe addicts in the abstract, she objected to the fact that staff directed derogatory terms like these to specific prisoners during confrontation sessions:

If I take you to group, I call you names, I say you a "dog." Then you have, "motherfucking this—sit here motherfucking, mopey-looking ass" or something like that. The name-calling, that's an issue for women that's an addict. 'Cause no addict, addicted women all their life been cussed out, name-called, and totally disrespected. That was the thing that I have a problem with, with the cussin'.

Meesha objected to the manner in which confrontation sessions were conducted for similar reasons:

> My interpretation of confrontations is to me, they are supposed to help a person, but it was twisted words. You don't tear a person really far down and make them look real ugly, you know, how you going to build a person up by tearing them down? This is something a lot of them is used to from childhood, being torn down. . . . That's ugly when you have to sit there and call people names to bring out their issues. . . . I mean, everybody might not be like that, but they [staff] do it [call people names]. They tear you down. You are used to being talked to like a dog when you on the street, and you don't want to hear that. That was when you were using, and you would have allowed anything just to get high. But you don't have to accept it now, but they [staff] still do it, and then they tell you things, and then they contradict themselves and you just look at them and say, "Which is which?" I don't know what to believe sometimes. I know what I believe within myself.

For Alicia and Meesha, the staff's use of expletives and degrading forms of address during the confrontation sessions was not only grossly inappropriate given the backgrounds of many of the women in the program, but it belied what they felt were the staff's personal biases toward prisoners. On one level, women who ripped and ran felt that the staff members did not really care about them as they periodically claimed during confrontation sessions. One prisoner explained:

> The impression that I get is that they don't want to be bothered. They don't want to listen. They always full of bullshit. . . . They don't have time to talk to you, but they always have time to be watching your visits and listening to your phone calls. They be all up in your business, but they don't really care about you.

On another level, many of them felt that the lack of concern and the name-calling were related to a larger bias staff held against them as poor, African American women. Melika elaborated on this in an interview:

MELIKA: I'm saying, and this is just my thing, but with the disrespect—so
much of it—the name-calling, cussin' people out, being up in their
business, and then leaving you just sit if you really need to get in to
talk to them, saying, you know, "Wait, we don't got time for your

problems now." That's discrimination in my book—I don't care if they black, brown, or white. They don't even treat us like we second-class citizens—

JM: Why do you think they act like that toward you?

MELIKA: 'Cause they got this image of us—you know, we all whores or we all jacking the welfare system or something and [with a mock British accent] that's not nice! That's not what polite people do. When the fuck was the last time you saw people like them holding court on [names a well-known drug corner in nearby city]?! They think we ghetto Blacks, even think that about white girls, so even the Black ones [counselors] think they too good for us.

The first stage in the moral career of women who rip and run involves their adamant rejection of the addict label. Although they were subject to severe punishments for doing so, they persisted in their noncooperation because they believed that the term "addict" was inaccurate when applied to their own drug use and experiences on the street. This group of prisoners was also suspicious of the staff's use of the term more generally since it appeared that staff used the label for ulterior purposes (most notably, to express their bias against poor, Black women).[15] Subsequently, they rejected the term "addict" when it was specifically applied to them, but they also rejected it on a more philosophical level because of its negative connotations. Their refusal to refer to themselves as addicts paved the way for the second, and final, stage in their moral careers.

Getting Over

The beginning of the end emerged during this group of prisoners' first few weeks in the program. With their refusal to identify themselves as addicts and their skepticism about the staff's motives during confrontation sessions, women who ripped and ran refused to make a good faith effort to follow the program's rules. Instead, they engaged in flagrant rule violations, intentionally defied staff dictates, and made a point to challenge the counselors during confrontation sessions. Although their behavior appeared inexplicable to many other prisoners who regarded the sanctions as too severe to be worth intentionally violating, they saw a method in their madness. One prisoner explained:

[PHW] brainwashes women, I've seen it happen. If you don't surrender to the process, you get punished. Well, I think for myself and I'd much rather have the punishment than their so-called therapy. I break rules, I know it's not what they want me to do. So, if I can break a rule, they don't control what's in my mind, see? I'm still in control. . . . Actually, when they yell louder, call me to the floor more, make me clean, take my visits, and all that, I can see this program for what it is—it's just like jail only they want to fuck with your head. Why would anyone surrender to that?

For this group, the concern that they would be "brainwashed" or otherwise controlled by the staff was greater than their fear of reprisals and sanctions. To avoid the institutional takeover of their self-identities, women who ripped and ran believed that they needed to prevent the staff from having any control over them. This often translated into intentionally undertaking behaviors that the staff regarded as deviant. By doing the opposite of what was expected of them, they "proved" to themselves that they had not been "brainwashed." In the vast majority of cases, the deviance took fairly innocuous forms (e.g., stealing an extra piece of fruit from the prison cafeteria, passing notes to inmates outside the program, faking illness with the intention of going to the medical office and chatting with other inmates, cheating on vocabulary tests, refusing to get out of bed or refusing to participate in therapy), but on occasion it was more serious (e.g., threatening suicide or other types of violence, fighting, serious property damage).

Minor forms of deviance served as a protective measure against institutional controls designed to transform the self. It did so by facilitating cognitive and physical spaces for self-reflection in which a prisoner was able to remind herself that she (and not the staff) was in control of her actions. A significant number of minor rule violations committed by this group of prisoners involved initiating communication with inmates outside the program. These exchanges helped women to validate both their sense of themselves and their criticisms of the disease concept. Even in cases where the rule violation was a solitary project, it often involved physically and mentally removing oneself from the day's proceedings in PHW (e.g., staying in bed or finding an excuse to visit the medical office). Both varieties of minor deviance generated private spaces in which prisoners could pursue critical thoughts about the program, challenge the staff's identity claims, and defend their vision of the self.[16] One prisoner who was mistakenly locked in her cell by a correctional officer explained the value of this particular type of rule violation:

When I came back from lunch I went and laid down which I wasn't supposed to do until 3:00 p.m. . . . Well, I guess they didn't know I was in there 'cause I fell asleep and when I got up I tried to get out the door and they had locked it. I mean it sounds weird, but they had locked me in and I was like so psyched. It was like I was gone. They wasn't gonna get to me 'cause they didn't know where I was. As soon as I thought that, I thought, "Oh my God, I can be who I want in here." You know, it's like you can think the stuff that you're not allowed to—I can't explain it. It's just that I could find my self, I mean that's weird, but it's like I was gone and in that room I found myself again.

Minor acts of deviance allowed women who ripped and ran to distance themselves from the program and, concomitantly, the program's claims about their identities. Indeed, they achieved a sort of separation from the thera-peutic discourse that eluded the group of women who surrendered. While the latter group was quick to follow program guidelines for thinking, feel-ing, expression, and behavior, the former remained aloof and, in so doing, retained their control over the narrative structure they used to describe their lives, as well as their definitions of self.

Major acts of deviance, including acts and threats of violence, were under-taken as a desperate measure designed to ensure expulsion from the program. Earlier in the chapter, I noted that modifications in the exit policy meant that prisoners who petitioned for transfer out of PHW could remain in the unit for as long as six weeks against their will. The vast majority of women who ripped and ran expressed an interest in dropping out of the program during the first week or two, and began to actively seek avenues of exit by the third week. When they learned they had to stay in the program several more weeks, a number became increasingly agitated and concerned that they would be "broken down" and "brainwashed" in that period. Melika explained that these concerns led to her decision to get into a fistfight with another prisoner:

It sounds crazy, but you've got to be here, you know, walk in my shoes to understand what it's like. What they make you feel like. Seriously, I mean, I was scared I was going to end up like those kiss-asses, brainwashed and all that shit. To be real honest with you, I did have a problem with that girl, she reported me to the staff for passing notes, but I didn't hit her 'cause of that. I'm not like one of those that gots to go around beating people up. I hit her 'cause I knew they'd kick me out and I needed to get out right away. . . . The whole time I was scared I'd start talking like them [women who surrendered].

The only way to get out of the program prior to the end of the mandatory orientation period was to be expelled by the staff. Every act of violence (as well as most serious threats) resulted in immediate expulsion from the program. Although program staff considered women who engaged in such behavior "mentally ill" or "lost causes," the prisoners' own statements suggest that the violence was situationally induced. It is worth noting that incidents of violence in PHW increased from two in the program's first year (before the thirty-day policy was in place), to ten in the second year, and to seventeen by the end of the third year. In most cases, seemingly inexplicable acts of violence were a rational response to a change in policy that forced women to stay in the program against their will. Fearing they would literally lose their self during the repeated confrontation sessions with staff, women who ripped and ran did whatever they could to get out of the program.[17]

The moral career of this group of prisoners ends with their premature departure from the program. Although staff subjected them to frequent and intense confrontations and levied all sorts of punishments in the interest of "breaking them down," in the end, staff were usually glad to see them go. Since these prisoners frequently challenged the legitimacy of addiction rhetoric and, by their rebellion, reminded other prisoners that alternatives to radical self-transformation exist, staff regarded them as a threat to the program's fragile moral order.[18] In their explanations to the remaining prisoners about why they chose to expel one of their peers, staff frequently used metaphors involving death and disease (e.g., "she's already walking with the dead," "there's no person there, only the disease"), suggesting that the expelled prisoners were beyond help and represented a threat to the remaining prisoners' chances for recovery. The departure of the women who ripped and ran, according to PHW's ideology, did not represent a failure of habilitation but a failure of self in that these women were considered beyond help.

For their part, all the women I talked to informally and during interviews expressed a sense of triumph when reflecting on their departure, and used phrases like "I got over," "I won," and "I didn't let them get to me" to express what was at stake when they resisted. Most of the women who dropped out of PHW had additional months added to their prison sentence, and several faced the prospect of serving an additional year or more (Jenna received three additional years). Despite the sentencing penalties, none of these women expressed any regrets. Meesha, for example, commented, "It's worth it to me not to become like them [women who surrendered]." Jenna summed up her feelings immediately after returning to the general prison population:

This is gonna really get ya. Now I really feel like doing drugs. More. I probably will. You know, I think they brainwash people. . . . They made me feel like coming over here and taking a hit of anything. . . . They're [staff] treating us like that and they're getting paid for us. That's just like a mirror image. I was getting paid for the girls who worked for me. I didn't treat them like shit . . . I didn't go around screaming and hollering. They were prostitutes. They were drug addicts. . . . I know I'm better than them [staff] 'cause I don't disrespect people 'cause of who they are or what they do and I don't allow anyone to disrespect me.

On the subject of the additional three years of prison time she received for refusing to stay in the program, Jenna commented:

My time is limited. Those suckers are gonna be here for God knows how long and they'll go to [therapeutic work-release] and they'll take a hit or do some kind of drug, and they'll be right back here next year. I'm not gonna make that mistake. I refused work release. And that's the first person you probably ever heard of that refused work release—of any kind. I refuse to enter a work release, 'cause you know, that's a trap. I don't want to be down there with all them girls, living in the same room, you know. I didn't want to hear their bullshit therapy talk.

Among women who ripped and ran, defending their sense of self from verbal attacks or various identity imputations (e.g., "You're an addict in denial") assumed precedence over everything else, including any interest in getting out of prison early. This group of women survived on the street by remaining in control of the situation, regardless of whether the situation involved law enforcement, the sale and distribution of drugs, or robbing local stores. PHW's demands that they "surrender themselves" and allow themselves to be "broken down" not only threatened their sense of themselves as autonomous subjects, but also were consistent with their definition of addicts. For them, addicts are people who lose control and allow themselves to be disrespected by others. Whether they are dependent on drugs or dependent on program staff, addicts are not in control of their worlds. In both worlds, addicts undergo a profanation of self that, in the eyes of women who rip and run, represents the ultimate loss of control. The moral career of this group of prisoners, then, is motivated by their interest in defending the self against disrespect, regardless of whether disrespect occurs on the street or in a treatment program.

Faking It to Make It

Women who ripped and ran were unique in PHW because they were willing to suffer whatever penalty befell them to defend their definition of self. Not all prisoners who had doubts about habilitation, however, perceived

themselves as having such a choice. A number of women in PHW anticipated severe penalties such as revocation of custody rights to a child, loss of
a spouse or partner, or additional time in prison if they failed to complete
PHW. Although they harbored similar doubts about the legitimacy of addiction discourse and resented claims staff made about the self, they did not
regard overt rebellion and premature departure from the program as a viable option. For example, Veronica was forty-three years old and had served
three years of an eighteen-year sentence for credit card fraud when she was
approached by prison administrators about entering PHW. Her judge and
the correctional authorities agreed to suspend thirteen years of her sentence
if she did two years in PHW and successfully completed the program. During an interview I conducted with her after she had been in the program for
fourteen months, she reflected on her decision:

> I didn't have a choice, really. I don't care how tough some of these women
> think they are, ain't nobody going to serve eighteen years just to prove a
> point. I don't like the program no better than some of them, but I'm in a situa-
> tion where I've got to strategize, got to stick it out, no matter how hard it gets.

Although Veronica's situation was unique with respect to the number of years
she faced in prison if she did not complete PHW, the majority of women
in PHW faced a similar dilemma. Many feared that social services would
take their children away if they did not make an effort to improve themselves
while in prison,[19] while others worried about employment prospects as an
"ex-con" and felt that completion of a drug treatment program would miti-
gate some of the stigma associated with having a criminal record. This group
of prisoners was faced with a difficult dilemma. On the one hand, they were
critical of (and even rejected) PHW's addiction philosophy. On the other
hand, they were committed to remaining in the program, often because the
sanctions for not doing so seemed too great to risk incurring.

These women pursued a third type of strategy that they referred to as "faking it to make it." "Faking it" references a style of participation in which prisoners appear to have surrendered to habilitation, while remaining privately
critical of program ideology and claims about the self. Unlike prisoners who
ripped and ran, this group did not publicly debunk the identity claims made
by the staff (although they occasionally challenged a staff member during
a confrontation) and many went on to graduate from the program. It is, by
far, the most common strategy pursued by prisoners in PHW. Based on participant observation and interview data, I'd estimate that approximately two-
thirds of women in the program are faking it at any given time. Women who

"faked it" constituted just over half (thirty-nine) of my interview respondents. The majority entered PHW voluntarily (although most reported doing so in the interest of sentence modification).[20] They were slightly more likely to graduate from the program than to drop out of it.

Despite their large numbers, staff did not acknowledge "faking it" as a viable strategy for negotiating the demands of habilitation. When asked, for example, about how often or how many prisoners "fake it," counselors gave answers similar to the one provided during my interview with the senior counselor:

> Nobody in here fakes it for any sustained amount of time, that's something that goes on in less rigorous treatment programs. If they are faking it, they can't keep up their fronts for too long . . . we'll find a way to break them down and get to what's going on with them.

Given their confidence in their professional capabilities (notably the ability to "get into" or "see inside" the minds of their charges), counselors did not believe that a strategy of "faking it" could be pursued over any length of time. Indeed, the practice of "breaking prisoners down" was intended to prevent prisoners from hiding their real selves from the program staff. Earlier I argued that staff believed they had insight into the "real" self when prisoners cried or expressed rage during the course of confrontation sessions. Although they acknowledged that the addict self is manipulative and deceitful, they vigorously defended their ability to see past the deception and "break down" the false representations created by the addict self. According to the counselors, there were two strategies at play in the program—surrendering to the process ("walking the walk") and walking with the dead.

Among prisoners, however, there was widespread acknowledgment of "faking it" as a strategy. Although Alicia ripped and ran, she explained to me how some prisoners settle on a strategy of "faking it":

> Some of them start out happy to be there. You got some that just have to be there, you got some that think it's the easy way out of jail, you got some that are really trying. You got a mixture, all different kinds. . . . But hearin' it every day, being in it, going through it . . . I think the women, they [counselors] strip them too far down to where they still don't—when you push somebody so far, they're going to push back eventually.

Other prisoners periodically expressed their annoyance toward women who "fake it" (e.g., "She's full of shit, she's just faking it") and questioned their trustworthiness (e.g., "If she can lie to the counselor's face about being whatever they want her to be, what makes me think she's not going to lie to my face?"). But they also acknowledged, as Alicia did in the above quote, that this particular group of women is confronted by a unique set of dilemmas. For example, although Mary Lou surrendered to the program and graduated from it, she noted that she did not have hostility toward women who faked it:

> I got along with them well. See people that, that understood me and I understood them are, we didn't have any animosity. It was like, they was straightforward, I was straightforward. I didn't beat around the bush. I didn't fake it to make it. Lots of them are constantly faking it to make it just to get out of the institution. I wasn't about that. I wanted recovery and I still want recovery so I didn't fake it to make it but I don't have problems with some of them that were forced into their situations by the staff, or the courts, or whatever, you know? So long as they didn't look down on me for my decision to get treatment.

To a large extent, other prisoners regarded women who faked it with both derision and sympathy. On the one hand, these women "rented out their heads" by allowing the staff to "disrespect" them during confrontation sessions despite their privately held criticisms of such disrespect. On the other hand, most prisoners acknowledged that they were all "renting out their heads" to one extent or another, since all faced a similar tension between accepting the staff's claims about the self (and thereby garnering some level of approval) and defending the self against disrespect. Ultimately, many prisoners came to regard prisoners who "faked it" with a begrudging level of approval. As Sam explained:

> We all bonded to one another to some extent 'cause we're fighting a battle. For some of us, it's a battle against the staff, others it's a battle against drugs, and others it's a battle against the amount of time to serve, but it don't matter 'cause we in the same trenches together and we're just all trying to make it out. One thing's for sure, we are not battling one another, not really.

In the sections that follow, I examine the moral career of the prisoners who "faked it to make it."

Questioning Therapeutic Truths

The first stage of the moral career of the prisoners who fake it involves critical analysis of the legitimacy of the disease concept, with particular focus on the accuracy of the staff's claims about their lives on the street. Unlike those who surrendered (who began their moral careers before they ever stepped foot inside PHW), prisoners who faked it did not typically commit to a particular strategy until well into their second month in the program. They resembled women who surrendered in that they did and said what the staff told them to, although a few initially protested some of the claims made by staff (particularly those involving their capabilities as mothers). Women who ripped and ran also undertook a critical examination of the staff's claims, though they did so right from the jump. For them, delegitimizing the disease concept merged with their early refusal to regard themselves as addicts. Women who faked it took a less radical approach during their first few weeks in the program. Most entered with a willingness to participate in treatment. Although they did not regard themselves as addicts and, in many cases, resented having to serve time in PHW, most decided at the outset to make the best of it. Kay explained:

> I didn't come in here with an attitude, you know, what good does it do? I'm in jail one way or the other, maybe I can learn something. Plus, I was pregnant when I first came in and I wasn't about to let them stress me and my baby out. So I said when I come over to the [PHW], I'm coming full force and I have.

The decision to make the best out of the program and not "have an attitude" was further solidified during the early stages of the orientation phase. Seeing other prisoners around them be confronted and punished for failing to learn program vocabulary or follow rules motivated this group of women to get through the program as quickly and painlessly as possible. For example, Kat entered PHW in the hopes of earning early release because she was afraid of getting into physical fights with inmates in the general population. Although her first impression of the program was negative, she decided to make the best of her situation and do the "easiest time" possible:

> Look, I wasn't serious about treatment. I was serious about getting the hell out of prison and while I was here, doing the easiest time I could. I sure as hell don't want to be getting into it out there [general population]. My first day here was real confusing. There was a lot to learn. There was a lot of things I couldn't do. A lot of things that, that I was just real confused why they would do the things they would do, why they would stand and yell at women. Like when they would "give information" I would see women hitting bricks and just doing different accountabilities and I would just be

like, what is this place, a nuthouse?[21] But I went along with it, 'cause I just wanted to get out as fast as I could and I knew that first day the way to do it was just to go along with whatever the staff said.

During the orientation phase of the program, they did their best to follow PHW's rules for conduct, learn the vocabulary, and narrate their life histories according to disease rhetoric.

The similarity between women who surrendered and those who faked it ended by the second or third month when confrontations with the counselors became more intense and increasingly degrading. Although both groups of women were angered by the identity claims made by the staff and responded by crying, yelling, or running into their cells, women who surrendered ultimately came to regard the confrontation sessions and claims as legitimate assessments of their "real" selves. They did so because they had become fully accustomed to conceptualizing their lives in terms of addiction discourse, so much so that the claims staff made about the self appeared to be true. Prisoners who fake it did not experience such a profound shift in their self-identities. Instead, they found one or more of the identity claims made during the confrontation sessions to be so offensive and degrading that it caused them to question the legitimacy of the program at a very fundamental level. Unlike women who ripped and ran, the claims women who faked it came to regard as offensive did not involve their drug use per se (most did not, for example, object to being called addicts), but other aspects of their lives such as motherhood, sexual identity, the social networks they belonged to, or how they made a living. Each of the women I interviewed recounted at least one identity claim that undermined any legitimacy they may have accorded to the program:

I'm a lesbian, always have been. . . . I really resented the things they said about my sexuality. They told me my sexuality was "sexual acting out" and said it was part of my disease. Well, I can see them talking about crime that way, but who I am as a person, that's just homophobia. It made me question everything. [Twenty-eight years old, African American]

I'll always remember it, what she said, "You're just a whore." In front of all these people, "You're just a whore." That really got to me, really got to me deep inside. On one hand they're telling me I can't see my boyfriend 'cause they think he's a negative influence and she tells me I'm nothing but a whore. It just really, you know, it just hurt a lot, but it was like I realized this is abuse. [Thirty-five years old, white]

Like women who surrendered, the prisoners who faked it experienced an epiphany of sorts during these confrontation sessions. They did not, however, "wake up" and recognize the veracity of addiction discourse and claims about the self. Instead, the experience of being called "degrading," "offensive," and "humiliating" names caused them to gain new insight into habilitation. During their first few weeks in the program, they described the program in fairly benign ways (e.g., "crazy," "a nuthouse," "silly"). Following a particularly severe confrontation session, these prisoners not only described the program in negative terms but they also came to regard it as harmful. Further, they systematically critiqued all or most of the claims staff members made about their lives. Rinda left the program after deciding that the confrontations were too much:

> They go through the process of strapping and tearing you down, breaking you down. But I feel like as though women don't have to be broke down like that, because by the time you get to jail they already broke down. Most of the time, the addict woman comes to jail. She done lost her home, she done lost her kid, she's probably out on the street trickin' . . . she's already down to nothing . . . and now we locked up. No visitation with their kids. They probably strung all over the place. . . . Emotionally, we already broke down, strucked out and desperate. So I think the name-calling and tearing them down part of it, I mean I feel as though, you have to do that to some people that may be in denial. But I think there's too much of it over there, that part. I have an issue with that. I think the men . . . you probably got to do that because the men no matter what has happened to him, he's been sexually abused or anything like that, he's gonna portray a macho image. So it's gonna take more tearing down and strapping him and putting him on the spot to get him to break down and get in touch with his real feelings. But you don't have to do that to a woman.

Latasha explained that being called degrading names caused her to question habilitation:

> It shook me up bad and I started thinking that they [staff] contradict themselves. Like the swearing, calling people names, treating you like you ain't even human, isn't that what they say addicts do to the people around them? Like addicts don't care about other people's feelings? It didn't seem like she cared about my feelings when she called me up to the floor and called me a "crack whore" and a "dope fiend." . . . I think the program has a lot of contradictions because, and I'm not trying to be smart, but they

really don't know what they're talking about. Like [senior counselor], she's never been on drugs or nothing and she can't really know about me 'cause she has never been me, she never been there, and you got to really be there to feel what it's really like to be me.

The experience of being called degrading and offensive names jolted this group of prisoners into critiquing the legitimacy of habilation as a treatment strategy. As the above statements reveal, they gained two critical insights about the program. First, they did not believe that the staff had access to any greater or more truthful insights about their lived experiences and selves than they did. Second, they regarded the frequent confrontation sessions as harmful to the women in the program.[22] These insights with respect to the program placed them in a unique position relative to their peers. Unlike women who surrendered, they became suspicious about the consequences of conformity for their self-identity (as one prisoner who faked it noted, "If I let counselors disrespect me how can I have any respect for myself?"). And unlike women who ripped and ran, their motivation to defend the self and avoid disrespect was secondary to their interests in "easy time" and getting out of prison early so that they could preserve ties to family, friends, and potential employers. Indeed, women who faked it were not interested in quitting the program or openly defying the staff like those who ripped and ran. How they resolved the tension between "easy time" and defense of the self constitutes the second phase of their moral career.

Managing the Rented Head

In the second stage of their moral careers, prisoners who fake it manage the tension between their desire to defend the self and their interest in completing the program by appearing to conform. In many ways, "faking it" represents a rather dubious compromise. By following the program's rules, appearing to accept the staff's claims about the self, and using the approved narrative structure to describe their lives, they reduced the number and intensity of confrontations with staff. In this way, faking conformity minimized the extent to which they were "disrespected" by the staff. Further, conformity was rewarded by the staff with more rapid promotion through the treatment program. At the same time, habitual use of the program's discursive categories and structure of narration became a bit of a slippery slope. Women who "faked it" were concerned that they might end up "brainwashed." To avoid this, they engaged in two sets of techniques (covert rule-breaking and "blocking") that allowed them to conceptually distinguish the "real" self from the "rented head."

The first technique, covert rule-breaking, is virtually identical to the rule-breaking strategy pursued by prisoners who ripped and ran. Women who faked it violated program rules not with the intention of getting caught by staff, but with an interest in demonstrating to themselves that the staff had not "broken them down." Toya explained why she covertly passed notes to inmates in the general population:

> It's my way of holding on to part of myself, you know, keeping in contact with people I respect and who respect me as I am. It keeps me real. I know I'm not becoming something they're telling me I am if I can just keep in contact with my home girls out there. They're important to me, you know. They won't let me change for the worse, only for the better. Writing to them keeps me sane.

Like prisoners who ripped and ran, these women violate the rules to express their real selves and demonstrate that they are in command of their thoughts and actions. Violating the rules creates a critical tension between the "real" self and the "rented head." With every rule violation, they brought their "real" self into their present circumstances, which prevented it from fading into the shadow generated by the "rented head."[23]

The second distancing technique was referred to as "blocking." Blocking was used by women who faked it as a means of psychologically removing themselves from the confrontation sessions. During encounter group and other confrontations, they looked directly at the counselor and expressed themselves appropriately when called on to do so (e.g., "Thank you for the information, I'll take a look at that"). They appeared to be listening very carefully to the statements the counselor was making and reflecting on these statements without reacting "negatively" (e.g., expressions of anger, sadness, or denial). In reality, they were virtually oblivious to what was being said:

> When I'm on the floor, Jill, I don't hear what they said. I totally block 'em out. I be all the way home somewhere. It don't bother me no more. [Thirty-one years old, African American]

> I don't hear a thing that they saying. I just nod and say, "Yes, thank you, you're right." Whatever it takes to get them off my back. I've got to ask someone afterwards what they were accusing me of. . . . I just go off into my fantasy world. Sometimes I think about my kids, or going someplace I really like, like down to the beach. I imagine myself there, playing in the ocean with my kids. [Forty years old, white].

Blocking requires a tremendous amount of concentration and, ironically, builds on some of the impression management skills PHW requires prisoners to learn. During confrontation sessions, prisoners are not allowed to respond to anything that was said (unless directed to do so) and cannot express a reaction of any kind. Counselors believed that by eliminating the possibilities for emotive expression, prisoners would learn to reflect on the information others told them about the self. Women who faked it became adept at managing their emotions during the confrontation sessions, but they were not engaged in serious reflection over the claims made about the self. In fact, they did not reflect on what was said at all.

All the techniques that embody the strategy of "faking it" (e.g., surface conformity, covert rule-breaking, and blocking) serve to distinguish the real self from the rented head. In this sense, women who fake it managed to construct front and back stages in a setting where the opportunity for privacy has been all but eliminated.[24] By dividing their lived experience in PHW into two categories—the enacted and the authentic—these prisoners are able to distance their "real" selves from the moral feelings of shame, humiliation, and anger during confrontation sessions. The self that is being profaned is not the real self, but the rented head. By periodically accessing their backstage (via covert rule-breaking), they reminded themselves of who they "really" are. The authentic self resides behind the scenes, expressed though forbidden conversations and in secret notes. Access to this self reinforces their belief that their conformity in the program is surface acting and not an expression of authenticity.

Losing Your Head

As a strategy for keeping the self protected from the long reach of habilitation, faking it was exceedingly difficult to maintain over the course of several months in the program. Restrictions on privacy, hours of required cleaning, lengthy group therapy sessions, unanticipated confrontations, the monotony of prison life, and limited sleep schedules proved exhausting to even the most resilient of prisoners. Indeed, it seemed that exhaustion could set in at any point during their time in PHW. Of the women I interviewed, many remembered their first bout of exhaustion as occurring shortly following their second month in the program, and they had more serious bouts as the months wore on. Many described losing their focus and feeling incapable of achieving the level of concentration necessary to block out what was said during confrontation sessions. They described themselves as feeling "confused" about their priorities, "frustrated" with the program, and filled with "disgust" and "hatred" toward themselves. After five and a half months in the program, Robin pulled me aside during a smoke break and asked if we could talk. I agreed and no sooner did we sit down in a corner of the recreation yard than Robin began sobbing uncontrollably.[25] After several minutes she said:

> I can' take it in here anymore. I don't know what I'm doing here. I don't know who I am or where I'm supposed to be. I've got to get out. They took my mother's time away.[26] I was supposed to visit with my son this weekend. I can't keep this up, I just can't. I feel like I'm fucking going nuts in here. I'm gonna lose my head.

Neka, after eight weeks in the program, recalled:

> I was thinking I'll be in here for a couple of months and play the game. I said I'll play the game, I'll go to work release, and I'll get out early. But then I just snapped. I was so tired I couldn't keep it up. . . . I'm nervous anyway, I'm real nervous and they just totally blew my mind. . . . I started to feel like I'm constantly being punished and I had to rebel against them, you know? I tried to sit down and think, why couldn't I make it? All those girls make it, all the time. Why couldn't I just do it? Starting hating myself for it, feeling like shit. . . . I was like, "Fuck you" to [a counselor]. And I had to say it 'cause I finally got so mad I couldn't hold it in. You know, and if I want to roll my eyes, I will roll my eyes.

For a few of the women who were faking it, feelings of exhaustion and confusion were accompanied by physical pain:

> I was on drugs for one year and couple months, and all the drugs I was on I looked like a queen, but the time I was over there [PHW], I looked like death walking. Look like you took your fist and beat me all in my eyes and my blood pressure went sky high. Every day I ran back and forth to the doctors. . . . If you kill me today and put me over there, my spirit would not stay there, that's how tough it is over there.

The exhaustion, confusion, and feelings of emotional and physical pain caused a number of women who were faking it to depart from PHW before graduating. Some of these women were expelled by the staff after a fit of rage (e.g., "It just went from there to there . . . and I was so mad I just kicked out the window") or after they were caught engaging in a serious rule violation (in one case, a woman smuggled four bags of heroin into the facility). Others petitioned their sentencing judges or the prison classification committee to transfer them out of the program. Those who left voluntarily did so because they experienced a change in their priorities. In the case of both Angel and Devon, the extra time in prison was worth it to avoid "losing their heads":

> Honestly, I hate prison but I hate [PHW] more. I'll probably do a few extra months but it's worth it to me. I was worried about it, scared I was going to lose my head. You know, they say, "Rent your head" and all that, well I was renting my head, faking it, letting them say whatever they wanted. Then I started feeling like, wait, I've seen girls get brainwashed in there and maybe this is not such a good idea. I left 'cause my head's not for rent no more! [Angel]

> I got out [of PHW] just in time is my feeling. All that happened to me when I went over there was that I was more of an emotional wreck when I came back [to prison] then when I went in there. It took me a couple months to get back on my feet. I put myself in AA and all the groups [offered in general population]. . . . I picked up everything, I just needed some time to regroup and get myself back on the right track and start working. [Devon]

For these women, fear of "losing one's head" and becoming "brainwashed" was motivation enough to abandon their interest in a sentence reduction. At the same time, many of these women no longer regarded PHW as "easy time." Instead, they came to regard the confrontation sessions, deprivations, punishments, and conformity performances as "harder time" than they would otherwise serve as general population inmates. As one prisoner phrased it, "I was sentenced to prison for my crime, not hell."

Other women who faked it were able to work through the exhaustion, confusion, and fear to successfully graduate from PHW. Carla, the prisoner profiled earlier who struggled to win over "the suits" during the press conference, was among those who faked it and went on to make it through the program. Many of these women were unable in our interviews to recount precisely what it was that allowed them to sustain the strength necessary to remain in the program. A few suggested that they were determined not to quit, while many others simply responded by shrugging and looking away as if they were embarrassed to talk about it. A year and a half after she graduated from PHW, Carla and I met in a small, public park located in a section of the city known for drug trafficking. Since her graduation, Carla had found two jobs (one as a maid in a downtown hotel and the other working as a crew member in a fast-food chain), moved into a tiny, one-bedroom apartment, and had resumed custody of all three of her children. As we talked, her children (ages ten, six, and four) screamed with glee as they played on a rusty jungle gym and chased one another around the picnic tables. When I asked Carla to reflect on her experiences in the program she sighed and mockingly wiped her brow. After a long pause she began:

> I don't like to think about it too much, but sometimes I find myself thinking about it all the time. . . . I basically see myself as a good person and I want to be a good person. I wanted to be a good person in there, I did for real. I wanted to do it, plug into the process after a while. To make it, make something of myself for a change. No more drugs, no more crime, no more disrespecting myself. I wanted, or I still want to get a nice job, live in a nice place, you know, with my kids. . . . I just couldn't, I never got it or I mean, I never got to be at peace with myself in there, so I don't know if you can talk about me like I'm successful. Like you're calling me successful 'cause I made it, but look at how I made it. I was faking it for a lot of times, doing what I had to do. And isn't that just what they say shows you're a bad person, still in your addiction? When you lie and manipulate and all that, is that what somebody who's good does? . . . I guess I still feel like I have doubts about the whole thing. I know, you know, I'm not stupid, I know that a lot of what they're doing in there is bullshit, just pure bullshit, but look at me [waves her arm around to indicate the area surrounding us]. Am I better off for graduating [PHW]? I'm clean and I've stayed clean and I don't sell no more drugs and I thank god for that, but I'm right back with the same problems, same people, and the same place. It's just all more of the same. It makes me wonder if I had really done it, really committed to it—not just talk the talk, but walk the walk, you know, if I'd still be here. Makes me wonder if there was something to what those counselors were saying after all.

Conclusion

Prisoners who resisted PHW's habilitation efforts were primarily motivated by the desire to defend the self from disrepute. Their refusal to surrender the self despite the overwhelming degree of control exerted within the program is related, in part, to the attitudes they maintained regarding drugs and drug treatment prior to entering the program, as well as to their ability to subvert the rules for the purposes of maintaining a sense of autonomy and self-determination. The majority of women who ripped and ran entered PHW with a positive view of drugs. They did not regard drug use as problematic or tiring, but instead saw it as a source of income and a tie to social networks. Further, they differentiated between the casual users they saw themselves to be, and addicts, whom they regarded as out of control. Unlike most of the women entering the program, this group of prisoners expressed hostility toward the disease narrative and claims about the addicted self. To avoid being "brainwashed" by the staff, they engaged in a strategy of "ripping and running," which involved breaking program rules in an effort to reinforce their definition of self. Reinforcing self-definitions was accomplished through prohibited conversations with inmates outside the program and through desperate measures such as violent behavior to ensure their immediate expulsion. Their relatively short tenure in the program combined with their adamant refusal to define themselves as addicts prevented their self-identities from being usurped by institutional control mechanisms.

Prior to entering PHW, prisoners who went on to fake it were not readily differentiable from those who surrendered or even those who ripped and ran. In fact, they could have gone either way given a different set of conditions. Two distinct sets of circumstances prevented them from undertaking either of the other two moral careers. First, they were unwilling or incapable of prematurely leaving the program. Many opted to remain in the program because the desire to get out of prison early superseded concerns about being referred to as an addict. Others worried that the failure to complete the program would threaten important relationships with members of the outside community. Subsequently, they were motivated by the desire to graduate from the program in a way that those who ripped and ran were not. Second, degrading claims about the self made by staff members during their second or third month in the program created a sense of resentment toward PHW (even among those who regarded their drug use as problematic). To achieve their desire to graduate from the program and at the same time not succumb to it, they engaged in two techniques (blocking and covert rule-breaking) to differentiate the "rented head" from the "real" self. Ultimately, however, many dropped out of the program after going through a period of confusion and deprivation in which they worried they would be "brainwashed." Others successfully managed to move back and forth from the rented head to the "real" self and graduated from PHW with their sense of self largely intact.

Resistance looks and feels different in PHW than it did when control in the prison was structured in terms of rehabilitative paternalism. Prisoners primarily strategized their time in the latter system by cultivating close relationships with high-ranking administrators, particularly the warden and the deputy warden. Rarely was resistance overt. Prisoners lobbied administrators to redefine or broaden their view of what women needed, and often this went toward gaining access to prescription drugs or garnering special favors within the prison. As one prisoner noted in chapter 1, it was a system of "vanilla power" in which staff treated prisoners as if they were children who were incapable of defining what was in their own interests. In this way they, like the subjects in Mary Bosworth's study of British women's prisons, exploited institutional constructions of their femininity primarily to gain some relief from the monotony and pains of prison life.[27] The most notable case of organized resistance in the former system came by way of the class action overcrowding lawsuit. This lawsuit was one of the rare instances in the prison's history where prisoners defined their needs in political terms, acted on those needs in an organized fashion, and saw results.

In contrast, prisoner resistance within the habilitative system often took on an explosive character. The system of control in PHW prevented prisoners from cultivating informal relationships with staff inside or outside the program. As a result, they were unable to rely on a staff member's discretion to make some of the rougher aspects of institutional life more bearable. Prisoners were left to their own devices and, not surprisingly, much of their resistance is individualized in character. Many petitioned judicial officials and the prison classification committee to transfer them back to the general population, while others took matters into their own hands and rebelled for the sake of articulating an autonomous self. Although there were occasions when prisoners in PHW threatened lawsuits, most of these threats went nowhere because the women who made them left or were kicked out of the program.[28]

While prisoners in PHW did complain about the "system," they were often not able to counter habilitation with a clear definition of their needs. Indeed, it was far more common for prisoners to speak in terms of what drug-involved women did *not* need. As several prisoners quoted in this chapter said, drug-involved women do not need to be further abused, disrespected, and broken down. That left them with little to direct their resistance toward. Habilitation makes the site of the battle the self, and in this sense, prisoners willingly took more time in order to preserve a sense of the self as respectable.[29] But this is not productive resistance. They did not actually "get over" on the system, because their resistance often conformed to the very stereotypes and myths about poor, African American women that the prison–industrial complex relies on to thrive and grow. In the end, their often-heroic efforts to defend the self left them with the kind of nagging questions that Carla (quoted above) finds herself thinking about everyday: am I any better off?

What If the Cure Is Worse Than the Disease?

The new penology is neither about punishing nor about rehabilitating individuals. It is about identifying and managing unruly
groups.
—Malcolm Feeley and Jonathan Simon, "The New Penology"

I ain't no princess, not a superstar, not going to make it big, you
know? I'm an addict, nothing changes that.
—PWH graduate, on why she relapsed following her release
from prison

When I returned to East State Women's Correctional Institution two years
after the conclusion of my original study, I was greeted at the front gate
by Lil' Toya, a prisoner who was still there serving time on her conviction
for possession of crack cocaine. "Welcome to hell," she said. Then, rolling
her eyes and nodding in the direction of a security camera lodged in the
corner of the ceiling, she commented, "You in prison now, Jill. They made
it for real since you been gone." The prison was a different place than
when it had opened its doors in 1992. Some of the changes to the physical
appearance of the facility had been implemented during the latter half of
my fieldwork. Others, like security modifications to the housing unit designated for "dangerous" prisoners and the installation of additional layers
of razor wire along perimeter fencing, were new. Deputy Warden Pearson
had retired and Warden Richardson was promoted to a prestigious position within the Department of Correction. His replacement was a former
deputy warden from the second-largest men's prison in the state. When the
new warden introduced himself to me, he observed, "[East State Prison]
has really come up. In the past it might have been thought of as a bad
career move to be warden of a woman's prison, now it's a way into a lead-
ership position with the DOC."

Beyond these changes, there were significant alterations to the prison's mission and organizational structure. The revised manual given to all incoming prisoners embraced the Department of Correction's responsibilization-inspired motto as its own, "If it's gonna be, it's up to me!" The same manual instructs prisoners, "Although staff has your best interests in mind, it is your responsibility to take control of your own life." Changes in rules and language suggested the formalization of staff–inmate relations. Prisoners were required to go through the chain of command if they had an issue they wanted to discuss with someone other than the correctional officer on duty. Internal documents like the orientation manual primarily referred to prisoners as "residents" or, less frequently, inmates. Prisoners were required to address staff members by their official titles (e.g., Officer Smith and Warden O'Malley) rather than by first names or personal monikers like "Mom." A new lexicon of discipline and control had also emerged. Inmates charged with rule violations were provided with formal disciplinary hearings and, if found guilty, were subject to "lockdown." Informally, correctional officers referred to inmates who engaged in repeated rule violations as "gangbangers" and "contracted out." Displays of disrespect directed at staff were referred to as "jailing" or "queening."[1] When staff admonished prisoners for inappropriate behavior, they said they were performing a "pull-up" and demonstrating "stern concern."

At first glance, it would seem that these changes were wholly within the "get tough" framework promoted by the Department of Correction. With its glittering razor wire and hi-tech surveillance devices, the prison looked and felt like a facility for men. By all appearances, East State no longer embraced the 19th-century concept of separate spheres in either its architecture or the surface rhythms of institutional life. There was nothing I saw upon my return to the prison that suggested that any vestiges of the old system of rehabilitative paternalism remained. Even the grainy, black-and-white photos of the original facility had been removed from the walls in the administrative wing. In this respect, the prison had achieved a sort of gender neutrality, one that was accomplished by aligning the women's facility more closely with the model used for men.

Nonetheless, punishment was not universally masculinized throughout the women's prison, nor was gender now irrelevant to the logic of penality. As I have endeavored to show throughout this book, the new penology reconfigured the ways that gender matters. Closer inspection of the prison reveals the influence of PHW's habilitative model, a gendered apparatus, on the whole of the institution's disciplinary structure and organizational culture. Referring to prisoners as "residents" was not part of the Department of

Correction's lexicon, nor was the term used in men's prisons throughout the state. This was directly imported from PHW, as were terms like "queening," "pull-up," and "stern concern." In fact, PHW's, and by extension, the Company's, leverage within the prison was considerable. By the time of the follow-up study, two Company employees were regulars at the warden's accountability meetings and had a vote on policies that affected not just PHW but prison policy more generally. PHW was in charge of 25% of the prisoner population and had ambitions to "habilitate" many more. Cross-training sessions run by the Company were part of the training all incoming correctional officers received. Among other things, new officers learned that up to 90% of women prisoners had drug problems serious enough to warrant placement in PHW's program and that their crimes were a function of "disordered selves." All of this had ramifications for the prison's control structure. In the era of rehabilitative paternalism, a prisoner who engaged in a rule violation might find herself having a heart-to-heart talk with the warden or his deputy regarding what caused her misbehavior. Depending on what the staff member felt she "needed," the prisoner may have been sent to Bible study, to a private session with a counselor, or to the nurse's office for medication. Alternatively, her offense may have been overlooked entirely. In the wake of "get tough," this kind informality and discretion diminished considerably. However, correctional officers did not merely file a disciplinary report on a prisoner accused of a rule violation. They "pulled her up" in order to express their "stern concern." In other words, they engaged in a similar set of confrontation and humiliation tactics that PHW counselors used during encounter groups.

On my first day back in the prison, I watched a male and a female correctional officer huddle over a prisoner whose back was literally pressed against the wall of the main hallway. Their faces were inches from hers as they loudly admonished her for leaving her cell block without permission. As I walked by I overheard the female CO say to the prisoner, "That was a real dope-fiend move." It was a phase I'd heard hundreds of times before within PHW. However, an interaction like this, in the prison's main hallway, would have been unthinkable just five years earlier.[2] Indeed, it was the use of derogatory names like "dope fiend" and "crack ho" that had fomented much of the prison staff's initial ire toward PHW. I later remarked on this to the new warden and he responded:

> What we call treatment the DOC calls "get tough" and it's virtually the same damned thing. We've got to call it by a different name because we're dealing with females and they're different in a number of ways from male offenders. If the DOC tells us to "get tough," we say they're insensitive to

women. If they bring caseworkers in here from social services and they tell us to hold women accountable, we do it. And you know what? As it turns out, you pretty much do the same thing to hold someone accountable as you do when you punish them.

The new warden's observations bring us to the heart of the question about gender and the new penology—in what ways does gender matter? From his vantage, treatment and punishment are "virtually" the same thing. The difference is in how control practices are named in men's and women's prisons, not in terms of the ends to which they are put. Contrast this with statements from prisoners like Red, Veronica, Alicia, and others who identify a "new kind of punishment" primarily in terms of its incursion into the private territories of the self (i.e., the new punishment "brainwashes" women and forces them to "rent out" their heads). The apparent contradiction in these claims is resolvable if we look to what the new penology is and what it is not. In Malcolm Feeley and Jonathan Simon's formulation, the new penology is not principally concerned with punishing or rehabilitating the individual offender. Rather, it is dedicated to identifying and controlling "unruly" categories of people.[3] Considered from this perspective, the warden's statement regarding treatment and punishment being the same makes sense. They are the same if we are referring to them in terms of their objectives. In the warden's words, the "get tough" era made the objective of control in both men's and women's institutions similar—to hold prisoners "accountable."

That men's and women's prisons share the same objective does not mean that they share the same techniques of control. If we accept Feeley and Simon's premise that the new penology is about identifying and managing unruly groups, it follows that the mechanisms of control may vary depending on the nature of the risk that various groups pose. Herein lies the significance of gender. From the perspective of state actors, men and women offenders represent different kinds of unruliness and, subsequently, pose different kinds of challenges for risk management. The anthropologist Lorna Rhodes's ethnography of control units in men's prisons reveals an institutional preoccupation with the rationality of male prisoners and a simultaneous commitment to inscribe control as tightly as possible on the body.[4] These institutions do not aim, even in a narrow sense, to reform the minds of the men they imprison. They are dedicated only to physical containment because the unruliness they are most concerned with is men's capacity for violence.

In contrast, women prisoners in East State and elsewhere are regarded as something less than rational actors.[5] In the era of rehabilitative paternalism, women prisoners were "good girls" who were generally not regarded as morally culpable for their crimes because they were the victims of bad men, or bad circumstances, or some combination of the two. In the wake of mass incarceration, prison staff identified a new prisoner in their midst, the "real criminal." Although they characterized her as more aggressive, angry, and manipulative than the "good girls," they did not ascribe the same rationality and volition to her as they did to male offenders. The new warden hints at this above when he says that women are "different" from men. To comprehend that difference, staff at the women's prison embraced the Company's disease concept and used it to interpret her criminal activity and drug use as symptoms of a disordered self. Her unruliness was linked not simply to her criminality, but also to her mothering skills, sexual practices, and dependency on men and the state. Managing the risks she posed meant inscribing control as tightly as possible on the self. In essence, gender informs institutional assumptions about prisoners' subjectivities and the risks they pose, and these assumptions are encoded into the prison's techniques of control. Subsequently, while both "treatment" and "punishment" aim to hold prisoners accountable, the women's prison achieves this by "breaking down" the self.

In drawing out the differences between how the new penology is interpreted and enacted across men's and women's prisons, I want to avoid overstating the case. At the turn of the 21st century, men's and women's institutions shared three very important similarities: the decline of the rehabilitative ideal, an increasingly punitive and coercive control apparatus, and a shift in the racial demographic of the prisoner population. When we focus on the similarities of men's and women's prisons, the significance of race comes sharply into view. Sociologist Loïc Wacquant and law professor Michelle Alexander argue that the new penology operates as a racial caste system, one that locks hundreds of thousands of African Americans out of economic opportunities, political participation, and social integration into mainstream, white society.[6] That the rehabilitative ideal disappeared at the moment when the number of African Americans surpassed the number of whites in the prison system is hard to dismiss as coincidence. From my study, the shift in the prison's racial demographic, coupled with overcrowding and disciplinary problems, changed the way that staff regarded prisoners. Race was central to the distinction they drew between "good girls" and "real criminals," and they routinely used prevailing racial stereotypes of African American women as "welfare queens" and "crack hos" to make two arguments about the changing character of punishment. The first was that overcrowding and high rates of prisoner recidivism were not indicators of organizational failure but, rather, symptoms of an "epidemic" whose source was impoverished, predominantly African American neighborhoods in a nearby city. Second, drawing heavily on the Company's disease model, prison staff came to see "real criminals" as broken beyond repair. Indeed, rehabilitation as an ideology of control might have survived in the face of internal problems like overcrowding and external pressures to "get tough" so long as the staff's socially constructed beliefs about the subjectivity and needs of women prisoners remained intact. But these beliefs underwent radical revisioning, and as the "good girl" disappeared from discursive representations of prisoners, so too did the staff's commitment to rehabilitation.

The latter point, regarding prisoners as "real criminals" who are incapable of rehabilitation, reflects the racial politics of the new penology and also demonstrates the influence of privatization and market logic. In terms of racial politics, mass incarceration was made possible by not one but two galvanizing tropes of the drug war: the "gangbanger" and the "crack ho." The gangbanger is feared for his capacity for impulsive violence, ruthlessness, and lack of remorse. His gendered counterpart, the crack ho, is feared for her sexual fecundity, lack of mothering skills, and dependency on state subsidies. Together each of these "real criminals" is portrayed as contributing to the moral and economic decline of impoverished, predominantly Black, urban neighborhoods, while their offspring of "crack babies" and "super-predators" are charged with threatening the stability and security of the white, middle and working classes. While the characters of "gangbanger" and "crack ho" are social constructions specific to the era of the drug war, the racial biases and fears they draw on date back to slavery. In both instances, racist constructions of young, Black men and women obscure the degree to which crime, poverty, and racial marginalization are a function of broader shifts in the political economy and of a social order that systematically privileges whites. In the current moment, these social constructions do something else as well. As Michelle Alexander argues, "In the era of mass incarceration, what it means to be a criminal in our collective consciousness has become conflated with what it means to be black."[7] The result is that the prison system becomes the major institutional site for the production of racial caste, in that it serves to permanently displace impoverished African Americans from mainstream society and the labor market. "Real criminals," who are, by definition, incapable of reform, are now subject to historically unprecedented levels of state surveillance and carceral control.

Market logic is at work here as well. One of the Company's key selling points in promoting its experimental drug treatment program to prison administrators and state officials was that habilitation would appreciably reduce the rates of prisoner recidivism and drug relapse, which, in turn, would solve the overcrowding crisis. Six years after PHW's debut in the prison, and three years after it picked up state funding, the prison was still overcrowded and the recidivism rate remained largely the same.[8] When I inquired about this, both the new warden and PHW's director explained to me that they were working with the state to provide women prisoners with "continuity of care," extending from the period of incarceration through the years following release. They emphasized that addiction is not a disease that can be cured. Rather, it is a disease that must be "managed" throughout the life course. PHW's program is "one link" in a larger chain of services that are needed to address the problem. Director Torrence noted:

> No one expected to get them in here [PHW] for twelve months, eighteen months, and then release them into the community and that's the end of it. They're in recovery in here. They're not cured. They need support and they're not going to get it going back to the communities they're going back to. To remain in recovery, it's not something they can do on their own.

The line staff I talked to were similarly pessimistic. More than one officer described it as a "vicious cycle" and reiterated that prisoners needed "after-care" programs following their release.

This theory of addiction and disorder served the Company well. It opened up a new market for drug treatment services in the burgeoning field of community corrections. In East State and elsewhere, the Company marketed a "therapeutic work release" program as the necessary complement to their prison-based programs, and it developed additional "aftercare" programs for parolees who had completed their time in work release. It used data the state had collected to show that while participation in PHW did not appreciably lessen women's rates of recidivism or drug relapse, time spent in both PHW and therapeutic work release did. Thus the longer a prisoner's exposure to habilitation, the better the odds for managing her disorder. Beyond opening up a new market, the disease model of addiction served to decouple evaluations of the drug treatment program's success from external measures like recidivism rates. The Company was able to successfully convince state officials that recidivism and relapse were "part of the process" of recovery. Instead of using recidivism and relapse data to evaluate the success of its drug treatment programs, it promoted internal measures like reductions in the rate of prisoner disciplinary infractions and survey data showing that prisoners possessed "greater awareness" of "addictive behaviors."

There is an interesting tension between the state's interest in holding prisoners "accountable" and the Company's claim that drug-involved offenders are largely incapable of self-regulation. In the orientation manual the prison distributes to all incoming prisoners, statements like "If it's gonna be, it's up to me!" exist alongside literature from PHW that describes addiction as a "disorder of the person." The manual's appendix includes a statement of PHW's philosophy as written by its "residents":

> Through these times of heartache and pain, we have learned to respect ourselves and have grown to love who we are. Our morals and standards are at their all time high. We are not total in being. We came to share in the belief that our trials and tribulations will bring us peace within ourselves and a life of integrity. We all have our faults, perfect we will never be. Coming together will pull us through. All that we can accomplish is not just for me, it's also for you. Sharing is caring. We talk the talk and walk the walk. Laugh and cry. All we have is hope in our eyes. There is a destiny that makes us Sisters.

In this statement, there is no mention of recovery or rehabilitation as a tangible end point or goal. Instead, prisoners hold out hope that maintaining high morals and standards will allow them to find inner peace in the face of "trials and tribulations." They echo PHW's ideology that they are not "total in being." Instead of self-regulation, they speak in terms of community regulation ("coming together will pull us through"), but it remains unclear in this passage who the community is that they are referring to: Is it their communities of origin? The correctional system? The Company's network of drug treatment providers?

This raises the question—what are the consequences of the new penology for women prisoners? In the analysis, I discussed the impact of habilitation on how prisoners navigated their sentences. For the most part, it shifted their focus away from strategizing ways to expedite their release from prison and toward defending a vision of the self as respectable. This was troubling on at least two levels. First, like prisoners in the community correctional program that Lynne Haney studied in her book *Offending Women*, women in East State were further disempowered within this new system of control.[9] While it was certainly not the case that women were empowered within the former system of rehabilitative paternalism, they were occasionally able to exploit the staff's use of "needs talk" to pursue larger political objectives like acquiring a law library and challenging overcrowded conditions as unconstitutional. Within the new penology, however, they were no longer able to speak in terms of their "needs" because addiction ideology held that they were unreliable narrators of those needs. For example, when a prisoner argued that she *needed* job training more than drug treatment, counselors told her that she was in "denial" about her addiction. Prisoners were similarly unable to engage in "rights" talk. Although they often claimed the program was "abusive," they were unsure whether they had a legal right not to have to endure it. One prisoner explained, "If they out of the blue hit us, that's abuse, and we can object because violence is illegal. If they call us crackheads and dogs, what can we do except try to get away from it? It's not illegal." As a result, the resistance prisoners pursued was narrow, individualized, and immediate in its scope. For the most part, prisoners just wanted to get out of PHW even if that meant extending the amount of time they did behind bars. They often did that using any means necessary, including violence. This disadvantaged them in that it meant they often lost good-time credit and the possibility of a release upon their minimum. Further, because displays of resistance often took dramatic turns, it served to confirm institutional constructions of them as unredeemable and disordered.

Second, although PHW was not successful in terms of convincing a majority of prisoners to "surrender to the process," it did have serious ramifications for how women defined themselves and how they understood their experiences, particularly with respect to poverty, violence, and sexual abuse. Carla, the prisoner whose story I profiled in the opening of chapter 6, told me that she had seriously begun to question whether she was the "good person" she thought herself to be before entering PHW. Although she was critical of certain aspects of the program's addiction ideology, she also wondered whether the impoverished circumstances she found herself in following her release from prison were the result of her being "in denial" about her "true self." Most of the women who were a part of this study report being plagued by doubts about the essential nature of their selves during some or all of their time in PHW. Their doubts about the self were linked to their fears about the future, particularly regarding their economic circumstances, their relationships with men, their ability to effectively parent and nurture their children, and their capacity to get away from the drugs, crime, and violence of the streets.

So what happened to the prisoners who were a part of this study after I left the field and many of them left the prison? When I returned to the prison in 2000, I was able to interview twenty-six women from the original study. Six years later, I remained in contact with just over a third of that group. Their stories speak to the implications of PHW and the new penology as mechanisms of state power directed primarily at poor, African American and Latina women.[10] By and large, these are not stories with happy endings. Alicia, the prisoner whose dramatic departure from PHW garnered the support of several COs and prison staff members, was murdered over a drug dispute two years after she had been released from prison. Ann, who had done two separate stints in prison and in PHW during the course of my research, died from a drug overdose along a section of an interstate highway known for drug sales and prostitution. That both women had relapsed on drugs following their release was common knowledge within the prison. Following news of their deaths (which occurred within a year of one another), PHW counselors and prison staff used the manner in which each woman died to emphasize to prisoners that they had only two options in life: "surrender to the process" or "walk with the dead." Many prisoners told me during the follow-up study that Alicia and Ann's deaths made it that much more difficult to raise objections to PHW's techniques of control or to request a transfer back to the prison's general population. As one prisoner remarked, "If you have kids, you really gonna think twice about leaving [PHW] now because it's like you're risking your life and, as a mother, you can't do that."

Among the women I interviewed, there was no clear pattern between their expressed willingness to "surrender to the process" and their subsequent success or failure on the street. For example, of those who resisted some or all of PHW's claims on the self, Veronica's story was unusual. She had originally been given an eighteen-year sentence for credit card fraud, but the judge offered to suspend thirteen years of it if she agreed to spend two years in PHW. She successfully graduated from the program but throughout it all remained critical of addiction ideology and the program's techniques of control. Several years following her release, she was able to open her own beauty salon and qualify for a loan to buy Section 8 housing. During our last interview, she pointed out that both the purchase of her house and the loan she used to start her business had been possible only because her conviction was for fraud rather than for a drug crime. More typical is Carla, who throughout all the years I have known her has struggled to make ends meet. After many years of "playing by the rules," economic circumstances got the better of her. By 2005, she was living in a three-bedroom row house located in a high-crime neighborhood with her three children, her older brother, his girlfriend, their newborn baby, and an elderly aunt. As a convicted felon, she was ineligible for subsidized housing, jobs programs, college loans, and welfare. She was earning minimum wage at a convenience store but admitted that she had recently started hustling drugs on the side in order to save up enough money to get her own apartment. She told me she was not using the drugs she was selling, and elaborated, "I'm not stupid, I have no interest in getting back into the life. I'm too old, I've got kids, and even if I didn't, I'll get caught. It's just that simple. It's exhausting, I get that. But however you look at it, I'm still having to hustle. There's no other way."

For other women, returning to "the life" was a function of economic circumstances as well as the lure of drugs. I found eight women from the original study selling sexual services along a well-known prostitution strip located less than two miles from the prison. Some were working on their own out of a corner bar, catering primarily to day laborers and construction workers. Others worked for a small network of pimps that operated out of a dilapidated motel that sold rooms by the hour. Women who appeared to have some control over their drug use worked the parking lot of a large truck stop. All but one of them asked not to be identified in the book's conclusion, preferring that their observations about PHW and the prison not be tainted by the fact that they returned to the streets. As one woman said, "Let my name out of that part. No one will listen to me because they'll say I'm just a crackhead."

The exception was Robin who was featured briefly in chapter 7 as one of the prisoners who was desperate to leave PHW because she felt like she was "going nuts" and was going to "lose her head." I found her through her pimp. When we spoke, she told me to come over to where she was staying, explaining that she wanted to "keep it real." Even though I had spent that summer doing research on the streets, the reality of Robin's situation was particularly difficult for me to witness. I found her in the upstairs bedroom of a two-story house with six other people, all of them huddled over a crack pipe. I barely recognized her. Robin had always been thin but now her slight frame was wasted to practically nothing. She had burns from the pipe around her mouth and lips. I asked if we should wait to do the interview but she insisted on doing it then. She was so high that I had trouble making sense of her responses to my questions. In her more lucid moments, though, she kept coming back around to the same point: "I'm an addict. I started using on the street but I became an addict in there [prison]." I believe that what she meant is that she had learned to identify as an "addict" in PHW. Prior to that, it was not a component of her self-identity.

This sentiment, about "becoming" an addict in prison, was not confined to Robin. Indeed, it was a theme that was particularly pronounced in my interviews with women who reported "surrendering to the process." For some of them, embracing the identity of "addict" strengthened their resolve to remain sober and "work the process." For example, five years following her release, Shawna was clean and sober and earning a living as a drug treatment counselor in a community-based program run by the Company. She credited PHW with "saving her life," and said that although she still experienced challenges in terms of her economic situation, she "used the process" to overcome the urge to "take the easy way out." Others, however, took their newfound identity as an addict to justify ongoing substance abuse. Leda, for example, had managed to stay sober for six months before relapsing on crack cocaine. When I asked her about it she told me that she had "made peace" with her "true self." She explained:

> People don't change. They're either bad or good, that's it. Heaven or hell. Not much to do about it once it's been set up. I'm an addict, the program made me realize that. I can be an addict if I don't use or I can be walking with the dead, but I'm always an addict. It's who I am. I'm a crack addict. Recovering, it's just a matter of time [before a relapse] because you are what you are. My using? I'm just finally getting honest. *Finally* [her emphasis]. I ain't no princess, not a superstar, not going to make it big, you know? I'm an addict, nothing changes that.

Regardless of whether these women were able to get off the streets and away from drugs, their experiences raise a crucial, final question—was the cure worse than the disease? When I present this research at academic and policy conferences, I am routinely asked if "punishment" in the form of "humane warehousing" is a preferable alternative to "treatment" in the form of PHW. The question is intended to be provocative, and often what animates it is the concern that by critiquing one of the very few alternatives to "get tough" punishment I am undermining efforts to challenge mass incarceration and the punitive character of contemporary penal regimes. I am sympathetic to this concern; however, I think the question itself is premised on a false dichotomy between treatment and punishment. There has been a long-standing tendency in both the research literature and in policy circles to frame "treatment" as a lesser (and preferable) form of coercion than "punishment." While that distinction may well have been analytically useful in the past, it no longer is today. Habilitation essentially collapses the distinction between treatment and punishment. As I have endeavored to demonstrate throughout the book, habilitation relies on a set of social technologies that aim to forcibly "break down" the self. From the perspective of many prisoners in this study, habilitation was the most coercive aspect of their prison experience not only because of its intensity and unrelenting character, but also because of the intrusiveness of its reach. Subsequently, habilitation is a new penology—one that is the gendered and racialized counterpart to coercive efforts to control and contain bodies in men's prisons. As such, it is necessary to consider habilitation on its own terms.

There are two angles from which to consider whether the "cure" of new penology is worse than the "disease" of drug abuse and crime. There is first the immediate, institutional context of the prison, and second, the broader socioeconomic contexts that women navigate in order to earn a living, raise their children, make community, experience love and pleasure, and pursue, in the words of one prisoner, a "little bit of happiness." In terms of the immediate context of the prison, PHW offers a lot to be desired as a particular kind of programmatic intervention. It forced many women to abandon educational and vocational opportunities that, while not a panacea, held out the possibility of tangible economic and social benefits. Beyond this, it compelled them to consider their lives through the narrow and distorting lens of addiction ideology. For the majority of prisoners I knew, drug use was not a relevant category in how they defined themselves, nor were terms like "criminal" or "addict." Even those who took pride in their work on the street as hustlers and dealers did not see themselves as only these things. Their definitions of self reflected the variety of roles they played and the social networks they belonged to. They were simultaneously mothers, workers, players, hustlers, students, wives, girlfriends, and "good people." A central problem with PHW as a drug treatment program was that it reduced their self-identities to one or two disreputable categories and denied them their complexity and their respectability.

That most of the women did not initially define themselves as addicts does not mean that they did not recognize drugs as a potential problem in their lives or that they were uninterested in seeking a way to either control or terminate their use. However, virtually all of the women in this study strongly rejected PHW's premise that they needed to be "broken down." They made a point of emphasizing that they entered prison with profound concerns about their physical safety, fear that their relationships with family and friends would erode, worried about children, confused about their legal status, and disoriented by the disruption in their routine. Encounter groups and confrontations with counselors added to the maelstrom and left them feeling humiliated, mortified, and demoralized. Greater emphasis on education and persuasion, rather than confrontation, humiliation, and coercion, might have allowed these prisoners to reconcile their own ideas about addiction and drug use with larger treatment narratives. The ability to negotiate and participate in a dialogue about their lives would likely have increased their commitment to the program and their chances of success. Of course, none of these changes would amount to much if the program continued to make use of the disease concept and claim that the disordered self can never be whole. Such a perspective left prisoners with little to hope for beyond, in Red's words, "some kind of civility." Given what they were up against in the broader social landscape, civility does not amount to a whole lot.

This brings me to the second angle from which to consider PHW and the new penology, and that is in terms of how this mechanism of governance is fitted within the contours of poor, undereducated, predominantly African American women's lives. If we take a broader perspective and consider state policies at the turn of the century, we see that the War on Drugs coincided with a War on Poverty, the hallmark of which was welfare reform measures that had the effect of barring millions of poor women from receiving a variety of state subsidies. While the War on Poverty is characterized by the retreat of the welfare state, the War on Drugs marks the advance of a penal leviathan. Based on this study, it is a leviathan that, without question, left women worse off than they were before. While most prisoners in my study found ways, however problematic, of making ends meet in the wake of economic restructuring and welfare's end, many were unable to conquer the challenges posed by the rise of a criminal justice state. As drug offenders, they were barred from the few forms of state support that remained (e.g., subsidized housing, college loans, small business development loans, and Temporary Aid to Needy Families), and as convicted felons, all faced an uphill battle in terms of finding steady work that covered the basics of food, rent, and diapers. Some women lost their children. At least four of the prisoners from the original study lost their lives to the streets. Most returned to the same communities and faced the same challenges that confronted them in the past: violence, drugs, poverty, and a pervading sense of hopelessness. As Red and so many other women from the follow-up study told me, they returned to those communities at a fundamental disadvantage. They were not referring to the economic, political, and social penalties that accrue to the status of being "convicted felons" so much as they were referring to the disadvantage conferred by the loss of something more basic—the integrity of the self.

The last time I saw Red was at a street festival. I had spent virtually every day of the last month looking for her. A few of my study participants told me that she was back to hustling but no one could confirm this and I could not find her in any of the places that I had grown accustomed to finding former prisoners. I did not go to the festival expecting to see her or anyone else from my study but there she was, sitting on a bench with a man who was rumored to be one of the area's most significant drug dealers. She smiled brightly as she recognized me and waved me over. She looked a little tired but generally good, just as I remembered her. As I approached, the man with her scowled at me and placed his arm firmly around her shoulders. Turning to him, she explained that I was writing a book that she was going to be in. "Why would anyone write a book about you." He said it as more of a statement than a question. She furrowed her brow and bowed her head. "Dunno," she said.

She looked very fragile just then. I took that as my cue to leave but before I did, Red and I made plans to meet the next day. Unfortunately, she never showed and I never heard from her again. I have thought of that last conversation with her many times over the intervening years and wondered what happened to her. Beyond that, I wonder what good is a state policy that, at best, only confers "some kind of civility" on its bearers.

For Red and many women like her, the cure of the new penology is worse than the entangling diseases of crime, poverty, and drug abuse. In the years leading up to the War on Drugs, most of the women in my study would not have been sent to prison for their crimes. Others, like Red, would have gone to prison but for considerably shorter periods of time than they are doing now. While there, they would likely have faced a less coercive control apparatus. In the 150 years since Gustave de Beaumont and Alexis de Tocqueville published *On the Penitentiary System in the United States and Its Application in France*, it has become abundantly clear that prisons are not institutions where social inequalities can be redressed or troubled souls healed. They seem, in fact, to do quite the opposite. Prisons exacerbate existing forms of social inequality and, in the process, threaten to erode the humanity of both the keepers and the kept. Observing aspects of this problem, de Beaumont and de Tocqueville argued, "If the penitentiary system cannot propose to itself an end other than radical reformation . . . , the legislature should abandon this system; not because the aim is not an admirable one, but because it is too rarely obtained."[11] I draw a similar conclusion here. Although state officials, prison administrators, and Company executives justified the new penology on the grounds that it served the needs of prisoners and the general public, in reality it did neither. By failing to help prisoners solve the crises in their lives, PHW was ultimately unable to serve the larger public's interest in reducing drug use and crime. Indeed, the only identifiable beneficiaries of the new penology were the Company (which profited from the sale of its services), state officials who looked "tough on crime," and prison administrators who were temporarily spared blame for institutional crises like overcrowding and recidivism. Providing a long-term, viable solution to a problem as complex as that presented by poverty and substance abuse is not something that prisons are well equipped to do. For that reason, the solution is not to tinker with the control apparatus of the prison but to abandon that apparatus altogether.

NOTES

NOTES TO THE PREFACE

1. Steinhauer, "Schwarzenegger Seeks Shift from Prisons to Schools."
2. Faler, "Bennett under Fire for Remark on Crime and Black Abortions."

NOTES TO THE INTRODUCTION

1. Names of persons, organizations, and places have been changed in order to ensure confidentiality. Although a number of prisoners insisted that I use their real names, I was prevented from doing so according to the stipulations of the Internal Review Board approval for this research. I tried to strike a balance by allowing prisoners, whenever possible, to select their own pseudonyms.
2. The decision to obscure the name of the prison and the state in which it is located is my own. Although the trend in ethnography of late has been to identify places on the premise that context matters, doing so in a prison is politically and ethically fraught. In particular, I am committed to protecting the identities of prisoners as well as state actors, a number of whom would otherwise be identifiable by virtue of their positions. Although I am often critical in this book of their decisions and actions, I greatly appreciate the trust they placed in me when they granted me access to the prison and the wider system in which it was located. I don't want to betray that trust by revealing any information that might compromise their careers or their reputations. Further, I am mindful that contemporary prison ethnographies represent a rare research genre. The decline of the prison ethnography is reflective of a broader trend that is itself a key feature of the new penology—the disappearance of social scientists from prisons and other correctional facilities (see Simon, "Society of Captives"). The disappearing act was not by choice. By century's end, a majority of states had adopted restrictive policies designed to severely limit researcher access to prisons and to control the kind of research that could be done therein. This, of course, can be interpreted as a backlash against earlier research that was not only critical of punishment practices but also named names. Although I absolutely agree with ethnographers who argue that context matters in developing analyses, in this particular situation I believe that preserving researcher access matters more. What is happening in the contemporary prison system is too important not to report on. Ultimately, I decided to obscure the name of the prison and of the state to leave the door open behind me for future researchers to enter. Whatever sacrifices I've made in the analysis as a result of that decision are minor compared to the larger implications of blocked access.
3. Also pseudonyms.

4. See Belknap, *Invisible Woman*; Becker and McCorkel, "Gender of Criminal Opportunity"; and Heimer and De Coster, "Gendering of Violent Delinquency."

5. In Red's case (which was by no means typical) the deal for successful completion of PHW included time off her minimum and the opportunity to serve a portion of her sentence in a community-based work-release facility.

6. For a comprehensive overview of therapeutic communities, see Kooyman, *Therapeutic Community for Addicts*; DeLeon, "Therapeutic Community for Substance Abuse"; and Sugarman, *Daytop Village*.

7. Gowan and Whetstone, "Making the Criminal Addict."

8. Red was eligible for time off her sentence because, unlike women convicted of drug crimes, her robbery convictions did not carry mandatory minimums.

9. The belief in a "real" and "empirical" self has persisted in American culture throughout much of the twentieth century. More recently, postmodernists have called into question the reality of the self, suggesting that hyperreality reduces the self to little more than multiple, fragmented representations. See Holstein and Gubrium, *The Self We Live By*.

10. Garland, *Culture of Control*; and Garland, *Punishment and Modern Society*.

11. Garland is not arguing, of course, that prisons necessarily engage in meaningful strategies to rehabilitate prisoners in practice. Studies like Irwin's *Prisons in Turmoil* suggest that rehabilitation as a practice waxes and wanes in institutional priority. Garland's point is that rehabilitation has operated as a legitimating device for a variety of control measures (ranging from chain gangs to group therapy) throughout much of the 20th century.

12. Foucault, *Discipline and Punish*.

13. Given the often-eclectic variety of crimes that states categorize as felonies, three strikes laws have produced some shocking outcomes. In California, one defendant who had prior convictions for burglary and robbery received a sentence of twenty-five years to life for his "third strike"—shoplifting golf clubs. See Zimring, Hawkins, and Kamin, *Punishment and Democracy*.

14. For more on federal drug laws and crack cocaine, see Bogazianos, *5 Grams*; Inciardi, *War on Drugs II*; and Reinarman and Levine, *Crack in America*.

15. Bureau of Justice Statistics, *Correctional Populations in the United States*.

16. King, "Rise and Rise of Supermax"; DiIulio, "Coming of the Super-Predators."

17. King, "Rise and Rise of Supermax"; Dowker and Good, "Proliferation of Control Unit Prisons in the United States"; Haney, "Infamous Punishment."

18. A comprehensive review of this research is impossible to include here, but one of the most detailed and nuanced studies to date is Rhodes, *Total Confinement*. See also King, "Rise and Rise of Supermax"; Dowker and Good, "Proliferation of Control Unit Prisons in the United States"; Haney, "Infamous Punishment"; and Perkinson, *Texas Tough*.

19. Feeley and Simon, "New Penology."

20. Ibid., 455.

21. Ibid.; Lynch, "Waste Managers?"; Blomberg and Cohen, *Punishment and Social Control*.

22. For example, see Miller, "Looking for Postmodernism in All the Wrong Places"; and Simon and Feeley's own acknowledgement, in "True Crime," that some of their pronouncements in the original article were premature.

23. Wacquant, *Punishing the Poor*; see also Gowan and Whetstone, "Making the Criminal Addict."

24. Britton, *At Work in the Iron Cage*; Rafter, *Partial Justice*; McCorkel, "Embodied Surveillance and the Gendering of Punishment"; Haney, "Homeboys, Babies, Men in Suits." For general discussion of gender regimes and gender organizations, see Acker, "Hierarchies, Jobs, Bodies"; and Connell, *Gender and Power*.

25. Rafter, *Partial Justice*; Freedman, *Their Sisters' Keepers*; Britton, *At Work in the Iron Cage*.

26. Kruttschnitt and Gartner, *Marking Time in the Golden State*.

27. Mauer, Potler, and Wolf, *Gender and Justice*.

28. Bureau of Justice Statistics, *Sourcebook of Criminal Justice Statistics*; Bureau of Justice Statistics, *Prisoners in 2009*.

29. Bloom, Chesney-Lind, and Owen report that increases in the number of women sent to prison in California are not caused by a worsening of women's crime participation but of the criminal justice system's more punitive response to women, particularly for those convicted of drug crimes. See *Women in California Prisons*. See also Mauer, Potler, and Wolf, *Gender and Justice*.

30. Chesney-Lind and Pollock, "Women's Prisons."

31. Rhodes, *Total Confinement*; Inderbitzin, "Look from the Inside"; Comfort, *Doing Time Together*; and Wakefield and Uggen, "Incarceration and Stratification."

32. Kruttschnitt and Gartner, *Marking Time in the Golden State*.

33. See also Owen, *In the Mix*.

34. The irony, of course, is that women are responsible for their own rehabilitation at a historical moment when opportunities to do so are limited. See also Bosworth, "Creating the Responsible Prisoner"; Pollack, "You Can't Have It Both Ways"; and Hannah-Moffat, "Losing Ground."

35. Rose, "Government and Control." See also Burchell, Gordon, and Miller, *Foucault Effect*.

36. Hannah-Moffat, *Punishment in Disguise*.

37. Ibid.; Hannah-Moffat, "Sacrosanct or Flawed." See also Pollack, "Taming the Shrew"; and Pollack, "I'm Just Not Good in Relationships." For more on the politics of need interpretation, see Fraser, *Unruly Practices*.

38. Haney, *Offending Women*.

39. See also McKim, "Getting Gut Level," an ethnography of a community-based drug treatment program for women offenders.

40. For a different take on what is happening currently in Canada, see Kilty, "It's Like They Don't Want You to Get Better." In this study, prison authorities rely on (over)prescription of psychotropic medications to manage women prisoners.

41. Haney, *Offending Women*, 52.

42. Ibid.

43. Some of the most interesting, theoretically sophisticated scholarship considers how the new penology functions to replace welfare as a technique for surveilling and controlling poor women. See Haney, "Gender, Welfare, and States of Punishment"; Hannah-Moffat, "Losing Ground"; and Roth, "Searching for the State."

44. Mauer and Huling, *Young Black Americans and the Criminal Justice System*.

45. Bureau of Justice Statistics, *Prisoners in 1996*.

46. Alexander, *New Jim Crow*; Wacquant, "Deadly Symbiosis."

47. Wacquant, *Punishing the Poor*.

48. Alexander, *New Jim Crow*.

49. For a fuller discussion of my experiences as an ethnographer in the setting, see McCorkel and Myers, "What Difference Does Difference Make?"

50. Haney, *Offending Women*; McKim, "Getting Gut Level."

NOTES TO CHAPTER 1

1. In January 1994, Prison Services Company provided medical services to ninety-one thousand inmates in seventeen states. It is a wholly owned subsidiary of a much larger health care company with annual revenues exceeding $5 billion.

2. By unfounding previously reported crimes, police departments reduce the overall crime rate and improve an important measure of success. Conversely, police can maintain an elevated crime rate by failing to unfound erroneous crime reports. They can then argue that high crime rates are the result of limited personnel and resources and thereby bolster their demands for more of both. See Lundman, *Police and Policing*; and Maxfield, Lewis, and Szoc, "Producing Official Crimes."

3. See Garland, *Punishment and Welfare*; Garland, *Culture of Control*; and Foucault, *Discipline and Punish*.

4. See Garland, *Punishment and Welfare*; Ignatieff, *Just Measure of Pain*; Foucault, *Discipline and Punish*; Rafter, *Partial Justice*; Simon, *Poor Discipline*; and Rothman, *Discovery of the Asylum*.

5. Numerous ethnographies, historical studies, and first-person accounts demonstrate that even when political and public support for rehabilitative measures is high, prison staff remain principally concerned with order and control, and are disposed to using varying degrees of punitiveness and coercion to accomplish these goals. For examples, see Dodge, *Whores and Thieves of the Worst Kind*; Conover, *Newjack*; Abbott, *In the Belly of the Beast*; Freedman, *Their Sisters' Keepers*; Hannah-Moffat, *Punishment in Disguise*; Irwin, *Prisons in Turmoil*; and Jacobs, *Stateville*.

6. On the rise of a "new penology," see Feeley and Simon, "New Penology"; Simon and Feeley, "True Crime"; Simon, "*Paramilitary Features of* Contemporary Penality"; and Pratt, "Return of the Wheelbarrow Men." Quote on "technical transformation" is from Foucault, *Discipline and Punish*, 233.

7. Feeley and Simon, "New Penology"; Rhodes, *Total Confinement*; Austin and Irwin, *It's About Time*.

8. Garland, *Culture of Control*. See also Simon and Feeley, "True Crime."

9. By 2000, the imprisonment rate was 450 per 100,000, which is just over five times the rate in 1972. See Garland, *Mass Imprisonment*.

10. Bureau of Justice Statistics, *Prisoners in 2006*; Sentencing Project, *Women in the Criminal Justice System*; Human Rights Watch, *Punishment and Prejudice*; Greene and Pranis, *Hard Hit*.

11. Garland, *Culture of Control*; Wacquant, "Deadly Symbiosis"; Beckett and Western, "Governing Social Marginality"; Wacquant, *Punishing the Poor*.

12. On "loose coupling" between policy and practice and the significance of local state actors, see Haney, "Homeboys, Babies, Men in Suits"; Thomas, "Aspects of Negotiated Order, Loose Coupling, and Mesostructure in Maximum Security Prisons"; Horowitz, *Teen Mothers*; and Hagan, "Social Organization."

13. For an elaboration of gendered organizational cultures in the prison system, see Britton, *At Work in the Iron Cage*.

14. Mirroring national trends, the population of women inmates in the state nearly tripled during the 1980s.

15. By the mid-1990s, the facility had been converted into an intake and treatment center for first-time drug and driving under the influence (DUI) offenders.

16. Feminist criminologists were among the first to observe that the "tough on crime" movement had important consequences for the gendered structure of the penal system. Meda Chesney-Lind and Joycelyn Pollock characterize this as "equality with a vengeance," while Dana Britton rightly observes that "equal treatment" is in fact "masculinization," since men's prisons serve as the baseline along which "equality" is brokered. See Chesney-Lind and Pollock, "Women's Prisons"; and Britton, *At Work in the Iron Cage*.

17. Rafter, *Partial Justice*; Freedman, *Their Sisters' Keepers*; Britton, *At Work in the Iron Cage*; Dodge, *Whores and Thieves of the Worst Kind*.

18. Dodge, *Whores and Thieves of the Worst Kind*; Colvin, *Penitentiaries, Reformatories, and Chain Gangs*; Rafter, *Partial Justice*; Freedman, *Their Sisters' Keepers*; Rothman, *Conscience and Convenience*.

19. Martinson, "What Works?" 22–54.

20. Martinson's findings have generated considerable debate and critique. See Inciardi, *War on Drugs II*.

21. This was slightly higher than the national average of 6% for actual expenditures in 1996. See Bureau of Justice Statistics, *State Prison Expenditures 1996*.

22. I was unable to verify these accounts of prison pregnancies or prostitution rings in the database of local newspapers, although this may be a function of limitations in the database.

23. See Dodge, *Whores and Thieves of the Worst Kind*; Rafter, *Partial Justice*; and Freedman, *Their Sisters' Keepers*.

24. Young, white women made up the greatest proportion of those sent to reformatories, while most Black women continued to serve their time in separate quarters within men's penitentiaries and in prison camps. This was based, in part, on the fact that Black women were disproportionately charged and convicted of felonies, but also reflected the popularity of eugenics and racist classification systems among reformers and criminal justice officials. See Rafter, *Partial Justice*.

25. Freedman, *Their Sisters' Keepers*; Rafter, *Partial Justice*.

26. Rafter, *Partial Justice*; Freedman, *Their Sisters' Keepers*; Dodge, *Whores and Thieves of the Worst Kind*.

27. See also Giallombardo's noted ethnography of a federal women's prison, *Society of Women*.

28. This is not to suggest that men's prisons have abandoned strictly punitive measures, only that the public face of the prison system has been organized in terms of reform rather than revenge. For greater elaboration, see Garland, *Culture of Control*; and Garland, *Punishment and Welfare*.

29. See Mills, "Situated Actions."

30. The deputy warden, who began her career in 1963 as a matron in the old facility, recalled that the use of familial references dated to "well before" her time in the institution. The number of years she worked in the facility eclipsed that of other senior staff members and the "old-timer" inmates I was able to interview.

31. See Ward and Kassebaum, *Women's Prison*; Giallombardo, *Society of Women*; Heffernan, *Making It in Prison*; and Owen, *In the Mix*. These authors focus primarily on the use of familial metaphors among inmates rather than between inmates and corrections staff. This appears to be an oversight, as reported comments from inmates and staff in their studies suggest that familial references are "in play" to describe staff–inmate relations as well as relations among inmates.

32. They frequently indicated that "approximately" 90% of the inmates in East State were victims of physical or sexual abuse. This figure came from a 1993 survey of inmates commissioned by the Department of Correction. I was unable to access the survey data and therefore cannot confirm the accuracy of administrators' claims. Nonetheless, a 1991 Bureau of Justice Statistics survey of women incarcerated in state prisons reported that just under half had experienced physical or sexual abuse. A number of commentators have suggested this figure is an underestimate. Bureau of Justice Statistics, *Women in Prison*. See McCorkel, "Justice, Gender, and Incarceration"; Richie, *Compelled to Crime*; and Human Rights Watch Women's Rights Project, *Sexual Abuse of Women in U.S. State Prisons*.

33. In *Total Confinement*, Rhodes makes a similar observation with respect to disputes between custody and mental health staff in men's prisons. A central debate animating contemporary discussions of control and treatment in men's maximum security prisons is whether troubled inmates have the capacity for self-control and can choose conformity over deviant behavior.

34. Rhodes offers a useful elaboration on this point in *Total Confinement*.

35. That very summer an inmate successfully escaped from the prison by slipping out of an unlocked door and climbing over the chain-link fence that surrounded the prison. Her escape prompted the installation of additional layers of razor wire.

36. This is entirely consistent with the rehabilitative functions of segregation and the silent system as they were outlined in Bentham's blueprint of the penitentiary. See Bentham, "Panopticon."

37. Foucault, *Discipline and Punish*, 26.

38. In contrast, there is very little effort to invoke a language of rights. This is particularly pronounced in the women's prison, where even inmates frame their demands in terms of needs. For a discussion of the gendered politics of need interpretation in the welfare system, see Fraser, *Unruly Practices*.

39. Rhodes, *Total Confinement*, 94.

40. During the early 1990s, there were as many religious programs in the prison as there were educational, vocational, and counseling programs combined.

41. McCorkel, "Justice, Gender, and Incarceration"; Lindquist, "Prison Discipline *and the Female Offender*"; Mann, *Female Crime and Delinquency*; Carlen and Worrall, *Gender, Crime, and Justice*.

42. See Bosworth's discussion of how women prisoners exploit norms of femininity as a form of resistance in *Engendering Resistance*.

43. Baskin et al., "Mental Health Services"; McCorkel, "Justice, Gender, and Incarceration"; Watterson, *Women in Prison*; and Kilty, "It's Like They Don't Want You to Get Better." The prevalence of prescription psychotropics at East State was not unusual. Many studies have reported similar levels in women's prisons across the country, and attribute it to the pervasive tendency to "psychiatrize" women's deviant behavior as well as to compensate for supervisory problems associated with understaffing.

44. The only vocational programs were food service, sewing, and horticulture. The description of food service training from the orientation manual for inmates describes it as, "You will cater banquets, outside events, and prepare meals for the staff."

45. This is consistent with studies that show resources are particularly limited in women's prisons because state prison systems operate on economies of scale. See McCorkel "Justice, Gender, and Incarceration"; Ross and Fabiano, *Female Offenders*.

46. Jacobs, *Stateville*; Irwin, *Prisons in Turmoil*.

47. Women's prisons have historically suffered from invisibility, but this has carried with it a fair degree of autonomy. See Kruttschnitt and Gartner, *Marking Time in the Golden State*; and Freedman, *Their Sisters' Keepers*.

48. Unless they were staffed by community volunteers or staff members who were willing to donate time.

NOTES TO CHAPTER 2

1. I was in attendance for the film and the controversy that ensued. The Company's report detailing the results of its own investigation was consistent with my observations.

2. Indeed, in the official minutes from that meeting, the recording secretary noted that "a representative from [PHW] did not attend. The Committee agreed that it is imparative [*sic*] for [PHW] to participate in these meetings. An invitation will be extended to one of the counselors to attend."

3. For more on criminal anthropology and scientific racism, see Rafter, *Criminal Brain*.

4. "Cesare Lombroso, the father of criminal anthropology, went to so far as to recommend death as a form of natural selection for certain categories of repeat criminal offenders." Ibid., 83.

5. Ayers, *Vengeance and Justice*; Colvin, *Penitentiaries, Reformatories, and Chain Gangs*; Fierce, *Slavery Revisited*; Lichtenstein, "Public and the Private in Penal History"; Sellin, *Slavery and the Penal System*.

6. Davis and Shaylor, "Race, Gender, and the Prison Industrial Complex"; Hallet, "Commerce with Criminals"; Feeley, "Entrepreneurs of Punishment"; Sudbury, "Celling Black Bodies"; Wacquant, "Four Strategies to Curb Carceral Costs."

7. Davis and Shaylor, "Race, Gender, and the Prison Industrial Complex"; Davis, *Are Prisons Obsolete?* Dyer, *Perpetual Prisoner Machine*.

8. Wood, "Globalization and Prison Privatization"; Bureau of Justice Statistics, *Census of State and Federal Correctional Facilities*.

9. Wacquant, *Punishing the Poor*.

10. Wood, "Globalization and Prison Privatization."

11. Schneider, "Public-Private Partnerships in the U.S. Prison System"; Dyer, *Perpetual Prisoner Machine*; Shichor, "Private Prisons in Perspective."

12. Justice Policy Institute, *Gaming the System*.

13. For example, Corrections Corporation of America charges prisoners at its facility in Lumpkin, Georgia, five dollars per minute to use the phone. This policy helped the prison earn between $35 and 50 million in net profits for the year. See Beadle, "Private Prison Charges."

14. The popularity of private prisons has receded in the wake of widely publicized problems with lax security and escapes, constitutionally inadequate health care, and very little in the way of demonstrable cost savings. Wood, "Globalization and Prison Privatization."

15. Holloway, "The Root."

16. Featherstone, *Narratives from the 1971 Attica Prison Riot*; Wicker, *Time to Die*; Useem and Kimball, *States of Siege*.

17. Ibid.

18. The numbers Dr. Nesbitt presented were as follows: In 1955 there were 550,000 beds in state psychiatric hospitals. By 1995, there were just 95,000 beds. He compared this to the

number of beds in prisons and jails. For 1972 he indicated there were 196,000 beds, and by 1995 this number had increased to 1.5 million beds.

19. Rhodes, *Total Confinement*; Arrigo and Bullock, "Psychological Effects of Solitary Confinement on Prisoners in Supermax Units"; Haney, "Infamous Punishment"; Human Rights Watch, *Human Rights Watch*.

20. Minkoff, "Integrated Treatment Model for Dual Diagnosis of Psychosis and Addiction." See also Inciardi, *War on Drugs III*.

21. Foucault, *Discipline and Punish*.

22. Although the Panopticon itself was never built, the logic of its design became the blueprint for early American penitentiaries.

23. Davis and Shaylor, "Race, Gender, and the Prison Industrial Complex"; Shichor, "Private Prisons in Perspective"; Genders, "Legitimacy, Accountability, and Private Prisons."

24. Alexander, *New Jim Crow*, 28.

25. Bogazianos, *5 Grams*. See also Alexander, *New Jim Crow*; and Reinarman and Levine, *Crack in America*.

26. Mauer, *Race to Incarcerate*; Alexander, *New Jim Crow*.

27. The leftist critique of rehabilitation emerged in the course of the prisoner rights movement during the late 1960s and early 1970s. In *Prisons in Turmoil*, Irwin argues that rehabilitation, particularly in the form of indeterminate sentences and high levels of discretion among correctional officers, contributed to racial inequality, racial animosities, and surges in prisoner-on-prisoner violence. See also Jackson, *Soledad Brother*.

28. Beckett, *Making Crime Pay*.

29. McCorkel, "Embodied Surveillance and the Gendering of Punishment."

30. Lockwood and Inciardi, "CREST Outreach Center"; DeLeon, "Therapeutic Community for Substance Abuse"; Weppner, *Untherapeutic Community*.

31. It remains unclear who initiated this discussion. In an early interview, the warden boasted that he had done so but later, after territorial battles emerged between prison staff and Company employees, the warden indicated that the program had essentially been foisted on him.

32. A 1998 survey found the number one reasons wardens said they supported privatization was to relieve overcrowding. See Bureau of Justice Assistance, *Emerging Issues in Privatized Prisons*.

33. Not only were women's needs rarely considered in the planning of treatment and vocational services, but women offenders were not themselves a locus of concern for policy makers in the state. This is consistent with research literature examining institutional treatment of women offenders within the criminal justice system. See McCorkel, "Justice, Gender, and Incarceration"; Richie, *Compelled to Crime*; Watterson, *Women in Prison*; Simon and Landis, *Crimes Women Commit and the Punishments They Receive*; Ross and Fabiano, *Female Offenders*; Heffernan, *Making It in Prison*; Giallombardo, *Society of Women*; and Morash, Haarr, and Rucker, "Comparison of Programming for Women and Men in U.S. Prisons since the 1980s." Indeed, the history of women's prisons is characterized by institutionalized patterns of neglect, racism, and gender discrimination. See Collins, *Imprisonment of African American Women*; Rafter, *Partial Justice*; and Kurshan, "Behind the Walls."

34. It was unclear from the commission's report the basis on which this assessment was made, but it was reported with regularity in a number of press releases and internal reports to Department of Correction officials, and in the grant application.

35. McCorkel, "Criminally Dependent?" Some of these agencies monitor police reports and court documents to ensure that welfare clients rendered ineligible for benefits as the result criminal convictions are no longer receiving those benefits. Other bridge agencies operate more broadly—they coordinate case files, placement options, surveillance, and processing of nonviolent drug offenders across criminal and family court systems, penal institutions, and social service agencies. See Swartz, "TASC."

36. The 1996 Personal Responsibility and Work Opportunity Reconciliation Act created a number of restrictions aimed at criminal offenders, including a lifetime ban on Temporary Aid to Needy Families benefits to those convicted of certain felonies (e.g., drug felonies). See Haney, "Gender, Welfare, and States of Punishment"; and McCorkel, "Criminally Dependent?"

37. There was one officer assigned to the unit per shift.

38. Sudbury, "Celling Black Bodies"; Davis, *Are Prisons Obsolete?* Dyer, *Perpetual Prisoner Machine.*

39. Garland, *Culture of Control*, 116; Feeley and Simon, "New Penology."

40. Garland, *Culture of Control*, 116.

41. For the most part, it did not take a lot of prompting to get officers to attend the sessions. As one officer explained to me, "An opportunity to be off-site *and* get paid? [his emphasis] Hell yeah, I don't care what the training is. It's a vacation from inmates!"

NOTES TO CHAPTER 3

1. An additional penalty for prematurely leaving the program was a mandatory stay in the prison's maximum security unit. The max unit imposed greater restrictions on movement, access to phones, cafeteria, visits, and yard time. Prisoners had to remain here until their case was reviewed and they were reclassified to another housing unit. This process could take as long as thirty days.

2. When I spoke to four of the correctional officers who were identified by several inmates as being in attendance that day, each denied participating in the event. Three of the officers said they had heard about a "demonstration" in the main hall but were not present for it, and the fourth said that she witnessed "a handful of inmates hugging an old friend," but did not see any officers clapping or shouting remarks at Alicia.

3. Advocates of the therapeutic community model believe that addiction is a disease "of the whole person." The aim of the therapeutic community is to habilitate rather than to rehabilitate because rehabilitation assumes a self that is whole and complete. Advocates argue that many drug addicts lack such a self. Lockwood and Inciardi observe, "Whereas rehabilitation emphasizes a return to a way of life previously known and perhaps forgotten or rejected, habilitation involves the clients' initial socialization into a productive and responsible way of life." "CREST Outreach Center," 68.

4. Belknap, *Invisible Woman*; Ross and Fabiano, *Female Offenders*; Britton, "Feminism in Criminology"; Chesney-Lind, "Challenging Girls' Invisibility in Juvenile Court."

5. Bureau of Justice Statistics, *Women in Prison*; Talvi, *Women behind Bars.*

6. American Civil Liberties Union, *Caught in the Net.*

7. Heimer et al., "Race and Women's Imprisonment."

8. These statistics are reproduced from annual reports compiled by the state Department of Correction.

9. The percentage of drug offenders serving prison time stabilized from 1990 to 2000. In 2000, drug offenders were approximately 16% of the prison population.

10. In 2000, one African American woman out of 284 was incarcerated in East State, compared to a rate of one in 1,448 among white women.

11. White women made up 35% of the female prisoner population. Less than 1% of the female prisoner population was listed as "other" (a category that included Latinas, Asians, and Native Americans). Although Latino/as represented only a small proportion of the general population of the state, these prison statistics should be regarded with caution. Staff were responsible for filling out demographic information on DOC population surveys, and they often miscategorized Latino/a prisoners as black or white depending on their skin tone.

12. Belknap, *Invisible Woman*; Young and Reviere, *Women behind Bars*; Bureau of Justice Statistics, *Sourcebook of Criminal Justice Statistics*.

13. On the increase in the number of women in prison due to drug war policies, see Chesney-Lind, "Rethinking Women's Imprisonment"; Chesney-Lind and Pollock, "Women's Prisons"; Owen and Bloom, "Profiling Women Prisoners"; Bush-Baskette, "War on Drugs as a War against Black Women"; Kruttschnitt and Gartner, "Women's Imprisonment"; and Kruttschnitt and Gartner, *Marking Time in the Golden State*. On the shift in the structure of illicit drug markets and women's increased participation, see Maher, *Sexed Work*; Sharpe, *Behind the Eight Ball*; and Becker and McCorkel, "Gender of Criminal Opportunity."

14. Human Rights Watch, *Punishment and Prejudice*.

15. Goode and Ben-Yehuda, *Moral Panics*.

16. As noted in chapter 1, "beefs" are verbal threats that occasionally escalate to physical confrontations and violence.

17. Collins, *Black Feminist Thought*; Roberts, *Killing the Black Body*. For how controlling images were directed against African American men during the drug war, see Alexander, *New Jim Crow*.

18. Collins, *Black Feminist Thought*, 67–68.

19. Kristen Myers defines "racetalk" as vocabulary and language that demeans based on race/ethnicity and works to preserve racial distinctions, hierarchies, and inequalities. See *Racetalk*. For more on its peculiar character in "color-blind" society, see Doane and Bonilla-Silva, *White Out*; and Wise, *Colorblind*.

20. Approximately three-quarters of PHW's counselors are African American. As the Committee's grant application makes clear, hiring African American and other minority counselors is part of PHW's effort to develop a "culturally specific" model of drug treatment.

21. I did not have access to demographic data for prison employees. During my time in the institution, I'd estimate that at least 50% of the correctional officers and 25% of support personnel were African American.

22. The counselor was transferred out of PHW to a drug treatment program in a maximum security men's prison shortly after this incident. Most of the counselors and two of the black correctional officers who were assigned to PHW regarded this as punishment for holding the groups.

23. "General pop" is slang for general prisoner population.

24. While white women were underrepresented in the prison population, they were overrepresented among those sentenced to community-based alternatives. During the years of this study they constituted 80–90% of women in community-based correctional settings.

25. For review of this research, see Alexander, *New Jim Crow*; and Human Rights Watch, *Punishment and Prejudice*.

26. Rafter, *Partial Justice*; Freedman, *Their Sisters' Keepers*.
27. Alexander, *New Jim Crow*; Wacquant, "Race as Civic Felony"; Garland, *Culture of Control*.
28. Rafter, *Partial Justice*; Freedman; *Their Sisters' Keepers*; Kruttschnitt and Gartner, *Marking Time in the Golden State*; Haney, *Offending Women*; Hannah-Moffat, *Punishment in Disguise*.
29. Twenty-four-hour lockdown means that prisoners are locked in their cells and cannot leave to go to the cafeteria, yard, school, or visiting room. It is typically used during periods of unrest in the prison, such as when inmates get into physical altercations with one another or with correctional officers.
30. They explained to me that because of the highly charged nature of their investigation, they needed to go above and beyond standard confidentiality protections.
31. This is reminiscent of Khalil Gibran Muhammand's argument on how discourses about race and crime become fused through early 20th-century collection of "racial statistics." See *Condemnation of Blackness*.
32. One of the galvanizing claims of the drug war was that crack cocaine was "more addictive" than other drugs, including powder cocaine. There is no scientific validity to this claim. See Reinarman and Levine, *Crack in America*; and Inciardi, Surratt, and Saum, *Cocaine-Exposed Infants*.
33. See Reinarman and Levine, *Crack in America*.
34. Ibid.; Flavin, *Our Bodies, Our Crimes*; Inciardi, Surratt, and Saum, *Cocaine-Exposed Infants*.
35. DeLeon, "Therapeutic Community for Substance Abuse," 302; Lockwood and Inciardi, "CREST Outreach Center," 61.
36. Barthwell et al., "Interventions/Wilmer"; Pan et al., "Some Considerations on Therapeutic Communities in Corrections."
37. For further discussion of these differences, see Bloor, McKeganey, and Fonkert, *One Foot in Eden*; DeLeon, "Therapeutic Community for Substance Abuse"; Sugarman, *Daytop Village*; Yablonsky, *Synanon*; and Jones, *New Treatment Approach*.
38. More specifically, ten of the twelve counselors were women, and eight of the twelve were African American.
39. There was a fair degree of diversity with respect to professional training and employment histories of the other counselors on PHW's staff. The senior counselor and another counselor, Elizabeth, each had their master's degree in social work. Elizabeth worked in residential treatment programs, methadone clinics, and "spirituality centers" most of her life (she boasted she was psychic with special healing powers), while the senior counselor's experience was limited to an internship she did with homeless adults in an urban area near the prison. Two counselors were former correctional officers. Joanne Torrence, the director, had over ten years of experience in drug and alcohol counseling, and a bachelor's degree in human services with a specialization in counseling. Tynice had been an inmate in the prison and by her admission, formerly addicted to crack cocaine. She successfully completed the Company's co-ed work-release therapeutic community and, after several years of sobriety, was recruited by the Company to become a counselor in PHW. Among those counselors who were employed briefly (nine months or less), James was formerly an elementary schoolteacher, Sharvas was an embalming apprentice (prior to that, a bank teller), Rose was a bartender, and Angie was a college student pursuing a bachelor's degree in criminal justice. With the exception of the director and two counselors who trained in the men's program for less than six months, none of the staff had previously worked in a therapeutic community.
40. The distinction between "book smart" and "street smart" counselors was a bit disingenuous, considering the employment histories of the staff (see above).

NOTES TO CHAPTER 4

1. Inmates could apply "good time" credits against their prison sentence to receive an early release.

2. The classic disease concept of addiction is highly controversial in the medical community because there is no empirical support for its central tenets. See Bourgois, "Disciplining Addictions"; Peele, "Introduction to Alcohol and Pleasure"; Neuhaus, "Disease Controversy Revisited"; and Conrad and Schneider, *Deviance and Medicalization.* A number of organizations including the American Psychiatric Association and the World Health Organization have instead adopted a dependency model for classifying drug abuse. This model suggests that dependency is characterized by one or more of the following conditions: (1) physiological impact including drug tolerance and withdrawal symptoms following use; (2) negative psychological impact including feelings of compulsion around the drug; and (3) negative social impact associated with use including the loss of employment, family, and housing.

3. A number of postmodern theorists argue that such a self no longer exists and many argue that it never did. See Lyotard, *Postmodern Condition*; Baudrillard, *Simulations*; Gergen, *Saturated Self*; Denzin, "Representing Live Experiences in Ethnographic Texts"; and Rose, *Inventing Our Selves.* For analyses of how the "real" self persists in experience and narrative, see Irvine, *Codependent Forevermore*; Maines, "Narrative's Moment and Sociology's Phenomenon"; Holstein and Gubrium, *The Self We Live By*; Plummer, *Telling Sexual Stories*; Somers, "Narrative Constitution of Identity"; McCorkel, "Going to the Crackhouse"; and Turner, "Real Self."

4. Sugarman, *Daytop Village;* Frankel, *Transforming Identities*; Gowan and Whetstone, "Making the Criminal Addict."

5. The emergence of a "therapeutic culture" is linked, in large part, to notions that the "real" self is hidden or inaccessible to the very persons embodied by it. Finding it requires outside intervention, often in the form of therapists, support groups, and organized retreats. See Irvine, *Codependent Forevermore*; and Davis, *Accounts of Innocence.*

6. Thanks to Robert Zussman for the observation that the counselors' central task is rendering the "internal external."

7. In Kilty's study, prison staff approached prisoners' failed selves as a foregone conclusion. Instead of engaging the self, they aimed only to manage emotion and behavior through prescription drugs. See "Governance through Psychiatrization."

8. See Foucault, *Discipline and Punish*; and Rothman, *Discovery of the Asylum.*

9. Given the myriad rules regulating conduct and expression in the program, all the women in the program were selected to be the targets of confrontation at one point or another.

10. PHW's cardinal rules include "no physical violence or threats of physical violence; no drugs, chemical, or alcoholic beverages; no stealing; no implicit or explicit sexual acts." Violation of any of these rules could result in immediate expulsion from the program.

11. PHW counselors referred to inmates in the program as "family" and encouraged them to do the same in reference to other PHW prisoners and staff members. This was an intentional reference to the prison's reformatory culture, though use of the term "family" rather than gendered referents like "Daddy" or "Mom" was designed, in part, to discourage the paternalism of the past.

12. "Dialogue" is a command issued by counselors that gives residents permission to speak during periods such as encounter group when they are not otherwise permitted to do so.

13. Hirsch, *Rise of the Penitentiary.*

14. The term "penitentiary" derives its meaning from Greek for "everything" and "a place of sight." For discussion of architecture and surveillance, see Foucault, *Discipline and Punish*; and Beaumont and Tocqueville, *On the Penitentiary System in the United States and Its Application in France*.

15. Barnes, *Repression of Crime*, 162.

16. Foucault, *Power/Knowledge*, 161.

17. In contrast to the prison facility within which it is part, PHW is essentially secular. Prisoners in the program are not required to participate in religious services, although the program does make an effort to accommodate their "spiritual needs" by allowing them to observe religious holidays and participate in Sunday services held in the general prison. Staff refer to a "higher power" during Alcoholics Anonymous and Narcotics Anonymous groups when they are reading from AA/NA literature, but in general, spirituality is considered a private matter in which staff rarely interfere.

18. Although counselors supplied the depiction of an eye and the poster's phrase, the color of the eye was selected by prisoners. That the eye was blue and not brown appears to be a comment on the racial character of institutional power. One of the women who was in the program when the signs were first commissioned commented, "Yeah, it's pretty much brown eyes watching in here, but some of us are down, you know, it's the big blue eye in the sky! The white man, you know?"

19. "Sexual acting out" included "implicit" and "explicit" sexual acts and was strictly forbidden in the program; in fact, it served as grounds for immediate expulsion even if the behavior was consensual.

20. Foucault, *Discipline and Punish*, 200–201.

21. In Foucault's historical account of asylums and medical clinics, he traces the emergence of a "language of seeing," which was used by early medical practitioners to understand what was happening inside the body by interpreting external, visible referents. "Surface signifiers" such as swollen glands, pedestrian limps, and nasal drip form a class of visually comprehensible symptoms, which act as stand-ins for internal processes. See *Birth of the Clinic*.

22. This is not dissimilar to Denzin's argument in *On Understanding Emotion* that emotions constitute the self, and Hochschild's claim in *The Managed Heart* that emotions are "signals" from the self.

23. Sugarman, *Daytop Village*; Kooyman, *Therapeutic Community for Addicts*; McKim, "Getting Gut Level."

24. Rhodes, *Total Confinement*.

25. Mead, *Mind, Self, and Society*.

26. Recent studies of women's prisons and community-based correctional programs that report on similar types of confrontation ceremonies include Haney, *Offending Women*; and McKim, "Getting Gut Level." For a notable contrast, see Kilty's 2012 study of the repression of feelings and emotions through prescription drugs in Canadian prisons for women, "It's Like They Don't Want You to Get Better."

NOTES TO CHAPTER 5

1. Much of the program's philosophy, as it is embodied in the training manual for counselors and in grant applications, is drawn directly from Daytop Village, one of the first and most influential therapeutic communities in the country. Daytop was founded in 1963 on Staten Island, New York. It began as a project of the New York Probation Department. For more on Daytop Village, see Sugarman, *Daytop Village*.

2. Bloor, McKeganey, and Fonkert, *One Foot in Eden*; Frankel, *Transforming Identities*; Silberman, *World of Violence*; Sugarman, *Daytop Village*; Weppner, *Untherapeutic Community*; Yablonsky, *Therapeutic Community*; Rice, *Disease of One's Own*.

3. Denzin, *Alcoholic Society*; and Denzin, *Alcoholic Self*.

4. Denzin, *Alcoholic Society*, 247.

5. Holstein and Gubrium, *The Self We Live By*; Irvine, *Codependent Forevermore*.

6. Yablonsky *Synanon*; Gowan and Whetstone, "Making the Criminal Addict."

7. In fact, PHW incorporated regular AA/NA sessions into its weekly group offerings.

8. This statistic is based on a survey of two hundred one-time PHW prisoners conducted by evaluators from a university research team.

9. Frankel, *Transforming Identities*; Alcoholics Anonymous, "What AA Is and Is Not."

10. Goffman, *Asylums*, 12.

11. Garfinkel, "Conditions of Successful Degradation Ceremonies."

12. Goffman, *Asylums*, 180.

13. I had supervised access to the records of women sent to PHW between June 1994 and October 1996.

14. In her ethnographic studies of community-based correctional programs that target incarcerated mothers and their children, Haney argues that motherhood is used as a gendered mechanism of control to organize women's desires and needs. Aiello makes a similar argument regarding programs that claim to "empower" women. In her study of jail, she finds that motherhood is a central means to punish women accused of violating institutional rules. See Haney, "Homeboys, Babies, Men in Suits"; Haney, *Offending Women*; and Aiello, "Mothering in Jail."

15. The crack baby was a galvanizing image that simultaneously legitimated the War on Drugs, the "get tough on crime" movement, and welfare cuts. There is a great deal of scholarship on how the myth of the crack baby was constructed, perpetuated, and used for political and cultural gains. Some of the best work includes Reinarman and Levine, *Crack in America*; Roberts, *Killing the Black Body*; Flavin, *Our Bodies, Our Crimes*; and Inciardi, Surratt, and Saum, *Cocaine-Exposed Infants*.

16. According to PHW's manual, branch groups are nonconfrontational groups where prisoners "share [their] innermost feelings, thoughts, and attitudes."

17. Ferraro and Moe argue that poor women engage in economic crime in order to enhance their children's well-being. See "Mothering, Crime, and Incarceration."

18. See also Reich, *Fixing Families*; Aiello, "Mothering in Jail"; and Haney, *Offending Women*.

19. Roberts, *Killing the Black Body*.

20. See Inciardi, Surratt, and Saum, *Cocaine-Exposed Infants*; Flavin, *Our Bodies, Our Crimes*; and Kennedy, "Children, Parents, and the State."

21. Roberts, *Killing the Black Body*; Roth, "Searching for the State"; Flavin, *Our Bodies, Our Crimes*.

22. Roth, "Searching for the State." This was an outgrowth of the 1997 Adoption and Safe Families Act.

23. Roth, "Searching for the State"; Flavin, *Our Bodies, Our Crimes*.

24. Roberts, *Killing the Black Body*, 156.

25. This is based on data collected by PHW during intake interviews with prisoners. Approximately 10% of PHW prisoners were serving time on prostitution-related charges during the period of study, 1994–1998.

26. There is a voluminous literature on victimization, gendered pathways to crime, and women's incarceration. For reliable overviews, see Richie, *Compelled to Crime*; DeHart, "Pathways to Prison"; Girshick, *No Safe Haven*; and Miller, *Getting Played*.

27. I rarely heard counselors speak about or punish prisoners for autoerotic practices, although cell mates periodically reported one another to staff for engaging in such activity. When counselors did discuss it, it was usually to verbally admonish women for "distasteful" and "compulsive" behavior. In staff meetings, such activity was framed as a "compulsive tendency" and "pleasure seeking" behavior, and was viewed as a derivation of addiction.

28. I never heard any counselor admonish another for homophobic remarks or otherwise indicate that gossip about prisoners' sexuality was inappropriate.

29. Kruttschnitt and Gartner, *Marking Time in the Golden State*; Ward and Kassebaum, *Women's Prison*; Giallombardo, *Society of Women*; Rafter, *Partial Justice*; Kunzel, *Criminal Intimacy*.

30. Kruttschnitt and Gartner, *Marking Time in the Golden State*. They find that the staff's preoccupation with prisoners' sexual practices and desires in the 1960s was premised on the belief that women needed to be "morally reformed." In the 1990s, it was because staff viewed such liaisons as a threat to the social order of the prison.

31. Haney characterizes this as the regulation of desire. See *Offending Women.*

32. See Roberts, *Killing the Black Body.*

33. I have elaborated elsewhere on how constructions of women drug offenders as "criminally dependent" were used to legitimate a shift in the prison's control structure. See McCorkel, "Criminally Dependent?"

34. Haney, *Offending Women*; Hannah-Moffat, *Punishment in Disguise*; McKim, "Getting Gut Level." See also Horowitz, *Teen Mothers.*

35. The 1996 Personal Responsibility and Work Opportunity Reconciliation Act included a lifetime ban on Temporary Aid to Need Family benefits for those convicted of certain felonies, including drug felonies. For more on how restrictions affected women in the criminal justice system, see Haney, "Gender, Welfare, and States of Punishment."

36. This ranged from boosting necessities like baby formula from drug stores and then reselling it on the street, to offering a range of services like child care and cosmetology from their residences.

37. By year three, prisoners could petition to interview for jobs outside the institution (the most common was at a meat processing plant) and for an apprenticeship as a nursing assistant.

38. This is similar to the community-based programs that Haney studied in which practical interventions like job training programs were abandoned in favor of therapeutic sessions examining prisoners' "dangerous" desires. See *Offending Women*. See also McKim, "Getting Gut Level."

39. The right people were usually those the staff regarded as "good Christians."

40. DeLeon, "Therapeutic Community for Substance Abuse"; Lockwood and Inciardi, "CREST Outreach Center"; Weppner, *Untherapeutic Community*; Bloor, McKeganey, and Fonkert, *One Foot in Eden*; Frankel, *Transforming Identities.*

41. DeLeon, "Therapeutic Community for Substance Abuse."

42. Conrad and Schneider, *Deviance and Medicalization.*

43. Gowan and Whetstone report a similar finding in "Making the Criminal Addict," their study of a therapeutic community program serving poor, predominantly African American men under correctional supervision.

44. According to the original design of the program, counselors were to hold individual counseling sessions with prisoners twice a month. Instead, counselors held private sessions

with prisoners only when they were interviewing them for admission to the program, during emergencies (e.g., illness or death of family members, HIV-positive diagnoses) and at their discretion.

45. Such interactions often involve closed awareness contexts wherein one actor (usually the layperson) does not have a complete account of how the other actor (usually the professional) regards his true identity. Such is the case when doctors avoid telling patients of fatal prognoses or when lawyers misrepresent the likely outcome of criminal cases to defendants. See Glaser and Strauss, "Awareness Contexts and Social Interaction"; and Blumberg, "Practice of Law as Confidence Game."

46. Rose, *Governing the Soul*; Rose, "Government and Control"; O'Malley, "Volatile and Contradictory Punishment."

47. Hannah-Moffat, *Punishment in Disguise*. See also Haney, *Offending Women*; and McKim, "Getting Gut Level."

NOTES TO CHAPTER 6

1. In all the years I attended these conferences, I never saw a graduate of PHW give one of the testimonials. This always struck me as a bit ironic since current prisoners were not in a good position to evaluate the program's "life changing" capabilities.

2. The term "suit and tie guys" was used primarily by women who had worked as street prostitutes. The phrase referred to the class and status of certain of their clientele. While "truckers" and "regular guys" referred to clients from working- and lower-class backgrounds, "suit and tie guys" designated middle- and upper-class men who wore suits and drove nice cars, and whom the women identified as doctors, lawyers, judges, and businessmen. Suit and tie guys were notorious among the women for wanting "freaky" sex that radically departed from the requests for "straight" intercourse and oral sex they typically received from truckers and regular guys. Although they often made more money with suit and tie guys, the majority of the women I spoke to said that such men made them "uncomfortable," "nervous," and "scared" because of the sexual acts they asked them to perform. Many feared that such men were "perverts" who would rape or otherwise physically abuse them.

3. The federal grant that had been awarded to the Committee to bring the drug treatment program into the prison stipulated that the program must be evaluated by "outside" researchers, meaning that neither the Department of Correction nor the Company could conduct an evaluation of the PHW. Part of the grant funds that the Committee received went to funding this outside evaluation. A research team from the state university, of which I was a part, conducted the evaluation. See McCorkel and Myers, "What Difference Does Difference Make?"

4. The reference is to the line "Life was is like a box of chocolates, you never know what you're gonna get" from the movie *Forrest Gump*.

5. I knew that the speech she gave was verbatim to the one she had rehearsed because I was among those who helped her practice her speech during the three days prior to the press conference.

6. Sykes, *Society of Captives*; Foucault, *Discipline and Punish*; Rhodes, *Total Confinement*.

7. In *Asylums*, Goffman refers to this process as the systematic mortification of the self. It includes replacing a person's name with a number, their clothing with a uniform, and denying him or her privacy and material possessions. See also Garfinkel, "Conditions of Successful Degradation Ceremonies"; Schmid and Jones, "Suspended Identity"; Silberman, *World of Violence*; and Rhodes, *Total Confinement*.

8. All organizations make demands on the self; however, total institutions become, in Goffman's words, "forcing houses for change" because of the intensity of the demands on the self and the absence of resources to counter institutional identity claims. See *Asylums*, 12. See also McCorkel, "Going to the Crackhouse."

9. Goffman, *Asylums*, 127; see also Schutz, *Phenomenology of the Social World*.

10. Goffman, *Asylums*, 164–165.

11. Ibid. It is important to note that Goffman is not so much arguing that inmates abandon their efforts to defend the self because they convert to the institution's view of themselves, but because it ultimately becomes impossible to defend an image of self that cannot be structurally sustained.

12. For examples see Schmid and Jones, "Suspended Identity"; Muedeking, "Authentic/Inauthentic Identities in the Prison Visiting Room"; and McCorkel, "Going to the Crackhouse."

13. Schmid and Jones, "Suspended Identity." 415.

14. See Hochschild, *Managed Heart*; Denzin, *On Understanding Emotion*; and Denzin, "A Note on Emotionality, Self, and Interaction."

15. Goffman, *Asylums*, 169.

16. Goffman, *Frame Analysis*; Goffman, *Presentation of Self in Everyday Life*. See also Holstein and Gubrium, *The Self We Live By*.

17. Graduates are slightly overrepresented among my interviewees. According to PHW's records, they graduated nearly 38% of the 226 women who entered the program between 1994 and 1997. This statistic was inflated to include women who did not actually graduate from the program but who left because they made bail or their sentence expired. Technically, according to the program's own criteria, the only persons who can be considered graduates are those who completed the fifth level of treatment. According to the statistics recorded by the university evaluation team, this number is just under 30%.

18. She tested positive for drugs on a urine screen.

19. Denzin, *Alcoholic Self*; Pollner and Stein, "Narrative Mapping of Social Worlds."

20. Ibid.

21. Denzin, *Alcoholic Society*.

22. Other women in the program had similar experiences. It is not the experience that distinguishes women who surrender from other prisoners, but their recognition that drug use worsened the situation and contributed to their weariness.

23. Goffman, *Asylums*.

24. Notably, all but one of PHW's counselors drank alcohol and several smoked cigarettes.

25. Prisoners in PHW were forbidden from taking any kind of medication without the express approval of the counseling staff. This included medicine prescribed by the prison medical staff, as well as that administered by physicians outside the prison.

26. In the above example, Red grew up in a working-class household where both parents were present and held relatively stable jobs. In contrast, Ice grew up in poverty. She had multiple caretakers throughout her childhood after her father disappeared and her mother was periodically institutionalized in prisons and mental hospitals.

27. Weppner, *Untherapeutic Community*; Bloor, McKeganey, and Fonkert, *One Foot in Eden*.

28. In order to progress through PHW, prisoners first had to demonstrate that they knew the program vocabulary by passing a written test; next, they had to use this vocabulary to express themselves during group therapy sessions; and finally, they had to be able to apply this language to narrate their own life histories. The failure to do so adequately

resulted in derision (e.g., confrontation sessions in which counselors referred to the target as a "dingbat" or "disrespectful creep") and punishment (e.g., writing one thousand sentences, or loss of precious few privileges such as phone time or visits with family members). Prisoners who did learn the vocabulary and made use of the narrative structure were promoted through the treatment program (promotion carried a few rewards such as an increase in phone time and more commissary privileges) and were confronted less frequently by the staff.

29. "Disintegrated" is a slang term for getting confronted by others and subjecting oneself to critique.

30. Goffman, *Asylums*.

NOTES TO CHAPTER 7

1. Levels of sentencing refer to the intensiveness of supervision. Level five is incarceration in one of the state's prisons, level four time refers to incarceration in a halfway house, and levels three through one indicate varying levels of probation and parole supervision.

2. A further complication involved the availability of beds for women in halfway houses. In most cases, a prisoner who was released on her minimum sentence or who received a sentence modification was stipulated to level four (community-based) custody. A number of women who received the modifications ended up remaining in prison because the state had not yet increased the number of community beds available to women.

3. Although I interviewed several inmates and two members of the prison staff who told me these things had happened to women they knew, I was never able to find anyone who would admit to being either a witness to or participant in such an event. Further, I never witnessed any such punishments. Forcing residents to wear diapers was a form of punishment used in Synanon, a therapeutic community that became infamous in the 1970s due to the bizarre behavior of its leader, Charles Dederich. PHW staff speculated that the "barking baby" rumors originated with members of the prison staff who might have regarded the therapeutic community modality as synonymous with Synanon. See Yablonsky, *Synanon*.

4. An additional change in the admission policy involved a modification of the original time remaining to serve on the incarceration portion of the sentence. In order to widen the net of inmates eligible for treatment, the program expanded the original requirement that inmates have twelve to fifteen months remaining on their sentences to a period ranging from six to eighteen months.

5. Court-mandated inmates faced an even greater set of obstacles to get out of the program. They had to petition both the sentencing judge and the prison classification board. The wait often took as long as two months while the judge, the classification committee, and PHW counselors determined the legitimacy of the inmate's complaints and whether she should be penalized for her actions. According to both counselors and inmates who had petitioned for transfer, judges usually penalized women who failed to remain in the program by extending the incarceration period (this could range from an additional three months to several years). In a handful of cases, judges found that the program was an unsuitable treatment modality for the petitioner (most often in cases where the petitioner was afflicted by serious medical problems or psychiatric diagnoses such as schizophrenia) and approved the transfer with no penalty.

6. Although many PHW prisoners continued to complain about disparities in the application of early release policies, all who entered after the first year did so with the understanding that these policies were vague and inconsistent.

7. Prisoners always spoke in the language of strategy. They did not see themselves as belonging to a certain "type." I have endeavored to preserve this convention in the analysis since people are rarely one type or another.

8. This was consistent with the program's control structure, which prevented the use of language and linguistic categories that departed from approved vocabulary terms and therapeutic rhetoric more generally.

9. It is also important to note that not all of the prisoners who left the program prematurely had pursued a strategy of ripping and running. A significant number of prisoners, even after they left or were kicked out of PHW, continued to subscribe to some aspects of the treatment philosophy or say that the program changed their self-definitions.

10. They make up approximately 30% of my respondents.

11. During the intake interview, each of these women admitted to either "having tried" or "used occasionally" substances such as alcohol, amphetamines, and marijuana. This use, though minor, was sufficient to meet PHW's criteria for admission. Notably, each was admitted during periods when PHW was having problems filling up beds in the program.

12. It is important to emphasize that the use of moral careers as a conceptual device renders prisoners' experiences and styles of participation in PHW overly rigid. I have employed this concept to demonstrate three distinct strategies of participation in the program and the implications such strategies had for self-identity. At the same time, however, it would be inappropriate to suggest that women entered the program as one of three distinct types. They each had their own distinct philosophies regarding drugs, treatment, and addiction before entering PHW, but these did not necessarily determine how they ultimately participated in the program.

13. Threatening suicide or violence toward another prisoner was a strategy that a number of prisoners pursued to get out of PHW as quickly as possible. Jenna told me she was "never suicidal" and "did what she had to do" to get out of PHW.

14. A slang term meaning twenty-four hours a day, seven days a week.

15. As I noted in a previous chapter, the majority of counselors and staff members in PHW are African American. Prisoners who were critical of the program frequently characterized staff members as racist and classist, pointing out that staff members were middle class and seeking the approval of white administrators and middle-class whites more generally.

16. For general discussion of "critical space," see McCorkel, "Going to the Crackhouse."

17. Although the evaluation team encouraged the staff to change the exit policy in order to reduce the amount of violence in the program, counseling staff continued to say that violent behavior was evidence of "psychiatric disorder," rather than a desperate measure to leave the program. To buttress their claims, they pointed out that the majority of women in the program never engaged in violence, despite the fact that a good number expressed an interest in leaving at one point or another during their residency.

18. Although women who surrendered regarded ripping and running in terms similar to the staff's (e.g., that the women who did it were "crazy" and "beyond help"), the women who ripped and ran did exert influence over other prisoners who had doubts about the program. Their stories will be examined below.

19. East State was one of a number of states around the country that began to aggressively terminate parental rights for mothers who had been convicted of drug crimes, particularly the rights to babies born in custody. See Kennedy, "Children, Parents, and the State"; and Roberts, *Shattered Bonds.*

20. Missing data do not permit a comparison of the total number sentenced to the program to those who entered voluntarily. Based on personal knowledge and available data from PHW case files, I estimate that approximately 60% of the women who "faked it" were sentenced into PHW and 40% entered voluntarily.

21. "Hitting bricks" referred to a form of punishment in which prisoners are made to stand facing a wall. They must rub the bricks with their hands until they are told by a staff member that they can stop.

22. Prisoners frequently commented in interviews that they feared some of the women in the program would try to commit suicide in response to being "broken down" in confrontation sessions. From 1994 to 1996, I was aware of a total of nine suicide threats, four of which resulted in women being placed on "suicide watch" in a separate correctional facility.

23. Goffman refers to these sorts of rule violations as "secondary adjustments." They are unauthorized practices that an individual uses to "get around the organization's assumptions of what he should do and who he should be." See *Asylums*, 107. I've noted elsewhere that PHW is designed to eliminate such opportunities. Nonetheless, prisoners find ways to exploit weaknesses in the surveillance structure in order to generate varying degrees of privacy. See McCorkel, "Going to the Crackhouse."

24. In *The Presentation of Self in Everyday Life*, Goffman conceptualizes the self as a performance that is simultaneously produced by its front stage effects (that which appears before an audience) and its backstage management (decisions the actor makes regarding what to reveal and what to conceal). In this sense, the self is always something more than that which appears on the front stage. To be deprived of the backstage, however, is to deny the self a fundamental aspect of its management and production.

25. When I present this research at academic conferences, I'm always asked if the interviews were a resource for prisoners to articulate and defend a definition of self that stood outside the disease narrative. This was definitely the case, particularly for prisoners who were "faking it to make it." The interview was a space that carried a guarantee of privacy from the eyes and ears of staff and other inmates.

26. "Mother's time" was an extended visit with one's children. It had to be earned and could be taken away for any violation of the program's rules.

27. Bosworth, *Engendering Resistance.*

28. Inmates often threatened to sue but the only time this threat was manifest was when an inmate's family actually contacted the ACLU following the showing of the film *Schindler's List.* (I discussed this incident in an earlier chapter.) This lawsuit never came to fruition, but inmates did see relief in that prison authorities and PHW officials acted on the complaint. Other than that particular incident, I know of no cases that were filed based on events within PHW. It bears noting that staff frequently prevented prisoners from going to the law library during their time in the program.

29. The sociologist Lynne Haney makes a similar finding in *Offending Women*, her study of community-based group homes for incarcerated mothers. She finds that prisoners in each of her field sites develop strong "anti-therapy" sentiments as the result of their experiences.

NOTES TO CONCLUSION

1. This was a new use of the term "jailing." During my first several years in the prison, I only heard the term used to describe sexual relationships between women. When I returned, the term was also used by staff to refer to women who did not comply with prison rules and norms. "Queening" was a term used by staff to refer to prisoners who they believed thought they were "entitled" to violate rules.

2. There were certainly instances of COs engaging in coercive behavior toward prisoners but this tended to be hidden. The incidents that occasioned the greatest amount of talk among prisoners involved sexual assault and threats of violence.

3. Feely and Simon, "New Penology," 455.

4. Rhodes, *Total Confinement*.

5. For examples, see ethnographies of women's prisons and community-based facilities by Haney, *Offending Women*; McKim, "Getting Gut Level"; and Kruttschnitt and Gartner, *Marking Time in the Golden State*.

6. Alexander, *New Jim Crow*; Wacquant, "From Slavery to Mass Incarceration."

7. Alexander, *New Jim Crow*, 193.

8. I am basing this latter point on Department of Correction data reporting the number of women entering prison for parole revocation.

9. See Haney's discussion in *Offending Women* of resistance in an institutional context devoted to regulating needs versus one that aims to regulate desires.

10. These data, because they are drawn from a convenience sample, are not a reliable guide to evaluating PHW's success or failure in terms of the percentage of women who relapsed or committed additional criminal offenses.

11. De Beaumont and de Tocqueville, *On the Penitentiary System in the United States and Its Application in France*, 89.

BIBLIOGRAPHY

Abbot, Jack Henry. *In the Belly of the Beast*. New York: Random House, 1981.

Acker, Joan. "Hierarchies, Jobs, Bodies: A Theory of Gendered Organizations." *Gender and Society* 4, no. 2 (June 1990): 139–158.

Aiello, Brittnie Leigh. "Mothering in Jail: Pleasure, Pain, and Punishment." PhD diss., University of Massachusetts–Amherst, 2011. ProQuest (AAT 3445141).

Alcoholics Anonymous. "What AA Is and Is Not." *AA.org*, http://www.aa.org/lang/en/subpage. cfm?page=221.

Alexander, Michelle. *The New Jim Crow: Mass Incarceration in the Age of Colorblindness*. New York: New Press, 2010.

American Civil Liberties Union. *Caught in the Net: The Impact of Drug Policies on Women and Families*. New York: American Civil Liberties Union, 2005.

Arrigo, Bruce A., and Bullock, Jennifer Leslie. "The Psychological Effects of Solitary Confinement on Prisoners in Supermax Units: Reviewing What We Know and Recommending What Should Change." *International Journal of Offender Therapy and Comparative Criminology* 52, no. 6 (December 2008): 622–640.

Austin, James, and John Irwin. *It's About Time: America's Imprisonment Binge*. Belmont, CA: Wadsworth, 2001.

Ayers, Edward L. *Vengeance and Justice: Crime and Punishment in the Nineteenth-Century American South*. New York: Oxford University Press, 1984.

Barnes, Henry Elmer. *The Repression of Crime: Studies in Historical Penology*. New York: George H. Doran Company, 1926.

Barthwell, Andrea, Peter Bakos, John Bailey, Miriam Nisenbaum, Julien Devereux, and Edward Senay. "Interventions/Wilmer: A Continuum of Care for Substance Abusers in the Criminal Justice System." *Journal of Psychoactive Drugs* 27, no. 1 (1995): 39–48.

Baskin, Deborah, Ira Sommers, Richard Tessler, and Henry Steadman. "Role Incongruence and the Gender Variation in the Provision of Prison Mental Health Services." *Journal of Health and Social Behavior* 30, no. 3 (September 1989): 305–314.

Baudrillard, Jean. *Simulations*. Translated by Paul Foss, Paul Patton, and Philip Beitchman. New York: Semiotext(e), 1983.

Beadle, Amanda Peterson. "Private Prison Charges Inmates $5 a Minute for Phone Calls While They Work for $1 a Day." *ThinkProgress.org*, November 16, 2011, http://thinkprogress.org/justice/2011/11/16/370173/private-prison-five-dollars-per-minute-phone-calls/?mobile=nc.

Becker, Sarah, and Jill A. McCorkel. "The Gender of Criminal Opportunity: The Impact of Male Co-offenders on Women's Crimes." *Feminist Criminology* 6, no. 2 (April 2011): 79–110.

Beckett, Katherine. *Making Crime Pay: Law and Order in Contemporary American Politics*. New York: Oxford University Press, 1997.

Beckett, Katherine, and Bruce Western, "Governing Social Marginality: Welfare, Incarceration, and the Transformation of State Policy." *Punishment and Society* 3, no. 1 (January 2001): 43–59.

Belknap, Joanne. *The Invisible Women: Gender, Crime, and Justice.* 4th ed. Belmont, CA: Wadsworth, 2011.

Bentham, Jeremy. "Panopticon." In *The Panopticon Writings*, edited by Miran Bozovic, 29–95. London: Verso, 1995.

Blomberg, Thomas G., and Stanley Cohen. *Punishment and Social Control.* New York: Aldine de Gruyter, 2003.

Bloom, Barbara, Meda Chesney-Lind, and Barbara Owen. *Women in California Prisons: Hidden Victims of the War on Drugs.* San Francisco: Center on Juvenile and Criminal Justice, 1994.

Bloor, Michael, Neil McKeganey, and Dick Fonkert, *One Foot in Eden: A Sociological Study of the Range of Therapeutic Community Practice.* New York: Routledge, 1988.

Blumberg, Abraham S. "The Practice of Law as Confidence Game: Organizational Cooptation of a Profession." *Law and Society Review* 1, no. 2 (June 1967): 15–40.

Bogazianos, Dimitri A. *5 Grams: Crack Cocaine, Rap Music, and the War on Drugs.* New York: New York University Press, 2011.

Bosworth, Mary. "Creating the Responsible Prisoner: Federal Admission and Orientation Packs." *Punishment and Society* 9, no. 1 (January 2007): 67–85.

——. *Engendering Resistance: Agency and Power in Women's Prisons.* Aldershot, England: Ashgate, 1999.

Bourgois, Philippe. "Disciplining Addictions: The Bio-politics of Methadone and Heroin in the United States." *Culture, Medicine, and Psychology* 24, no. 2 (June 2000): 165–195.

Britton, Dana M. *At Work in the Iron Cage: The Prison as Gendered Organization.* New York: New York University Press, 2003.

——. "Feminism in Criminology: Engendering the Outlaw." *Annals of the American Academy of Political and Social Science* 571, no. 1 (September 2000): 57–76.

Burchell, Graham, Colin Gordon, and Peter Miller, eds. *The Foucault Effect: Studies in Governmentality.* Chicago: University of Chicago Press, 1991.

Bureau of Justice Assistance. *Census of State and Federal Correctional Facilities, 2005.* Washington, DC: U.S. Department of Justice, 2008.

——. *Correctional Populations in the United States, 2010.* Washington, DC: U.S. Department of Justice, 2011.

——. *Emerging Issues in Privatized Prisons.* Washington, DC: U.S. Department of Justice, 2001.

——. *Prisoners in 1996.* Washington, DC: U.S. Department of Justice, 1997.

——. *Prisoners in 2006.* Washington, DC: U.S. Department of Justice, 2007.

——. *Prisoners in 2009.* Washington, DC: U.S. Department of Justice, 2010.

——. *Sourcebook of Criminal Justice Statistics, 2002.* Washington, DC: U.S. Department of Justice, 2003.

——. *State Prison Expenditures 1996.* Washington, DC: U.S. Department of Justice, 1999.

——. *Women in Prison.* Washington, DC: U.S. Department of Justice, 1994.

Bush-Baskette, Stephanie R. "The War on Drugs as a War against Black Women." In *Crime Control and Women: Feminist Implications of Criminal Justice Policy*, edited by Susan Miller, 113–129. Thousands Oaks, CA: Sage, 1998.

Carlen, Pat, and Anne Worrall, eds. *Gender, Crime, and Justice.* Philadelphia: Open University Press, 1987.

Chesney-Lind, Meda. "Challenging Girls' Invisibility in Juvenile Court." *Annals of the American Academy of Political and Social Science* 564, no. 1 (July 1999): 185–202.

———. "Rethinking Women's Imprisonment." In *The Criminal Justice System and Women*, edited by Barbara Price and Natalie Sokoloff, 105–117. New York: McGraw-Hill, 1995.

Chesney-Lind, Meda, and Joycelyn Pollock. "Women's Prisons: Equality with a Vengeance." In *Women, Law, and Social Control*, edited by Alida Merlo and Joycelyn Pollock, 155–176. Boston: Allyn and Bacon, 1995.

Collins, Catherine Fisher. *The Imprisonment of African American Women: Causes, Conditions, and Future Implications.* Jefferson, NC: McFarland, 1994.

Collins, Patricia Hill. *Black Feminist Thought: Knowledge, Consciousness, and the Politics of Empowerment.* New York: Routledge, 1991

Colvin, Mark. *Penitentiaries, Reformatories, and Chain Gangs: Social Theory and the History of Punishment in Nineteenth-Century America.* New York: St. Martin's Press, 1997.

Comfort, Megan. *Doing Time Together: Love and Family in the Shadow of the Prison.* Chicago: University of Chicago Press, 2007.

Connell, R. W. *Gender and Power.* Stanford: Stanford University Press, 1987.

Conover, Ted. *Newjack: Guarding Sing Sing.* New York: Vintage Books, 2001.

Conrad, Peter, and Joseph W. Schneider. *Deviance and Medicalization: From Badness to Sickness.* Philadelphia: Temple University Press, 1992.

Davis, Angela Y. *Are Prisons Obsolete?* New York: Seven Stories Press, 2003.

Davis, Angela Y., and Cassandra Shaylor. "Race, Gender, and the Prison Industrial Complex." *Meridians* 2, no. 1 (Spring 2001): 1–25.

Davis, Joseph E. *Accounts of Innocence: Sexual Abuse, Trauma, and the Self.* Chicago: University of Chicago Press, 2005.

De Beaumont, Gustave, and Alexis de Tocqueville. *On the Penitentiary System in the United States and Its Application in France.* Translated by Francis Lieber. Carbondale: Southern Illinois University Press, 1964.

DeHart, Dana D. "Pathways to Prison: Impact of Victimization in the Lives of Incarcerated Women." *Violence against Women* 14, no. 12 (December 2008): 1362–1381.

DeLeon, George. "The Therapeutic Community for Substance Abuse: Perspective and Approach." In *The American Drug Scene: An Anthology*, edited by James A. Inciardi and Karen McElrath, 301–308. Los Angeles: Roxbury, 1995.

Deleuze, Gilles. *Negotiations.* Translated by Martin Joughin. New York: Columbia University Press, 1997.

Denzin, Norman K. *The Alcoholic Self.* Newbury Park, CA: Sage, 1987.

———. *The Alcoholic Society: Addiction and Recovery of the Self.* New Brunswick, NJ: Transaction, 1993.

———. "A Note on Emotionality, Self, and Interaction." *American Journal of Sociology* 89, no. 2 (September 1983): 402–409.

———. *On Understanding Emotion.* San Francisco: Jossey-Bass, 1984.

———. "Representing Live Experiences in Ethnographic Texts." In *Studies in Symbolic Interaction Vol. 12*, edited by Norman K. Denzin, 59–70. Greenwich, CT: JAI Press, 1991.

DiIulio, John J., Jr. "The Coming of the Super-Predators." *Weekly Standard* 1, no. 11 (November 1995): 23–28.

Doane, Ashley W., and Eduardo Bonilla-Silva, eds. *White Out: The Continuing Significance of Racism.* New York: Routledge, 2003.

Dodge, L. Mara. *Whores and Thieves of the Worst Kind: A Study of Women, Crime, and Prisons, 1835–2000.* DeKalb: Northern Illinois University Press, 2002.

Dowker, Fay and Glenn Good. "The Proliferation of Control Unit Prisons in the United States." *Journal of Prisoners on Prisons* 4, no. 2 (1993): 95–110.

Dyer, Joel. *The Perpetual Prisoner Machine: How America Profits from Crime.* Boulder, CO: Westview Press, 2000.

Faler, Brian. "Bennett under Fire for Remark on Crime and Black Abortions." *Washington Post,* September 30, 2005.

Featherstone, Richard A. *Narratives from the 1971 Attica Prison Riot: Towards a New Theory of Correctional Disturbances.* Lewiston, NY: Edwin Mellen Press, 2005.

Feeley, Malcolm M. "Entrepreneurs of Punishment: The Legacy of Privatization." *Punishment and Society* 4, no. 3 (July 2002): 321–344.

Feeley, Malcolm, and Jonathan Simon. "The New Penology: Notes on the Emerging Strategy of Corrections and Its Implications." *Journal of Criminology* 30, no. 4 (November 1992): 449–474.

Ferraro, Kathleen J., and Angela M. Moe. "Mothering, Crime, and Incarceration." *Journal of Contemporary Ethnography* 32, no. 1 (February 2003): 9–40.

Fierce, Milfred C. *Slavery Revisited: Blacks and the Southern Convict Lease System, 1865–1933.* New York: City University of New York Press, 1994.

Flavin, Jeanne. *Our Bodies, Our Crimes: The Policing of Women's Reproduction in America.* New York: New York University Press, 2009.

Foucault, Michel. *The Birth of the Clinic: An Archaeology of Medical Perception.* Translated by A. M. Sheridan Smith. London: Routledge, 1973.

———. *Discipline and Punish: The Birth of the Prison.* Translated by Alan Sheridan. New York: Random House, 1977.

———. *Power/Knowledge: Selected Interviews and Other Writings, 1972–1977.* Edited by Colin Gordon. London: Harvester, 1980.

———. "Technologies of the Self." In *Technologies of the Self: A Seminar with Michel Foucault,* edited by Luther H. Martin, Huck Gutman, and Patrick H. Hutton, 16–49. Amherst: University of Massachusetts Press, 1988.

Frankel, Ruth. *Transforming Identities: Context, Power, and Ideology in a Therapeutic Community.* New York: Peter Lang, 1989.

Fraser, Nancy. *Unruly Practices: Power, Discourse, and Gender in Contemporary Social Theory.* Minneapolis: University of Minnesota Press, 1989.

Freedman, Estelle B. *Their Sisters' Keepers: Women's Prison Reform in America, 1830–1930.* Ann Arbor: University of Michigan Press, 1981.

Garfinkel, Harold. "Conditions of Successful Degradation Ceremonies." *American Journal of Sociology* 61, no. 5 (March 1956): 420–424.

Garland, David. *Culture of Control: Crime and Social Order in Contemporary Society.* Chicago: University of Chicago Press, 2001.

———, ed. *Mass Imprisonment: Social Causes and Consequences.* Thousand Oaks, CA: Sage, 2001.

———. *Punishment and Modern Society: A Study in Social Theory.* Chicago: University of Chicago Press, 1993.

———. *Punishment and Welfare: A History of Penal Strategies.* Brookfield, VT: Gower, 1985.

Genders, Elaine. "Legitimacy, Accountability, and Private Prisons." *Punishment and Society* 4, no. 3 (July 2002): 285–303.

Gergen, Kenneth J. *The Saturated Self: Dilemmas of Identity in Contemporary Life.* New York: Basic Books, 1991.

Giallombardo, Rose. *Society of Women: A Study of Women's Prisons.* New York: John Wiley and Sons, 1966.

Girshick, Lori B. *No Safe Haven: Stories of Women in Prison.* Boston: Northeastern University Press, 1999.

Glaser, Barney G., and Anselm L. Strauss. "Awareness Contexts and Social Interaction." *American Sociological Review* 29, no. 5 (October 1964): 669–679.

Goffman, Erving. *Asylums: Essays on the Social Situation of Mental Patients and Other Inmates.* New York: Doubleday, 1961.

——. *Frame Analysis: An Essay on the Organization of Experience.* Boston: Northeastern University Press, 1974.

——. *The Presentation of Self in Everyday Life.* New York: Doubleday, 1959.

Goode, Erisch, and Nachman Ben-Yehuda. *Moral Panics: The Social Construction of Deviance.* Oxford, England: Wiley-Blackwell, 1994.

Gowan, Teresa, and Sarah Whetstone. "Making the Criminal Addict: Subjectivity and Social Control in a Strong-Arm Rehab." *Punishment and Society 14, no. 1* (January 2012): 69–93.

Greene, Judith, and Kevin Pranis. *Hard Hit: The Growth in the Imprisonment of Women, 1977–2004.* New York: Women's Prison Association's Institute on Women and Criminal Justice, 2006.

Hagan, John. "*The Everyday and Not So Exceptional in the Social Organization of Criminal Justice Practices.*" In *Everyday Practices and Troubled Cases: Fundamental Issues in Law and Society Research,* edited by Austin Sarat, Marianne Constable, David Engel, Valerie Hans, and Susan Lawrence, 109–125. Evanston: Northwestern University Press, 1998.

Hallet, Michael. "Commerce with Criminals: The New Colonialism in Criminal Justice." *Review of Policy Research* 21, no. 1 (January 2004): 49–63.

Haney, Craig. "Infamous Punishment: The Psychological Consequences of Isolation." *National Prison Project Journal* 8, no. 2 (Spring 1993): 3–7, 21.

Haney, Lynne A. "Gender, Welfare, and States of Punishment." *Social Politics* 11, no. 3 (Fall 2004): 333–362.

——. "Homeboys, Babies, Men in Suits: The State and the Reproduction of Male Dominance." *American Sociological Review* 61, no. 5 (October 1996): 759–778.

——. *Offending Women: Power, Punishment, and the Regulation of Desire.* Berkeley: University of California Press, 2010.

Hannah-Moffat, Kelly. "Losing Ground: Gendered Knowledges, Parole Risk, and Responsibility." *Social Politics* 11, no. 3 (Fall 2004): 363–385.

——. *Punishment in Disguise: Penal Governance and Federal Imprisonment of Women in Canada.* Toronto: University of Toronto Press, 2001.

——. "Sacrosanct or Flawed: Rise, Accountability, and Gender-Responsive Penal Politics." *Current Issues in Criminal Justice* 22, no. 2 (November 2010): 193–215.

Heffernan, Esther. *Making It in Prison.* New York: John Wiley and Sons, 1972.

Heimer, Karen, and Stacy De Coster. "The Gendering of Violent Delinquency." *Criminology* 37, no. 2 (May 1999): 277–318.

Heimer, Karen, Kecia R. Johnson, Joseph B. Lang, Andres F. Rengifo, and Don Steman. "Race and Women's Imprisonment: Poverty, African American Presence, and Social Welfare." *Journal of Quantitative Criminology* 28, no. 2 (June 2012): 219–244.

Hirsch, Adam J. *The Rise of the Penitentiary: Prisons and Punishment in Early America.* New Haven: Yale University Press, 1992.

Hochschild, Arlie Russell. *The Managed Heart: Commercialization of Human Feeling*. Berkeley: University of California Press, 1983.

Holloway, Lynette. "The Root: Inmate Health Care Another Kind of Prison." *NPR.org*, June 8, 2011, http://www.npr.org/2011/06/08/137055836/the-root-inmate-health-care-another-kind-of-prison.

Holstein, James A., and Jaber F. Gubrium, *The Self We Live By: Narrative Identity in a Postmodern World*. New York: Oxford University Press, 2000.

Horowitz, Ruth. *Teen Mothers: Citizens or Dependents?* Chicago: University of Chicago Press, 1995.

Human Rights Watch. *Human Rights Watch World Report*. New York: Human Rights Watch, 1997.

———. *Punishment and Prejudice: Racial Disparities in the War on Drugs*. New York: Human Rights Watch, 2000.

Human Rights Watch Women's Rights Project. *Sexual Abuse of Women in U.S. State Prisons*. New York: Human Rights Watch, 1996.

Ignatieff, Michael. *Just Measure of Pain: The Penitentiary in the Industrial Revolution, 1750–1850*. New York: Pantheon Books, 1978.

Inciardi, James A. *War on Drugs II: The Continuing Epic of Heroin, Cocaine, Crack, Crime, AIDS, and Public Policy*. Mountain View, CA: Mayfield, 1992.

———. *The War on Drugs III: The Continuing Saga of the Mysteries and Miseries of Intoxication, Addiction, Crime, and Public Policy*. London: Allyn and Bacon, 2002.

Inciardi, James A., Hilary L. Surratt, and Christine A. Saum. *Cocaine-Exposed Infants: Social, Legal, and Public Health Issues*. Thousand Oaks, CA: Sage, 1997.

Inderbitzin, Michelle. "A Look from the Inside: Balancing Custody and Treatment in a Juvenile Maximum-Security Facility." *International Journal of Offender Therapy and Comparative Criminology* 51, no. 3 (June 2007): 348–362.

Irvine, Leslie. *Codependent Forevermore: The Invention of Self in a Twelve Step Group*. Chicago: University of Chicago Press, 1999.

Irwin, John. *Prisons in Turmoil*. Boston: Little, Brown, 1980.

Jackson, George. *Soledad Brother: The Prison Letters of George Jackson*. Chicago: Lawrence Hill Books, 1970.

Jacobs, James B. *Stateville: The Penitentiary in Mass Society*. Chicago: University of Chicago Press, 1978.

Jones, Maxwell. *The Therapeutic Community: A New Treatment Approach in Psychiatry*. New York: Basic Books, 1953.

Justice Policy Institute. *Gaming the System: How the Political Strategies of Private Prison Companies Promote Ineffective Incarceration Policies*. Washington, DC: Justice Policy Institute, 2011.

Kennedy, Deseriee A. "Children, Parents, and the State: The Construction of a New Family Ideology." *Berkeley Journal of Gender, Law, and Justice* 26, no. 1 (Winter 2011): 78–138.

Kilty, Jennifer M. "Governance through Psychiatrization: Seroquel and the New Prison Order." *Radical Psychology* 2, no. 7 (2008): 24.

———. "'It's Like They Don't Want You to Get Better': Psy Control of Women in the Carceral Context." *Feminism and Psychology* 22, no. 2 (May 2012): 162–182.

King, Roy D. "The Rise and Rise of Supermax: An American Solution in Search of a Problem?" *Punishment and Society* 1, no. 2 (October 1999): 163–186.

Kooyman, Martien. *The Therapeutic Community for Addicts: Intimacy, Parent Involvement, and Treatment Success*. Lisse, Netherlands: Swets and Zeitlinger, 1993.

Kruttschnitt, Candace, and Rosemary Gartner. *Marking Time in the Golden State: Women's Imprisonment in California*. Cambridge: Cambridge University Press, 2005.

——. "Women's Imprisonment." In *Crime and Justice: A Review of the Research, Volume 30*, edited by Michael Tonry, 1–81. Chicago: University of Chicago Press, 2003.

Kunzel, Regina. *Criminal Intimacy: Prison and the Uneven History of Modern American Sexuality*. Chicago: University of Chicago Press, 2010.

Kurshan, Nancy. "Behind the Walls: The History and Current Reality of Women's Imprisonment." In *Criminal Injustice: Confronting the Prison Crisis*, edited by Elihu Rosenblatt, 136–164. Boston: South End Press, 1996.

Lichtenstein, Alex. "The Public and the Private in Penal History." In *Mass Imprisonment: Social Causes and Consequences*, edited by David Garland, 171–178. Thousand Oaks, CA: Sage, 2001.

Lindquist, Charles A. *"Prison Discipline and the Female Offender." Journal of Offender Counseling, Services, and Rehabilitation* 4, no. 4 (1980): 305–318.

Lockwood, Dorothy, and James Inciardi. "CREST Outreach Center: A Work Release Iteration of the TC Model." In *Innovative Approaches in the Treatment of Drug Abuse: Program Models and Strategies*, edited by James Inciardi, Frank Tims, and Bennett Fletcher, 61–69. Westport, CT: Greenwood Press, 1993.

Lundman, Richard. *Police and Policing*. New York: Holt, Rinehart, and Winston, 1980.

Lynch, Mona. "Waste Managers? The New Penology, Crime Fighting, and Parole Agent Identity." *Law and Society Review* 32, no. 4 (1998): 839–869.

Lyotard, Jean-François. *The Postmodern Condition: A Report on Knowledge*. Translated by Geoff Bennington and Brian Massumi. Minneapolis: University of Minnesota Press, 1984.

Maher, Lisa. *Sexed Work: Gender, Race, and Resistance in a Brooklyn Drug Market*. Oxford: Oxford University Press, 1997.

Maines, David R. "Narrative's Moment and Sociology's Phenomenon: Toward a Narrative Sociology." *Sociological Quarterly* 34, no. 1 (March 1993): 17–38.

Mann, Coramae Richey. *Female Crime and Delinquency*. Birmingham: University of Alabama Press, 1984.

Martinson, Robert. "What Works? Questions and Answers about Prison Reform." *The Public Interest* 35 (Spring 1974): 22–54.

Mauer, Marc. *Race to Incarcerate*. New York: New Press, 2006.

Mauer, Marc, and Tracy Huling. *Young Black Americans and the Criminal Justice System: Five Years Later*. Washington, DC: The Sentencing Project, 1995.

Mauer, Marc, Cathy Potler, and Richard Wolf. *Gender and Justice: Women, Drugs, and Sentencing Policy*. Washington DC: The Sentencing Project, 1999.

Maxfield, Michael, Dan Lewis, and Ron Szoc. "Producing Official Crimes: Verified Crime Reports as Measures of Police Output." *Social Science Quarterly* 61, no. 2 (September 1980): 221–236.

McCorkel, Jill. "Criminally Dependent? Gender, Punishment, and the Rhetoric of Welfare Reform." *Social Politics* 11, no. 3 (December 2004): 386–410.

——. "Embodied Surveillance and the Gendering of Punishment." *Journal of Contemporary Ethnography* 32, no. 1 (February 2003): 41–76.

——. "Going to the Crackhouse: Critical Space as a Form of Resistance in Total Institutions and Everyday Life." *Symbolic Interaction* 21, no. 3 (November 1998): 227–252.

——. "Justice, Gender, and Incarceration: An Analysis of the Leniency and Severity Debate." In *Examining the Justice Process*, edited by James Inciardi, 157–76. New York: Harcourt Brace. 1996.

McCorkel, Jill, and Kristen Myers. "What Difference Does Difference Make? Position and Privilege in the Field." *Qualitative Sociology* 26, no. 2 (June 2003): 199–231.

McKim, Allison, "'Getting Gut Level': Punishment, Gender, and Therapeutic Governance." *Gender and Society* 22, no. 3 (June 2008): 303–323.

Mead, George Herbert. *Mind, Self, and Society.* Chicago: University of Chicago Press, 1934.

Miller, Jody. *Getting Played: African American Girls, Urban Inequality, and Gendered Violence.* New York: New York University Press, 2008.

Miller, Lisa L. "Looking for Postmodernism in All the Wrong Places." *British Journal of Criminology* 41, no. 1 (2001): 168–184.

Mills, C. Wright. "Situated Actions and Vocabularies of Motive." *American Sociological Review* 5, no. 6 (December 1940): 904–913.

Minkoff, Kenneth. "An Integrated Treatment Model for Dual Diagnosis of Psychosis and Addiction." *Hospital and Community Psychiatry* 40, no. 1 (October 1989): 1031–1036.

Morash, Merry, Robin Haarr, and Lila Rucker. "A Comparison of Programming for Women and Men in U.S. Prisons since the 1980s." *Crime and Delinquency* 40, no. 2 (April 1994): 197–221.

Muedeking, George D. "Authentic/Inauthentic Identities in the Prison Visiting Room." *Symbolic Interaction* 15, no. 2 (Summer 1992): 227–236.

Muhammad, Khalil Gibran. *The Condemnation of Blackness: Race, Crime, and the Making of Modern Urban America.* Cambridge: Harvard University Press, 2010.

Myers, Kristen A. *Racetalk: Racism Hiding in Plain Sight.* Lanham, MD: Rowman and Littlefield, 2005.

Neuhaus, Charles. "*The Disease Controversy Revisited*: An Ontologic Perspective." *Journal of Drug Issues* 23, no. 3 (1993): 463–478.

O'Malley, Pat. "Volatile and Contradictory Punishment." *Theoretical Criminology* 3, no. 2 (May 1999): 175–196.

Orwell, George. *Nineteen Eighty-Four.* New York: Penguin, 1977.

Owen, Barbara. *In the Mix: Struggle and Survival in a Women's Prison.* Albany: State University of New York Press, 1998.

Owen, Barbara, and Barbara Bloom. "Profiling Women Prisoners: Findings from National Surveys and a California Sample." *Prison Journal* 75, no. 2 (June 1995): 165–185.

Pan, Hao, Frank Scarpitti, James Inciardi, and Dorothy Lockwood. "Some Considerations on Therapeutic Communities in Corrections." In *Drug Treatment and Criminal Justice*, edited by James A. Inciardi, 30–43. Newbury Park, CA: Sage, 1993.

Peele, Stanton. "Introduction to Alcohol and Pleasure: A Health Perspective." In *Alcohol and Pleasure: A Health Perspective*, edited by Stanton Peele and Marcus Grant, 1–7. Philadelphia: Brunner/Mazel, 1999.

Perkinson, Robert. *Texas Tough: The Rise of America's Prison Empire.* New York: Metropolitan Books, 2010.

Plummer, Ken. *Telling Sexual Stories: Power, Change, and Social Worlds.* London: Routledge, 1995.

Pollack, Shoshana. "'I'm Just Not Good in Relationships': Victimization Discourses and the Gendered Regulation of Criminalized Women." *Feminist Criminology* 2, no. 2 (April 2007): 158–174.

———. "'Taming the Shrew': Regulating Prisoners through Women-Centered Mental Health Programming." *Critical Criminology* 13, no. 1 (January 2005): 71–87.

———. "'You Can't Have It Both Ways': Punishment and Treatment of Imprisoned Women." *Journal of Progressive Human Services* 20, no. 2 (2009): 112–128.

Pollner, Melvin, and Jill Stein. "Narrative Mapping of Social Worlds: The Voice of Experience in Alcoholics Anonymous." *Symbolic Interaction* 19, no. 3 (Fall 1996): 203–223.

Pratt, John. "The Return of the Wheelbarrow Men; or, The Arrival of Postmodern Penality?" *British Journal of Criminology* 40, no. 1 (January 2000): 127–145.

Rafter, Nicole. *The Criminal Brain: Understanding Biological Theories of Crime.* New York: New York University Press, 2008.

———. *Partial Justice: Women in State Prisons, 1800–1935.* Boston: Northeastern University Press, 1985.

Reich, Jennifer A. *Fixing Families: Parents, Powder, and the Child Welfare System.* New York: Routledge, 2005.

Reinarman, Craig, and Harry G. Levine, eds. *Crack in America: Demon Drugs and Social Justice.* Berkeley: University of California Press, 1997.

Rhodes, Lorna A. *Total Confinement: Madness and Reason in the Maximum Security Prison.* Berkeley: University of California Press, 2004.

Rice, John Steadman. *Disease of One's Own: Psychotherapy, Addiction, and the Emergence of Co-dependency.* New Brunswick, NJ: Transaction Books, 1996.

Richie, Beth E. *Compelled to Crime: The Gender Entrapment of Battered Black Women.* New York: Routledge, 1996.

Roberts, Dorothy. *Killing the Black Body: Race, Reproduction, and the Meaning of Liberty.* New York: Vintage Books, 1999.

———. *Shattered Bonds: The Color of Child Welfare.* New York: Basic Civitas Books, 1997.

Rose, Nikolas. *Governing the Soul: The Shaping of the Private Self.* London: Free Association Books, 1999.

———. "Government and Control." *British Journal of Criminology* 40, no. 2 (2000): 321–339.

———. *Inventing Our Selves: Psychology, Power, and Personhood.* Cambridge: Cambridge University Press, 1996.

Ross, Robert, and Elizabeth Fabiano. *Female Offenders: Correctional Afterthoughts.* Jefferson, NC: McFarland, 1986.

Roth, Rachel. "Searching for the State: Who Governs Prisoners' Reproductive Rights?" *Social Politics* 11, no. 3 (Fall 2004): 411–438.

Rothman, David J. *Conscience and Convenience: The Asylum and Its Alternatives in Progressive America.* Boston: Little, Brown, 1980.

———. *The Discovery of the Asylum: Social Order and Disorder in the New Republic.* Boston: Little, Brown, 1971.

Schmid, Thomas J., and Richard S. Jones. "Suspended Identity: Identity Transformation in a Maximum Security Prison." *Symbolic Interaction* 14, no. 4 (Winter 1991): 415–432.

Schneider, Anne Larason. "Public–Private Partnerships in the U.S. Prison System." *American Behavioral Scientist* 43, no. 1 (September 1999): 192–208.

Schutz, Alfred. *The Phenomenology of the Social World.* Translated by George Walsh and Fredrick Lehnert. Evanston: Northwestern University Press, 1967.

Sellin, J. Thorsten. *Slavery and the Penal System.* New York: Elsevier, 1976.

The Sentencing Project. *Women in the Criminal Justice System.* Washington, DC: The Sentencing Project, 2007.

Sharpe, Tanya Telfair. *Behind the Eight Ball: Sex for Crack Cocaine Exchange and Poor Black Women.* New York: Haworth Press, 2005.

Shichor, David. "Private Prisons in Perspective: Some Conceptual Issues." *Howard Journal of Criminal Justice* 37, no. 1 (February 1998): 82–100.

Silberman, Matthew. *A World of Violence: Corrections in America*. Belmont, CA: Wadsworth, 1995.

Simon, Jonathan. "Paramilitary Features of Contemporary Penality." *Journal of Political and Military Sociology* 27, no. 2 (Winter 1999): 279–290.

———. *Poor Discipline: Parole and the Social Control of the Underclass, 1890–1990*. Chicago: University of Chicago Press, 1993.

———. "The 'Society of Captives' in the Era of Hyper-Incarceration." *Theoretical Criminology* 4, no. 3 (August 2000): 285–308.

Simon, Jonathan, and Malcolm Feeley. "True Crime: The New Penology and Public Discourse on Crime." In *Punishment and Social Control: Essays in Honour of Sheldon L. Messinger*, edited by Thomas Blomberg and Stanley Cohen, 147–180. New York: Walter de Gruyter, 1995.

Simon, Rita, and Jean Landis. *The Crimes Women Commit and the Punishments They Receive*. Lexington, MA: Lexington Books, 1991.

Somers, Margaret R. "The Narrative Constitution of Identity: A Relational and Network Approach." *Theory and Society* 23, no. 5 (October 1994): 605–649.

Steinhauer, Jennifer. "Schwarzenegger Seeks Shift from Prisons to Schools." *New York Times*, January 6, 2010.

Sudbury, Julia. "Celling Black Bodies: Black Women in the Global Prison Industrial Complex." *Feminist Review* 70 (2002): 57–74.

Sugarman, Barry. *Daytop Village: A Therapeutic Community*. New York: Irvington, 1983.

Swartz, James. "TASC—The Next 20 years: Extending, Refining, and Assessing the Model." In *Drug Treatment and Criminal Justice*, edited by James A. Inciardi, 127–148. Newbury Park, CA: Sage, 1993.

Sykes, Gresham M. *The Society of Captives: A Study of a Maximum Security Prison*. Princeton: Princeton University Press, 2007.

Talvi, Silja J. A. *Women behind Bars: The Crisis of Women in the U.S. Prison System*. Emeryville, CA: Seal Press, 2007.

Thomas, Jim. "Some Aspects of Negotiated Order, Loose Coupling, and Mesostructure in Maximum Security Prisons." *Symbolic Interaction* 6, no. 2 (Fall 1984): 243–260.

Turner, Ralph H. "The Real Self: From Institution to Impulse." *American Journal of Sociology* 81, no. 5 (March 1976): 989–1016.

Useem, Bert and Peter Kimball. *States of Siege: U.S. Prison Riots, 1971–1986*. New York: Oxford University Press, 1991.

Wacquant, Loïc. "Deadly Symbiosis: When Ghetto and Prison Meet and Mesh." *Punishment and Society* 3, no. 1 (January 2001): 95–133.

———. "Four Strategies to Curb Carceral Costs: On Managing Mass Imprisonment in the United States." *Studies in Political Economy* 69 (Autumn 2002): 19–30.

———. "From Slavery to Mass Incarceration: Rethinking the 'Race Question' in the U.S." *New Left Review* 13 (January/February 2002): 41–60.

———. *Punishing the Poor: The Neoliberal Government of Social Insecurity*. Durham: Duke University Press, 2009.

———. "Race as Civic Felony." *International Social Science Journal* 57, no. 183 (March 2005): 127–142.

Wakefield, Sara, and Christopher Uggen. "Incarceration and Stratification." *Annual Review of Sociology* 36 (2010): 387–406.

Ward, David, and Gene Kassebaum. *Women's Prison: Sex and Social Structure*. Chicago: Aldine, 1965.

Watterson, Kathryn. *Women in Prison: Inside the Concrete Womb*. Boston: Northeastern University Press, 1996.

Weppner, Robert S. *The Untherapeutic Community: Organizational Behavior in a Failed Addiction Treatment Program*. Lincoln: University of Nebraska Press, 1983.

Wicker, Tom. *A Time to Die: The Attica Prison Revolt*. New York: Quadrangle, 1975.

Wise, Tim. *Colorblind: The Rise of Post-Racial Politics and the Retreat from Racial Equity*. San Francisco: City Lights Books, 2010.

Wood, Phillip J. "Globalization and Prison Privatization: Why Are Most of the World's For-Profit Adult Prisons to Be Found in the American South?" *International Political Sociology* 1, no. 3 (September 2007): 222–239.

Yablonsky, Lewis. *Synanon: The Tunnel Back*. Baltimore: Penguin Books, 1965.

———. *The Therapeutic Community*. New York: Gardner Press, 1989

Young, Vernetta D., and Rebecca Reviere. *Women behind Bars: Gender and Race in U.S. Prisons*. Boulder, CO: Lynne Rienner, 2006.

Zimring, Franklin E., Gordon Hawkins, and Sam Kamin. *Punishment and Democracy: Three Strikes and You're Out in California*. New York: Oxford University Press, 2001.

Jill A. McCorkel is Associate Professor of Sociology and Criminology at Villanova University. Her work has appeared in several leading journals, including *Social Problems*, *Journal of Contemporary Ethnography*, *Journal of Offender Rehabilitation*, and *Social Politics*. She lives in Philadelphia.